DIPLOMACY AND ENTERPRISE

DIPLOMACY
AND ENTERPRISE

BRITISH CHINA POLICY 1933-1937

Stephen Lyon Endicott

UNIVERSITY OF BRITISH COLUMBIA PRESS

DIPLOMACY AND ENTERPRISE
British China Policy 1933-1937

UNIVERSITY OF BRITISH COLUMBIA PRESS

This book has been published with the help of a grant from the Social Science Research Council of Canada, using funds provided by the Canada Council.

Canadian Shared Cataloguing in Publication Data
Endicott, Stephen Lyon.
    Diplomacy and enterprise: British China policy, 1933-1937 / Stephen Lyon Endicott.—
    1. Great Britain — Relations (general) with China. 2. China — Relations (general) with Great Britain. I. Title.
DS740.5.G5E549   382.0942051
ISBN 0-7748-0036-4

International Standard Book Number 0-7748-0036-4

Printed in Canada

For Lena

Contents

Photographic Credits

Plate 3 is from the Radio Times Hulton Picture Library. Plate 4 is reproduced by courtesy of Victor Rose, plate 6 by courtesy of Sir William Keswick, plate 8 by courtesy of Miss Edith Hardy and Lady Pratt, and plate 9 by courtesy of John Swire and Sons Limited. Plates 10, 11, and 12 are reproduced by courtesy of World Wide Photos, and plate 14 is from Central Press Photos. Plates 17, 18, and 19 are facsimiles of Crown-copyright records in the Public Record Office and appear by permission of the Controller of Her Majesty's Stationery Office, London.

Illustrations

Following page 128

Abbreviations

All papers are in the Public Record Office, London, unless otherwise noted.

ADM	Admiralty Papers
BT 11	Board of Trade Papers
BT 59	Board of Trade Papers, Department of Overseas Trade
CAB 2	Cabinet, Committee of Imperial Defence
CAB 4	Cabinet, Committee of Imperial Defence
CAB 21	Cabinet, Secretariat
CAB 23	Cabinet, Minutes of Decisions
CAB 24	Cabinet, Memoranda
CAB 27	Cabinet, Committee Meetings, Minutes
CAB 29	Cabinet, Conferences
CAB 63	Cabinet, Sir Maurice Hankey Papers
Cadogan Papers	FO 800 series
Cadogan Papers, Diary	Cadogan Trustees, London
Chatfield Papers	Southampton University Library, Southampton
DBFP	*Documents on British Foreign Policy, 1914-1939*, 2nd Series, Vols, 8-10. London: H.M.S.O., 1960, 1965, 1970
DGFP	*Documents on German Foreign Policy, 1918-1945*, Series C, Washington, D.C.: Government Printing Office, 1949-64.
DOT	Department of Overseas Trade
ECGD	Export Credit Guarantee Department
FO	Foreign Office, Political Correspondence, 371 series
FO 366	Foreign Office, Chief Clerk's Office
FO 369	Foreign Office, Consular Department
FO 405	Foreign Office, Confidential Print, China
FO 410	Foreign Office, Confidential Print, Japan
FO 676	Foreign Office, Peking Legation Archives
FO 800	Foreign Office, Private Office Papers
FRUS	*Foreign Relations of the United States: Diplomatic Papers, 1933-37*. Washington, D.C.: Government Printing Office, 1949-54
G.C. Papers	China Association, General Committee Papers, Hatton Garden, London
H.C. Deb.	House of Commons Debates
H.L. Deb.	House of Lords Debates
IMTFE	International Military Tribunal, Far East, Imperial War Museum, London
Lothian Papers	Scottish Record Office, Edinburgh
Maze Papers	School of Oriental and African Studies, London
Simon Papers	FO 800 series
Simon Papers, Diary	Port of London Authority, London
Swire Papers	John Swire and Sons, London
T 160	Treasury Papers, In-Letters
T 172	Treasury, Chancellor of the Exchequer's Office
T 188	Treasury, Leith-Ross Papers, Treasury Chambers, London
WO	War Office Papers

In the notes, the abbreviations of PRO manuscript materials of the Foreign Office are followed by numbers indicating the PRO volume number, the department number, and the piece or file number.

Preface

The external policy of a government is never far removed from its domestic political concerns. What is often masked, however, is the extent to which private economic power is translated into public political policy. When the government of an advanced industrialized state intervenes to help its private interest groups make gains in other parts of the world, pains are taken to legitimize such action as part of the national interest, and means are found to suppress the resentments which such activities inevitably generate in the Third World. The problems which flow from these aspects of international relations are at the heart of the debates about containment and revolution which have dominated many of the political actions of the advanced industrialized countries in the years since World War II.

The history of Anglo-Chinese relations in the turbulent pre-war decade of the 1930's provides some compelling insights into these persistent problems. Through government sponsored negotiations for tied loans, by attempts to create multinational corporations, by providing financial and political advisers to the Chinese government, as well as by maintaining a long established naval-military presence in the area, certain British policymakers hoped to check the discontents underlying Chinese nationalism and blunt the thrust of a rival Japanese imperialism. These efforts by the British imperial government to help private British venture capital in China proved unsuccessful in the long run. The heyday of British hegemony in world affairs had passed. But British leaders, with Neville Chamberlain as chancellor of the Exchequer and later as prime minister at their head, were prepared to take considerable risks and apparently never gave up trying to make gains in China as long as even the slightest hope for success existed.

Because the influence of corporations has been "more or less camouflaged," many scholars have separated political and economic factors in international politics and have upheld the view that the desire for "greatness and glory which animates the leaders of men" has the decisive importance which outweighs the economic influences on the course of events.[1] The impression given by a study of British China policy before World War I by Professor Nathan Pelcovits is that British merchants and British officials were almost always on opposite sides of the fence over the issues raised in Anglo-Chinese relations.[2] The present study presents a different perspective. Based on the circumstances of the 1930's, the new evidence reveals a much closer relationship between the private economic and public political factors in British politics. It is true that the British Foreign Office continued to annoy British traders by keeping them at arm's length. But it was the British Treasury, with its own distinct viewpoints about the Far East, in tune with private interests, that took effective charge of China policy away from the Foreign Office. Taking advantage of the split in the Whitehall bureaucracy (which it helped to create), a well-organized business élite pressed its demands. By convincing the cabinet that the interests of the British China Houses coincided with the national interest or, alternatively, by threatening to withdraw from China, this pressure group undermined the prime political aim of the government which according to a cabinet decision of July 1934 had been to seek Japanese friendship and keep the peace whatever the cost to China. The China lobby in Britain succeeded in persuading the government to substitute instead an opposite policy of checking the Japanese influence in China by having closer relations with Chiang Kai-shek in Nanking and preserving South China as a British sphere of interest.

The suggestion that this movement in foreign policy was determined by an interlocking of business and political interests raises difficulties of proof and interpretation, and the connections which linked the China lobby to the effective centre of political power must be shown. In addition, it must be demonstrated that significant demands were accepted by the politicians and that the operation resulted in changes in policy which would not otherwise have occurred. It must also be determined whether merchant adventurers were using the government to forward their private interests or to what extent the government was using the entrepreneur to advance a public interest. The influence which particular private interests, no matter how powerful, can exert on a government structure such as exists in a mature state like Britain depends on many objective circumstances. No simple formula or single cause can explain the workings of British diplo-

---

[1]Raymond Aron, *Peace and War* (New York: Doubleday, 1966), p. 266. See also Eugene Staley, *War and the Private Investor* (Chicago: University of Chicago Press, 1935, reprinted 1967), pp. 100, 360 and D.C.M. Platt, *Finance, Trade and Politics in British Foreign Policy* (Oxford: Clarendon Press, 1968), p. 284.

[2]N. A. Pelcovits, *Old China Hands and the Foreign Office* (New York: King's Crown Press, 1948), pp. viii-x, 300-302.

macy and enterprise in China. But the making of British China policy, which exhibited a close interlocking of economic, political, and strategic interests, does seem to suggest that the historian might well spend less time trying to decide whether it is economic or political factors which determine foreign policy making and more attempting to discover whose economic interests are effectively linked to which political forces and to what strategic end.

Compared to events which were unfolding in Europe it might be thought in retrospect that for British officials the years 1933 to 1937 were a time of relative calm in the Far East. There can be little doubt that the rise of Nazi Germany, the Italian aggression in Abyssinia in defiance of the League of Nations, and the civil war in Spain were the foremost items in the minds of people concerned with foreign policy in England. But this did not mean, as some have suggested,[3] that there was little time or inclination to think out any deliberate course of action to meet problems in the Far East. The evidence preserved in the British archives, even if the subject is largely absent from the published memoirs of cabinet ministers, strongly suggests that throughout the 1930's the cabinet felt a heavy responsibility for British interests in East Asia; indeed the members of the British government "were constantly looking over their shoulders" to see what was happening in China.[4]

Many unpleasant dilemmas for British policy makers arose in the Far East in the 1930's. Continuous diplomatic and military pressure on China by the Japanese threatened to weaken or destroy British interests in China. Were Britain to join Japan in the pacification and rehabilitation of the China market as some advocated, strategic worries about defending her interests would be reduced. But in this case Britain would forfeit Chinese good will and face moral condemnation by the international community. Any effort to block the powerful Japanese military machine single-handedly was out of the question, especially in view of the threat posed by the resurgence of Germany. But reliable allies to check Japan were not readily available. China was politically divided and militarily weak; the United States seemed invulnerable to Japanese attack and introverted by isolationist sentiment; the Soviet Union, although now a fellow member of the League of Nations and seriously threatened by Japan, was communist led and viewed with suspicion by conservative politicians. If Japan pressed on unchecked, China might fall into the arms of Soviet Russia and eventually go communist. Alternatively, if left without allies, some feared

[3]Evan Luard, *Britain and China* (London: Chatto and Windus, 1962), p. 47.
[4]William N. Medlicott, *British Foreign Policy Since Versailles* (London: Methuen, 1968), p. 156.

that China might join Japan in a pan-Asian movement in which a renewed "yellow peril" would drive out all European interests. Any faltering in China, moreover, might lead to serious consequences for imperial interests throughout Asia.

In their inner councils, British statesmen could not always agree on policy to deal with this confusing situation; at times their actions were contradictory and in the end their choices proved unsuccessful, but there was no lack of thought or concern. The strongest personality in the British cabinet was Neville Chamberlain, who came to reject a purely defensive outlook on the Far East. Through bold strokes of initiative masterminded by Sir Warren Fisher, the formidable permanent under-secretary of the Treasury and head of the civil service, Chamberlain's viewpoint eventually gained the upper hand. It is the evolution of the Chamberlain-Fisher policy, oscillating between friendship with Japan and economic advance in China, its triumph over the far eastern experts of the Foreign Office, and the consequences of that triumph, which form the main core of interest in these years of British policy in the Far East.

Gaps in the documentary record exist but they have been partially filled by interviews with surviving participants. In this respect my thanks are due to W. J. Keswick of Jardine, Matheson Co., for a long and informative interview; to Mr. Arthur Dean and Mr. James Scott, directors of John Swire & Sons, for their interviews and for permission to examine and quote from the company's extensive archive relating to Butterfield and Swire Co.; to Mr. Frances Gardener, retired Shanghai executive of the Asiatic Petroleum Co., and Dr. R. W. Ferrier, historian of British Petroleum who helped arrange the interviews; to W. J. Reader, historian of Imperial Chemical Industries; to Sir Laurence Collier, retired, Foreign Office and Diplomatic Service; and to Mr. Derek Bryan, formerly of the China Consular Service.

I wish to acknowledge with gratitude the financial support of the Canada Council which enabled me to carry out my research in Britain. While I am indebted to many people, I should like to thank especially Professor J. L. Cranmer-Byng and Professor H. I. Nelson, Chairman of the International Studies Programme of the University of Toronto, and Dr. Jane Fredeman of the University of British Columbia Press for their friendly criticism, scholarly advice, and valuable suggestions on the preparation of the manuscript. Needless to say, none of these people should be held responsible for my conclusions about a subject which remains a centre of controversy.

My thanks are due to the Keeper of Public Records at the Public Record Office and the Curator of Historical Records at the Scottish Record Office for permission to quote from unpublished material in their hands.

Also I am indebted to *Pacific Affairs* for extracts from my article, "British Financial Diplomacy In China: the Leith-Ross Mission 1935-1937," which appeared in Vol. 46, No. 4 (Winter 1973-74), and to the following people for permission to make use of unpublished material in their possession: the Librarian, Cambridge University, for the Baldwin and Templewood papers; E. S. Bush, secretary of the China Association; Professor David Dilks for the Cadogan diaries; the Librarian, British Museum, for the Cecil of Chelwood papers; Lady Chatfield for the Chatfield papers; Viscount Simon for the Sir John Simon papers; the School of Oriental and African Studies for the Maze papers; Ms. Marjorie Ellmer for the Conference of Missionary Societies archives and Rev. N. C. Pateman of the China Inland Mission; V. H. Rose for the Archibald Rose papers; the Rt. Hon. Malcolm MacDonald for the Ramsay MacDonald papers; the Keeper, Bodleian Library, for the E. J. Nathan papers; and Mr. Kenneth Younger, Royal Institute of International Affairs, for the Institute of Pacific Relations sub-committee minutes.

S. L. E.

Atkinson College,
York University, Toronto.

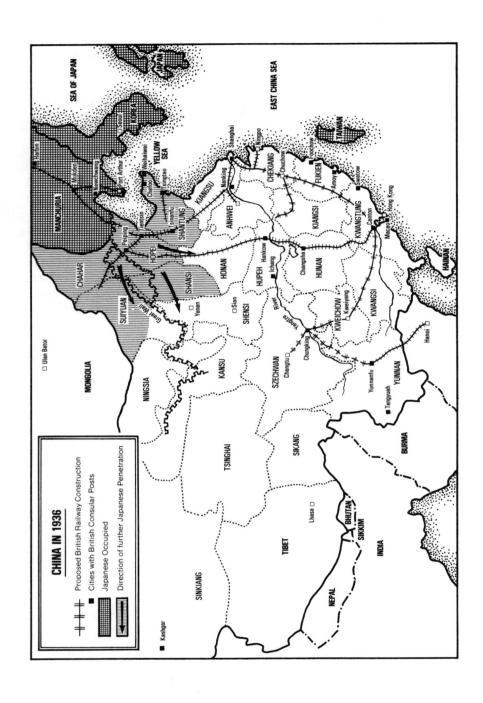

CHINA IN 1936

Proposed British Railway Construction
Cities with British Consular Posts
Japanese Occupied
Direction of further Japanese Penetration

SEA OF JAPAN

EAST CHINA SEA

JAPAN

Seoul

KOREA

Harbin

MANCHURIA

Mukden

Newchwang

Port Arthur

Weihaiwei

Chefoo

Tsingtao

YELLOW SEA

Tientsin

Peping

Shanhaiwei

CHAHAR

SUIYUAN

Great Wall

HOPEI

SHANTUNG

SHANSI

Yenan

Sian

SHENSI

HONAN

KIANGSU

Nanking

Shanghai

Ningpo

CHEKIANG

Chuchow

Ichang

Hankow

HUPEH

ANHWEI

KIANGSI

FUKIEN

Foochow

Amoy

Swatow

TAIWAN

KWANGTUNG

Canton

Hong Kong

Macao

HAINAN

Changsha

HUNAN

Kweiyang

KWEICHOW

KWANGSI

Yangtze River

Chengtu

Chungking

SZECHWAN

Yunnanfu

Tengyueh

YUNNAN

Hanoi

BURMA

Ulan Bator

MONGOLIA

NINGSIA

KANSU

TSINGHAI

SIKANG

Lhasa

TIBET

BHUTAN

SIKKIM

INDIA

NEPAL

Kashgar

SINKIANG

1

British Views of "The China Problem"

The vision of a vast, semi-modernized market for trade and investment coloured the reporting of British observers in China to a remarkable degree in the 1930's. This bias strongly influenced their projections and analyses of trends in that country. In spite of the many uncertainties—such as civil war, drought, floods, famine, absence of a standard currency, communism, foreign aggression, native resistance, and massive poverty—British officials maintained a perennial optimism about the future of British trade. London traders and manufacturers were even urged by the United Kingdom government to make every effort "and, if necessary, sacrifices" to maintain their precarious positions in China.[1] The implication appeared to be that a better day was just around a trade corner.

Questions uppermost in the minds of British investigators of the China scene were of a political and economic nature. They wondered if the Nanking régime had the capacity and determination needed to launch China onto the path of economic modernization with appropriate laws, adequate financial institutions, and efficient governmental practices. Although a few observers believed emphatically that it would not be possible to remake China in the Western image because the ethnocentric Chinese were too arrogant to see and to try "better ways," the prize to be won by integrating China into the Western-oriented world market tended to banish doubts about the feasibility of making the necessary transformations. Close attention was paid to Chiang Kai-shek, the leader of the Nationalist party, who was considered to be especially friendly to Britain, in the hope that he

[1]F. Barber (Board of Trade), Notes, 11 May 1937, FO 20995/2718.

might prevail over turbulent internal opposition and provide the framework of law and order necessary for sound trading.

One of the most intractable problems for British diplomacy in the Far East lay in the attempt of successive British governments to treat China simultaneously as a semi-colony under foreign tutelage and as a sovereign, independent nation. This was a combination of irreconcilables. The origins of the British dilemma over China's international status lay in the treaty system which was established after China's defeat by Britain in the Opium Wars of 1839-41 and 1857-60. No study of British China policy in the twentieth century can ignore that treaty background, because the elements of colonialism imposed at that time were not fully removed until the establishment of the People's Republic in 1949, and even then Hong Kong remained a British colony on the coast of China.

The principal characteristics of the old treaty system were the treaty ports, extraterritoriality, and the 5 per cent tariff. The treaty ports were designated places or concessions where foreigners could reside and trade and, most important, receive the protection of their own warships. Britain normally maintained a larger fleet on the China Station than any of the other powers. A commander-in-chief once boasted to the Shanghai Chamber of Commerce that the officers and men in the Royal Navy's Yangtse Flotilla exceeded the total number of fellow countrymen employed in trade pursuits on that river.[2] The commander-in-chief of the China Station of the Admiralty was the senior officer of a British military presence which by the 1930's included six battalions of British and Colonial troops (totalling about 7,600 men) and associated naval, military, and secret intelligence services.[3] The role of the navy and army marines was both preventive and punitive. They had delicate duties as a supplement to diplomacy in smooth-

---

[2]Vice-Admiral Sir Arthur Duff, reported in *British Chamber of Commerce Journal*, Shanghai, no. 20 (December 1920): 4, Rose Papers, Victor Rose, Framlingham, Suffolk.

[3]A. Duff Cooper (War Office) in answer to parliamentary question, 313 *H.C.Deb.*, 16 June 1936. Although still not officially admitted, Secret Intelligence Service activities did take place, as fragmentary notations in the Foreign Office records bear witness. Information which the S.I.S. intercepted was referred to in the Foreign Office as coming from "highly secret but impeccable sources." The Japanese diplomatic code had been broken by the S.I.S. and intercepts were "the most important and fragile of our unofficial weapons"; recipients of such information had instructions to burn their letters after perusal. Japanese versions of diplomatic conversations were also used to keep check on the adequacy and accuracy of the reporting of British diplomatic officials. In the Foreign Office, Clifford J. Norton, private secretary to the permanent under-secretary, Sir Robert Vansittart, was the liaison with the S.I.S. See Minute and Outfile, "most secret," to Sir Hughe Knatchbull-Hugessen (Nanking), 19 March 1937, FO 20994/F1677g and Norton, Minute, 19 May 1937, FO 20988/F205.

ing the channels of trade for British merchants in China. If a British firm were having labour troubles, a gunboat would be sent to the area as "a precautionary measure" because it made it "easier for consul and others concerned to deal with a difficult situation."[4] In order that their presence might not pass unnoticed by the local residents, it was a comparatively commonplace event on the China Station for naval vessels to salute each other with seventeen or twenty-one gun salvos as they steamed into port. Even when things were quiet, the British Chambers of Commerce recorded their appreciation of the fact that the sight of gunboats "going about their lawful occasions" was a constant comfort and a sure shield in case of need for "our brethren in the remoter outports."[5] The activities of the China Squadron were an example of "gunboat diplomacy," defined by James Cable in his recent study as

> the use or threat of limited naval force, otherwise than as an act of war, in order to secure advantage, or to avert loss either in the furtherance of an international dispute or else against foreign nationals within the territory or jurisdiction of their own state.[6]

The legal basis for the insistence of the treaty powers on the right of their warships to visit inland ports in China lay in a "very liberal interpretation"[7] of Article 52 of the Sino-British Treaty of Tientsin (1858), which reads as follows:

> British ships of war coming for no hostile purpose, or being engaged in pursuit of pirates, shall be at liberty to visit all ports within the dominions of the Emperor of China, and shall receive every facility for the purchase of provisions, procuring water. . . . The commanders of such ships shall hold intercourse with the Chinese authorities on terms of equality and courtesy.

Even though the Admiralty took full advantage of the possibility of stationing gunboats as far as fifteen hundred miles up the Yangtze River, it realized that in the not-too-distant future the Chinese would attempt to restrict the operations of foreign warships and seek to revise the old treaties. The Admiralty also held the view that it was not a practical proposition to

---

[4]Admiralty to Foreign Office, 1 August 1934, encl., "Proceedings," from Admiral Sir Frederick Dreyer, 1 April to 3 May 1934, FO18118/F4699.

[5]Sir Alexander Cadogan (Peking) to Sir John Simon (foreign secretary), 18 June 1915, encl., Hankow British Chamber of Commerce, Minutes of Annual Meeting, FO 19333/F3928.

[6]James Cable, *Gunboat Diplomacy* (London: Chatto and Windus, 1971), p. 21.

[7]Naval Intelligence Department, Memorandum, "Rights of Foreign Warships in Chinese Waters," 24 November 1932, ADM 116/2984.

say that trade could be successfully kept alive and healthy by means of forcible naval protection in the heart of a foreign country. For these reasons the Admiralty believed the sole point of punitive action against pirates, bandits, or other "outrages . . . when there is deliberate and wanton destruction of property" was to prevent recurrence of the action by forcing Chinese authorities to assume the responsibility which "properly belongs to them" for affording adequate protection.[8] Under the hold which Chiang Kai-shek had established on the Yangtze, the British rear-admiral, Yangtze Flotilla, found that relations with the Chinese had improved and that any suggestion he made as to the need of a Chinese gunboat at any place "has been instantly met."[9] However, in case of unsettled conditions, British military authorities were willing to supply free of charge (but at no extra cost to the army) armed guards for the 150 British merchant ships which plied Chinese waters. Also they held a "Yangtze River Force" of marines (rifle company, a machine-gun platoon, and a battery of Lewis guns) in reserve at Shanghai which could be sent up river on a cruiser at short notice.[10]

Although the China Fleet was of some use in dealing with the Chinese, British naval and military commanders were increasingly uncomfortable over the unsound position of isolated garrisons and ships in Central and North China in case of a challenge from Japan. The reaction of Admiral Sir Frederick Dreyer, commander-in-chief from 1933 to 1935, to this problem was to try to get on friendly personal terms with the Japanese. He organized four gala fleet visits to Japan during which he expressed his admiration for Japan's achievements and on one occasion proposed a toast to "the continued glory of the Imperial Japanese Navy."[11] This was too much for his chief-of-staff, Commodore George P. Thomson, a submarine expert, who returned home to be transferred to another station.[12] Dreyer himself was replaced in 1936 by the vice-chief of naval staff at the Admiralty, Vice-Admiral Sir Charles Little, who held different views about cooperation with Japan. Also under no illusions about the superior local strength of the Japanese navy, Little maintained that in case of war with

[8]Ibid., Memoranda "A" and "B," "Protection of British Lives and Property in China. Instructions to Commander-in-Chief, China," 25 January 1933, ADM 116/2984.

[9]Admiralty to Foreign Office, encl. from Rear-Admiral Richard A. S. Hill, 10 January 1934, FO 18117/F187.

[10]Memorandum, 4 February, 1932, WO 106/110.

[11]Dreyer to secretary of the Admiralty, 30 June 1934, ADM 116/2994. In his memoirs, *The Sea Heritage* (London: Museum Press, 1955), Dreyer gives earnest but unconvincing disclaimers about his pre-war attitude to Japan.

[12]N. S. Brown (Shanghai) to J. Swire and Sons, 2 November 1934, Swire—1082.

Japan the function of the submarines of the China Station would be to damage the Japanese fleet and try to hold Hong Kong and Singapore until the arrival of the main fleet.[13] In spite of the difficulties which seemed to lie ahead for the China Station, none of the British authorities were prepared to acknowledge, at least publicly, that the days of the China Fleet were numbered, and in fact new keels continued to be laid for the shallow draught gunboats needed to patrol the commercial routes of the Yangtze River where Britain still had extraterritorial rights and privileges to protect.

Extraterritoriality, the second main feature of the treaty system, meant that foreigners were subject to the jurisdiction only of their own national courts, which functioned on Chinese soil, and that no Chinese laws, except those expressly accepted, were binding on them. It was the British consuls, found at over twenty different posts across the country, from Shanghai to Kashgar in Sinkiang Province and from Mukden in the north to Tengyueh in Yunnan Province, who acted as the judges and governors of British subjects who traded or resided within their jurisdictions. The China consular service, which was a separate entity, like the Levant service, until it was amalgamated with the general service in 1935, had been known as an élite corps which had special aptitudes and qualities. In recent years, however, the prestige of the China service had declined because it was difficult to find first class recruits. Young Englishmen who headed the civil service examination lists did not fancy a country where living conditions were so difficult. T. A. Dunlop, the inspector-general of consulates, confirmed in 1937 that conditions in China made the consul liable to wear out at an earlier age than in other countries. Over the previous twenty-five years eight had died at their posts, three committed suicide, four retired from ill-health and died shortly afterwards, three had to be certified and sent to an asylum, four were invalided out of the service, ten were "compulsorily" retired for various reasons such as "eccentricity" (including two who married Chinese women), one died in a motor accident, five had a serious breakdown or illness which impaired their efficiency, and nine resigned. The attrition rate was about two per annum.[14]

The focal point for this exacting service, which comprised 20 per cent of Britain's world consular force, was at Shanghai, near the mouth of the Yangtze River. The consulate-general there was considered to be the most important consular post in the world, rivalled only by New York. According to Dunlop, the consular grounds with their "solid Victorian buildings and spacious green lawns" gave the "striking impression of British stability and

[13]Little, Minute, 19 March 1935, Chatfield Papers.
[14]Thomas A. Dunlop, 16 December 1937, FO 369/2461/K14807 and K13117.

opulence" and testified adequately to the importance of British interests in Shanghai.[15]

The commercial aspects of the British mission in China were co-ordinated at Shanghai by an energetic man, Louis Beale, who headed the commercial-diplomatic service. Beale demanded that his department should make itself "the guide, the propagandist and the inspiration" of British trade in China. To the delight of British traders, who commended his fanatic zeal, Beale believed Britain should go ahead with might and main to carve out for herself a large share of the economic fabric of China or else be squeezed out by Japan.[16] This crusading official had not been posted to China until 1932, at the age of fifty-three, after serving as trade commissioner in Winnipeg and Wellington and working for a while in the Department of Overseas Trade in London. Beale made an eight month long tour of Britain in 1935, conducting almost a thousand interviews with industrialists, bankers, and politicians and urging "a very considerable expansion of [U.K.] trade and industry in China,"[17] which was an indication of the British government's interest in promoting the China market.

The third pillar of the treaty system was the tariff, whereby, until she unilaterally abrogated the agreement in 1926, China bound herself not to levy more than a 5 per cent customs duty and an inland revenue tax of not more than 2½ per cent on imports and exports. Apart from the fact that this was a very low customs duty permitting easy foreign penetration of the Chinese marketplace, there had also grown up a foreign-staffed customs service to collect and administer the revenue, which provided many opportunities to meddle and pry into China's internal affairs.

During the great Taiping Rebellion (1850-1864), the existing Chinese customs service broke down, and local Chinese authorities at Shanghai, on consultation with foreign consuls, more or less voluntarily and without treaty obligation appointed foreign inspectors who were supposed to act as servants of the Chinese government. Thus it came about that the Chinese Maritime Customs Administration became one of those Chinese organizations (others included the Salt Gabelle and the Postal Administration) with which the British authorities had a semi-official relationship. The Chinese Maritime Customs was headed by a British inspector-general, who main-

[15]Ibid., Report, 18 May 1937, FO 369/2460/K5963.
[16]Edward M. B. Ingram (Peking) to Simon, 5 January 1933, encl. from Beale, FO 369/2304/K285; G. W. Swire (Shanghai) 24 February 1934, Swire Papers—D.N.O.E., copy to Foreign Office, FO 18046/F2266; Sir Edward Crowe (D.O.T.) to Foreign Office, encl. from Beale, 14 November 1933, FO 18096/F231.
[17]Beale to Cadogan, 21 June 1935, Cadogan Papers, FO 800/293.

tained a London office with a full-time non-resident secretary.[18] In addition to placing Britain in a position to know some of the innermost policies of the Chinese government, there was another reason why a partially foreign-staffed customs service (see Table 1) had long been "a cardinal point of British policy in China."[19] It was that if the foreign merchant had had to deal with a purely Chinese administration, there would have been no guarantee that a uniform tariff would be enforced at all ports, and trade would have been "strangled by obstruction, inefficiency and corruption."[20]

The presence of foreign customs commissioners also benefited the Chinese central government in various ways. The system provided a buffer against demands of provincial secessionist movements, and the employment of foreigners resulted in an efficient collection of revenue at a cost of about 8 per cent. On the secure surplus revenues thus provided, China's credit position and borrowing capacity both at home and abroad were kept intact for many years. Following the loan agreements of 1896 and 1898, which were secured on customs revenue, the Chinese government had given an assurance that as long as British trade predominated in China there would be a British inspector-general.

Developments in the first quarter of the twentieth century, however, had undermined the British position, and by the 1930's the inspector-general's post was in jeopardy as British predominance in the China trade began to give way to foreign competitors. (See Table 2.) Also, although the first inspector-general, Sir Robert Hart, who held the position from 1868 to 1911, had not attempted to ignore or displace Chinese authority, his successors, Sir Francis Aglen and A. H. F. Edwardes, had tried to deny the Chinese government the right to handle and control expenditure of their own revenues, turning the customs administration into an "adjunct of Legation Street."[21] The result was that the Chinese Nationalist Party (Kuomintang) had stopped all recruitment of foreign personnel in 1928. In the face of Japanese jealousy and with no treaty requirement that the Chinese recruit foreigners or have a British subject as inspector-general, the British government was forced to give considerable thought to means

[18]On taking office as non-resident secretary in 1933, J. H. Macoun wrote that, apart from routine matters, his duty was to call on the Foreign Office, the Hong Kong and Shanghai Bank, the British and Chinese Corporation, and the Department of Overseas Trade, since it was useful "to be in close touch with official, banking and commercial people in London who exercise influence in matters connected with China." Maze Papers, 9: 433-34.

[19]Foreign Office, Memorandum, 11 July 1935, T 188/67.

[20]Sir John Pratt, Memorandum, 10 August 1936, FO 20253/F4902.

[21]T. V. Soong, quoted by Sir Frederick Maze, Memorandum, 24 January 1936, Maze Papers, 9:470.

for securing a suitable successor to the aging Sir Frederick Maze, who had assumed the post in 1929. In the words of Sir Warren Fisher, permanent under-secretary at the Treasury, it was "immensely important alike as a symbol and from an immediately practical point of view" that an Englishman should continue to have the post.[22]

In addition to treaty ports, extraterritoriality, and the tariff which stemmed directly from the Treaties of Nanking (1842) and Tientsin (1858) and loan agreements which placed the maritime customs and salt administrations under foreign supervision, there was the Protocol of Peking of 1901, following the suppression of the Boxer uprising, which gave foreign powers the right to garrison unlimited numbers of soldiers in North China. The erosion of Chinese independence was intensified during the scramble for railway concessions prior to World War I, when the country was divided into unofficial spheres of influence by Russia, Japan, Germany, Great Britain, and France.

When China came into World War I on the side of the Allies in 1917, a grateful British government, hard pressed in Europe, assured the government in Peking of Britain's friendship and support and promised to "do all that rests with them to ensure that China shall enjoy in her international relations the position and regard due to a great country."[23] Accordingly, at the Paris Peace Conference, Britain tacitly affirmed China's independence and status as a sovereign nation by sponsoring her as a full member of the League of Nations.

When the Treaty of Versailles with Germany was being negotiated, however, no attention was paid to China's claims, and former German rights in Shantung were handed over to Japan. There followed in 1919 the great outburst of Chinese feeling known as the May 4th Movement. From then on, the growing force of Chinese nationalism made it obvious to all that the vast superstructure of foreign privileges was a source of irritation and offence to Chinese opinion which could not safely be ignored. The Kuomintang (Nationalist) party of Sun Yat-sen revived and forged an alliance with the new-born Chinese Communist party. Thereafter, revolutionary nationalism began to transform the balance of political power within China.

Aware of the militant mood of the Chinese nationalists and alarmed by Japan's predatory designs on China, as shown by the Twenty-One Demands of 1915, the powers, led by the United States and Great Britain, agreed on a policy of heeding China's national aspirations. They promised

---

[22]Fisher to J. D. G. Fergusson, 27 June 1936, T 188/67.
[23]Memorandum, 3 April 1933, FO 17079/F2152.

tariff reform and the eventual surrender of extraterritorial privileges. The agreement among the powers, defining their policy as an "open door in China" and enunciating the principle of "equal opportunity for trade," was embodied in the Nine Power Treaty signed in Washington in February 1922.[24] The political basis of the Nine Power Treaty was a resolution drafted by Mr. Elihu Root of the American delegation by which the powers professed themselves ready "to respect the sovereignty, the independence and the administrative integrity of China."[25]

The Nine Power Treaty was intended by the Western powers as an instrument to check Japan and mollify Chinese opinion. The Washington conference did lead to settlement of the Shantung question in China's favour, but the Nine Power Treaty itself was not ratified until 1925, and the carrying out of most of the promises made at Washington was postponed. As a result of this procrastination, Britain, which had been the chief architect of the treaty system and its main defender, was singled out for attack by boycotts and shipping strikes organized by the Kuomintang-Communist alliance. The other nations, in Britain's view, ostentatiously drew aside. In these circumstances the British government decided that the time had come to implement the promises made to China in 1922, and on 18 December 1926 it communicated a declaration to that effect to the powers.

The *December Memorandum*, conceived by its authors to be in the spirit of the Washington Nine Power Treaty, reaffirmed the need to abandon foreign tutelage and to go as far as possible toward meeting the legitimate aspirations of the Chinese nation. The British government proposed to modify its traditional attitude of rigid insistence on the strict letter of treaty rights. Also, it would not insist on establishment of a strong central government before re-negotiation of treaties.

By the time the *December Memorandum* was issued, the nationalist movement had "reached its most dangerous stage"[26] with attacks on British property and personnel. Therefore, without waiting for actual negotiations, the British made proposals to Chinese authorities in both North and South China. By giving away shadows, British officials hoped to retain substance. Among the matters dealt with were the retrocession of British concessions at some treaty ports, the renegotiation of terms for continued British use

[24]The treaty did nothing to disturb the *status quo* of vested interest; see H. B. Morse and H. F. McNair, *Far Eastern International Relations* (Shanghai: Commercial Press, 1928), p. 1010.

[25]Cited in H. F. McNair and D. Lach, *Modern Far Eastern International Relations*, rev. ed. (New York: Van Nostrand, 1955), p. 182.

[26]Pratt, Memorandum, 3 April 1933, FO 17079/F2151.

of the Weihaiwei naval base, Chinese representation on the municipal council of the International Settlement at Shanghai, the admittance of a Chinese court into the settlement, the return of control of the maritime customs revenues (with retention of a British inspector-general), the return of the Boxer indemnity for use in China, and tariff autonomy.

Although the British government landed a large force of marines in Shanghai early in 1927 to safeguard British interests from attacks by Chinese revolutionary nationalists, their new political policy was successful. Backed by a pledge of $30 million in Chinese National Currency from Shanghai bankers,[27] Chiang Kai-shek began to purge the Kuomintang of its revolutionary elements, and the most valuable British treaty rights were maintained. With the establishment of the Nationalist government in Nanking in 1928, hostility to Great Britain virtually disappeared, and a group of London companies were able to send Sir Frederick Whyte to China to become adviser to the national government of China.[28] Anglo-Chinese negotiations on extraterritoriality began shortly after Britain recognized the Nanking régime as the government of all China in December 1928. It was deliberate British policy to go ahead of the other powers to avoid once more being made the sole target of nationalist agitation. But negotiations were suspended soon after an outbreak of civil war between Chiang Kai-shek and the northern warlords in 1930.

When the Japanese seized Manchuria in September 1931, many on the British side were relieved to find Chinese attention diverted in other directions. Owing to Britain's dual attitude to China's international status, the Foreign Secretary, Sir John Simon, could avoid seeing any question of principle involved in the conflict between China and Japan over Manchuria in the years 1931-33. In a speech to the League of Nations on 7 December 1932, Simon maintained that there were rights and wrongs on both sides. Because of Japan's special treaty rights in China, which were analogous to Britain's, it was not, according to Simon, a simple question of aggression and he "did not desire to be the judge on either side." But the

---

[27]CN Currency was the money authorized and circulated in those parts of China under the control of the Nanking government headed by Chiang Kai-shek. T. V. Soong approached both Chinese and foreign bankers in Shanghai to raise financial support for Chiang Kai-shek. See Colonial Office to Foreign Office, 5 November 1934, FO 18122/F6568, pp. 19-20 and T. Shaw (Shanghai) to J. Swire and Sons, 31 December 1926, Swire—China and Japan, vol. 42.

[28]The fact that each of ten companies paid £500 annually for Whyte's mission "to explore possibilities and to seize or create opportunities" and continued to pay his salary after he became adviser to the Chinese government was not publicly known. See David Landale (Matheson and Co.) to G. W. Swire, 26 March 1928, and Landale to C. Scott (J. Swire and Sons), 13 March 1929, Swire—1185.

failure to solve the Manchurian crisis on the basis of Chinese sovereignty (owing to the fact that thirty million Chinese lived there, if for no other reason) was a serious blow at the general post-war collective security system which it had been Britain's aim to establish.

Britain's respite from the pressures of Chinese nationalism was temporary, however, as the Japanese soon began to make more active use of the special privileges and military occupation rights which the foreign powers had jointly imposed on China in the past in order to improve their position in North China. Apart from military weakness, the uncomfortable fact was that Britain had no strong political or moral grounds upon which to complain of Japanese infringements of Chinese sovereignty. In a brilliant critique of his country's "hesitant, divided, illogical and incoherent" attitude to China, a member of the British diplomatic service was later to liken it to an abortive hybrid sired by Palmerston and born of the League of Nations. It was "neither efficiently hard-boiled nor sincerely half-baked." A good case could have been made for excluding China from the League of Nations because she did not satisfy the definition of a nation; a good case could be made for granting her the rights of a nation. But no case could be made for adoption of two opposite policies at the same time.[29] This type of argument, however, found few ardent supporters within British officialdom.

Britain's ambivalence about the international status of China and her occasional determination to treat China as an unorganized or dependent territory was well understood and exploited by Japan. The latter contrived more than one incident to demonstrate that, when faced with disorder in China, Britain would take forceful, unilateral action to protect British lives and property without regard to Chinese sovereignty.

Perhaps the most famous Japanese provocation was the S.S. *Shuntien* piracy in 1934. The new Butterfield and Swire liner was on passage from Taku to Chefoo in the Yellow Sea when it was taken by internal piracy on 17 June 1934. When it was learned that five British subjects (including two Royal Navy officers), one Japanese, about twenty Chinese, and considerable property had been loaded onto eight or nine junks, the British minister, without the concurrence of the Chinese government or clearing the proposed action at Whitehall, authorized the penetration of Chinese airspace by British naval aircraft. With the majority of the British China fleet about 180 miles distant at Weihaiwei, a force of six vessels, headed by the aircraft carrier H. M. S. *Eagle*, went to the suspected scene

---

[29]Douglas MacKillop (Shanghai) to Sir Archibald Clark Kerr, 12 April 1938, FO 800/299.

of the piracy. Aerial reconnaissance to a depth of forty miles at right-angles to the Chinese coast was carried out in violation of Chinese airspace, and a group of junks in the mouth of the Yellow River was bombed and machine-gunned, with casualties among the Chinese. When the British captives were freed, the navy's "shares" rose "very high indeed in Shanghai"[30] as a result of wide publicity by the unsuspecting British. Later however, British officials had reason to believe that there had been Japanese complicity in organizing the piracy. Witnesses reported that the Japanese "captive," Mr. Yamamoto, had "volunteered" to be taken on the pirate junks and had been at liberty while in the pirates' lair.[31]

Japanese purposes were clearly well served during the *Shuntien* affair by Britain's strong justification of military operations within Chinese territory. According to the British rationalization, it was desirable to inform Chinese authorities of such action but "*not* necessary or desirable to seek their formal permission or concurrence." Britain had always maintained the right to send naval and military forces anywhere in China for the protection of British lives and property, and now that naval vessels carried aeroplanes as part of their armament, "it seemed natural and proper that we should equally maintain our right to use such aeroplanes without restriction" for defensive purposes.[32] It was usually in just this same fashion that Japan justified her own "defensive" actions on a larger scale in Manchuria and North China.

In the face of such situations, the experts of the Far Eastern Department of the Foreign Office were forced to the conclusion that Britain's definition of China's status required amendment. By 1937 and perhaps earlier, they favoured abolition of extraterritoriality in China and reliance, as in other countries, on normal diplomatic representations to protect British interests. If public opinion was not prepared to go that far, then the Foreign Office recommended that the cabinet should at least authorize the use of a 1931 draft treaty on extraterritoriality as the basis for giving up these rights while retaining as many safeguards as possible in Shanghai.[33]

British companies in China, however, were still opposed to any "benevolent non-interference" in the internal affairs of China. Conditions there, from a Western point of view, were still irregular and often chaotic. Any

---

[30]Dreyer to secretary of the Admiralty, 8 July 1934, ADM 116/3069.
[31]Sir John Brenan (Shanghai) to Cadogan, July 1934, ADM 116/3253; also FO 18150, file 3679 and WO 106/110.
[32]Cadogan to Simon, 25 June 1934, FO 18150/ file 3679.
[33]Memorandum on Extraterritoriality in China, Cabinet Paper 153 (37), CAB 24/269.

indication that the Foreign Office was prepared to renegotiate treaty rights was called a policy of drift and indifference to vulnerable British interests.

The conversion of the Foreign Office to a root and branch solution to extraterritoriality also did not impress the cabinet. All the familiar arguments for keeping China in her semi-colonial status were aired at the cabinet meeting of 16 June 1937.[34] Leading British residents would be "horrified at the idea of handing the International Settlement over to the Chinese." The Foreign Office painted the Nanking administration "in too favourable a light." The Chinese legal code was admirable, but it was not honestly administered. Though the end of extraterritoriality was inevitable, as in Egypt, "we should walk very warily"; it might just let the Japanese in more firmly. Also, the "main economic need of China was the investment of foreign capital," and the abolition of extraterritoriality would "reduce the confidence of foreign investors." Any changes might be "disastrous to our trade and embarrassing to the Chinese themselves, who preferred the safety of Shanghai to the precarious conditions outside." And so the arguments went on, without a murmur of contradiction, even by the foreign secretary. The cabinet decided not to take any initiative until the Chinese government started pressing the question again.

By its stand-pat attitude on the unequal treaties, the British government deprived itself of one of the few favourable political opportunities it had to put the Japanese position in China off balance. An offer to give up extraterritoriality would have cost Britain very little; the Soviet Union had renounced the old system, and the Germans were thriving in China without it.

China's internal development also presented many complexities to British policy makers. Throughout these years foreign service officers succeeded in collecting large quantities of valuable information on China's domestic politics which was subsequently summarized and analysed in the Far Eastern Department. Consular officials reported on Chinese personalities and movements of Chinese officials, on changes in taxation and land laws, on developments in judicial, police, prison, educational, and civic reforms, on traffic in arms and opium, on military, commercial and industrial intelligence, as well as on the activities and movements of foreign officials in China. With twenty or more consular observation posts sending reports independently of each other, it was to some extent possible to double-check for accuracy, to cross-examine judgments and detect omissions. But this wealth of information did not prevent Foreign Secretary Simon

[34]CAB 23/88; CAB 24 (37) 3. The question went to the cabinet after the United States requested an exchange of views, Cordell Hull, *Memoirs* (New York: Macmillan, 1948), 1: 566; *FRUS*, 1937, 4:639; FO 405/276, no. 58.

from complaining to cabinet colleagues that it was difficult to really know what was going on "inside the anthill."[35] It was especially difficult to reach any firm convictions with respect to the prospects for a stable central government. It was to this all-important question, in a country that contained a quarter of the human race, that British observers devoted their keenest attention.

China's long and relatively stable political order, based on a centrally appointed scholar-official class and the local landed gentry, had broken down only in the late nineteenth century. But after the anti-Manchu revolution of 1911, the country had been wracked by protracted civil wars. As contending provincial warlords struggled for personal power, the situation became more and more confusing. After the establishment of the Nationalist government in 1927, however, British officials thought a new consensus was emerging, and they hoped that a central government for all of China would soon be consolidated.

China, however, as the decade of the 1930's opened, was still an area the size of Europe divided into half a dozen major alignments: Manchuria under Chang Hsueh-liang, commonly referred to as the "young marshal," until he was replaced there by the Japanese in 1931; Honan, Shensi and Kansu in the northwest under Feng Yu-hsiang; the lower Yangtze provinces under Chiang Kai-shek; Kwangtung and Kwangsi in the south under Marshals Li Tsung-jen and Chen Chi-tang; Hunan, Hupei, Szechuan, Yunnan, and Kweichow in central and southwest China under semi-independent chiefs; and communist-led soviet areas in various provinces.[36]

Under such conditions in the past, British merchants had wanted, in the name of realism, to deal separately with local governors and not bother with any pretense about there being a national capital which needed to be bolstered. But now they were largely in agreement with British officials that Chiang Kai-shek should be supported, even though the fiat of and tax returns to his "central" government seldom extended further than his armies could march. The reason for this change of heart was partly the practical consideration that Chiang controlled Nanking and commanded the lower Yangtze where foreign interests were concentrated. Also, in spite of its weaknesses, it was only by working through a central government that the separatist policies of Japan in Manchuria and North China, and, more remotely, the Soviet Union in Outer Mongolia and Sinkiang, could be combatted. And lastly, Chiang was thought to be the outstanding indi-

[35]Minutes, Committee of Imperial Defence (C.I.D.), 9 November 1933, CAB 2/6.
[36]Memorandum, "Political Survey of Republican China," 12 February 1935, FO 19307/F940.

vidual in a country where "personalities not principles" were the most powerful factor in politics.[37] It was to the growing power and influence of this remarkable man that British observers attached the greatest hopes for political stability.

The personal qualities of Chiang Kai-shek made "an obviously good impression" on the succession of British ambassadors of the 1930's who kept in frequent touch with him.[38] He was "a nice-looking, fit-looking soldier, of few words," who apparently used neither alcohol nor tobacco. He was a strong man who pursued a consistent policy. His "ultimate objective" was to establish himself as "virtual dictator and unchallenged head of party, Government and State."[39] Such a man had to be admired for his "dynamic leadership."[40] His second wife, Soong Mei-ling, who usually interpreted at interviews, was considered a political asset to Chiang. Ambassador Cadogan described her as being amiable, intelligent, subject to wild enthusiasms, and "extremely voluble in almost faultless American."[41] During interviews, Chiang Kai-shek often asked many questions and his quick movements suggested impatience. The interviewer was aware that he had to make his points short and clear-cut or risk losing the generalissimo's attention. But there seemed to be general agreement that Chiang had "amazing judgment, ingenuity and genius for success" when dealing with his rivals and with popular moods.[42]

As might be expected, there were conflicting opinions and unfriendly reports about Chiang Kai-shek. Sir Miles Lampson, the British minister until 1934, generally admired Chiang's "courage and determination," but he suggested on at least one occasion that Chiang was establishing "something like a fascist dictatorship."[43] A man as close to Chiang as W. H. Donald, his Australian-born personal adviser, felt that, as a national leader, Chiang was not of the "intrinsically heroic mold" which the times required. For all his good intentions, Chiang was too weak and at the mercy of a horde of dishonest or unreliable underlings.[44] There was much truth in these assertions, but within a few years Chiang's detractors were confounded by his rise to become supreme leader of the nation—acclaimed as such briefly even by his long-time rivals, the Chinese Communists.

[37]Ingram (Peking) to Simon, 10 February 1933, FO 17060/F952.
[38]Cadogan to Vansittart, 3 June 1934, FO 800/293.
[39]Cadogan to Simon, 9 November 1934, FO 18048/F6712.
[40]Archibald Rose (B-A Tobacco Co.) to Lord Lothian, 14 November 1934, Lothian Papers, GD 40/17/285.
[41]Cadogan to Vansittart, 3 June 1934, FO 800/293.
[42]"Political Survey of Republican China."
[43]Sir Miles Lampson to Simon, 30 January 1934, FO 18116/File 170.
[44]Cadogan to Simon, 23 August 1935, quoting W. H. Donald, FO 19307/F5493.

Friendliness to foreigners and their property was an aspect of Chiang which was particularly appreciated by British officials. Chiang had succeeded in having the Kuomintang reinterpret its ideas of anti-imperialism. While Sun Yat-sen was alive, the Kuomintang had regarded the reconstruction of China as impractical as long as foreign imperialist exploitation remained. Under Chiang's régime, however, political activities, slogans, and processions against foreign imperialism were considered both "useless and dangerous."[45] Arms and laws were required. The imperialists, Chiang claimed, feared a strong, united central government; and a sound body of laws would not only protect private property and lives but would also remove the foreigners' excuses for preventing the abolition of the unequal treaties. Following this policy, the Kuomintang claimed to have passed an average of one hundred clauses of new laws per day in the course of a single year. Chiang, it was clear, had firmly committed the Kuomintang to reconstruction without proclaiming class war and to domestic pacification before resistance to foreign foes.

In spite of Chiang's reassuring political stance, the façade of law-making and constitution-writing left British observers unimpressed. In summarizing these activities the Far Eastern Department noted that they created "a perfect maze of words signifying . . . little or nothing."[46] Nevertheless the Kuomintang had established a government structure which in its formal appearance was not entirely dissimilar to Western models. (See Chart 1.) In addition to the central apparatus with its cabinet portfolios, there were twenty-four provincial governors who at least nominally were members of the Kuomintang and nominally owed their allegiance to and received their appointments from Nanking. This appearance of central authority made it possible for Chiang and foreigners alike to maintain the pretense that Nanking was already a truly national government.

Flimsy though his constitutional façade might be, Chiang Kai-shek was energetic in using the resources of central China and the prestige which the national government derived from recognition by the powers in order to undermine his rivals. Japanese expansion into the northeast, with which Chiang was seeking to come to terms, had already neutralized some of the northern provincial warlords. By his "bandit suppression" or anti-communist campaigns in central China, Chiang was successful in penetrating many of the other provinces with his well-equipped, German-trained army. He defeated a southern separatist régime in Fukien province early

---

[45]P. Cavendish, "Anti-imperialism in the Kuomintang 1923-1928," in Jerome Ch'en and N. Tarling, *Studies in the Social History of China and South-East Asia* (Cambridge: Cambridge University Press, 1970), pp. 23-56.

[46]Ronald Hall, Minute, 9 February 1935, FO 19306/F760.

in 1934, and later that year Mao Tse-tung's Soviet government was dislodged from Kiangsi province. As the Chinese Communist party trekked across China on its Long March to a new base in the northwest, Chiang seized the opportunity to establish his authority in Kweichow, Yunnan, Szechuan, and Shensi provinces. By mid-1936 Kwangtung's military governor went into exile after being out-manoeuvred by Chiang, and with Canton firmly in Chiang's control the power base of the mandarins in the Kwangtung-Kwangsi southwest Political Council, the most powerful and persistent critics of Nanking from within the Kuomintang, was at last broken.

According to accounts reaching British ears, Chiang used diverse systems and tactics to strengthen his authority at the county and village levels. Administrative reform through special commissioners and the revival of the *pao-chia* or ten-family guarantee system to control population movement were combined with moral exhortation by the launching of a New Life Movement in 1934. Quoting the canons of Confucianism, Chiang declared that the people must adopt a spirit of diligence, thrift, asceticism, and endurance to counteract the state of "ruin, dissolution and collapse."[47] Political terrorism was also part of his arsenal to pacify the country. One of the vehicles for such activity was the Blue Shirt Society, organized among young men who admired fascism and who "advocated assassination and terrorism." The Blue Shirts swore personal allegiance to Chiang and were used ruthlessly to "eliminate radicalism of all description" and also to "assassinate personal or political enemies."[48] On more than one occasion Chiang Kai-shek denied the existence of his fascist Blue Shirt party, but from the special branch reports of the Shanghai Municipal Police, British ambassadors had no doubt of its existence. They offered no judgments but felt that it was a matter "of great interest" since it was directed by Chiang Kai-shek himself.

In spite of these measures for tighter control from the centre, British officials noted that civil disorders continued at a high level, and the financial resources and efficiency of the national government did not improve noticeably. Personal corruption and self-seeking were rampant. As John Chaplin of the Far Eastern Department read incoming reports on the

[47]Cadogan to Simon, 10 July 1934, FO 18152/F4157; also A. L. Scott, "Revival of Confucianism," 14 February 1935, FO 19320/F991; John Alexander (Tientsin), "Memorandum on the Pao-Chia System," 3 October 1935, FO 676/223.

[48]Information on the Blue Shirts is in various files; for 1933, FO 17142/File 6170; "Annual Report on China, 1934," para 21, FO 19325; for 1935, FO 19325/File 375; Clark Kerr Papers, FO 800/299. For a recent discussion of Chiang's terror tactics see Lloyd Eastman, "Fascism in Kuomintang China: The Blue Shirts," *China Quarterly* 49 (March 1972): 1-31.

subject, he concluded that corruption was so pervasive that talking to the high officials of China about dishonesty in government was like "wind in the horse's ear."[49] While it has since become widely accepted by Western scholars that Kuomintang political cliques were building personal fortunes, British officials believed, even at that time, that the Chiang, Kung, and Soong families were using their official positions to engage in "scandalous speculations in exchange, Government bonds and cotton yarn" and to accumulate wealth for deposit in such banks as the National City Bank of New York.[50]

In areas where the peasants had turned to the Communists, the national government had to meet special problems. This theme was explained to members of the British cabinet by Sir Frederick Leith-Ross, chief economic adviser to the government, upon his return from China in 1936 after nearly a year's visit. According to Leith-Ross, the Communist leaders showed "considerable enlightenment" in their administration of rural areas. They divided up the land in economic holdings and raised the standard of living "at the expense, of course, of the landlords." When government troops restored control, the landlords came back and, with the help of local magistrates, tried to restore all the paraphernalia of the old régime. This created bitter discontent. The national government was trying to cope with the situation, but conditions varied greatly from province to province, and Leith-Ross thought it would be difficult to adopt any uniform plan, especially as any reforms in land tenure "will be opposed by the vested interests . . . among whom the local military leaders are generally to be found."[51]

By any ordinary standards, the background of massive peasant discontent, ruthless factionalism and corruption within the ruling élite, tendencies to regional autonomy, and the pressure of foreign aggression would have meant that prospects for a stable, central government headed by a personal military dictatorship were not impressive. However, British officials in China were not prone to adopt a gloomy attitude. The views of British officials on this score were conditioned by two factors: comparisons with the previous twenty years of warlordism in China and the absence of any suitable alternative to Chiang. Chiang Kai-shek, in their view, had shown himself to be "a more enlightened patriot than any other similar military leader"; he had collected around him a number of able and

[49]Minute, 27 December 1935, FO 19248/F7936.

[50]Leith-Ross, "Notes," 19 December 1935, FO 19248/F7936; G. S. Moss (Hankow, confidential), 28 June 1935, FO 19307/F5493; Leith Ross, "Record of Conversation with Dr. Stampar," 19 June 1936, FO 20250/F3599; Cyril Rogers (Bank of England) to Clark Kerr, 3 March 1938, FO 800/274, no. 100.

[51]Leith-Ross, "Notes," 25 July 1936, FO 20218; C.P. 251 (36), 29 September 1936, CAB 24/264.

intelligent men, and it was considered that the "political aims of his Government" were "in advance of anything which China has seen before."[52] Based on the premise that Chiang was not an ordinary warlord, British officials, unlike their more pessimistic American colleagues,[53] were cautiously optimistic that China would become a united and well-ordered country. It was on the basis of this perspective that the British government tried to encourage or create openings for British enterprise in the Chinese economy.

Accurate and up to date information about the trend of China's economy, no less than her political development, was important to Britain because, as a *Times* leader correctly declared on 5 May 1935: "More British money is invested in China than in any other foreign [i.e., outside the British Empire] country and British industries supply the greatest share of Chinese imports of manufactured goods." The Foreign Office lacked any precise accounting of British investments in China, but the sum generally quoted in interdepartmental correspondence was £300 million (U.S. $1,500 million). More conservative estimates placed it at £250 million. But such information as was available gave British officials the impression of an "overwhelmingly preponderant interest of the United Kingdom" in China proper as compared to other countries.[54]

Available knowledge about the state of the Chinese economy was not such as to inspire confidence, at least not at first sight. The verdict of the famous British economist, Sir Arthur Salter, who visited China in 1931 and again in 1933-34, first as a League of Nations expert and then as an adviser to the Chinese government,[55] was that the general trend of China's economic system, six years after the Kuomintang took power, was still "downward." Salter's report, "China and the Depression," was read care-

---

[52]Ibid.

[53]See Dorothy Borg, *The United States and the Far Eastern Crisis of 1933-1938* (Cambridge, Mass.: Harvard University Press, 1964), especially chapter 2 and James Thomson, *While China Faced West* (Cambridge, Mass.: Harvard University Press, 1969), pp. 27-34.

[54]Charles W. Orde, Minute, 23 January 1934, FO 18078/F414. See Table 6 for trend and distribution of British investment in China.

[55]Salter recalled his visit to China in *Slave of the Lamp* (London: Weidenfeld and Nicholson, 1967) and wrote that he felt uncomfortably that Chiang was looking for a "simple magic formula" from an economist, "without the tiresome balancing of the material resources available" (p. 110). Salter became professor of politics at Oxford in 1934; he was also a member of the cabinet's confidential Economic Advisory Committee, composed of eight other influential economists, including J. M. Keynes, Sir Josiah Stamp, and G. D. H. Cole (Cab 46[34], 12 December 1934, CAB 23/80). According to Salter, the advice of the EAC was so secret it was unable to influence City opinion or overcome the equally secret advice being given to the government by the Bank of England.

fully by both business and government in Britain. By way of comparison, India, with similar congestion of population but fewer natural resources, had, according to Salter, "attained a standard of living more than twice as high as that of China." In China, a general distress had been caused by abnormal floods and external and civil wars. In addition, "symptoms of a general decline" were to be seen in the diminution of small ownership, the breakdown of the landlord and tenant system, the abnormal fall in the value of land, the forced economy in the use of fertilizers, the reduced transport of goods, the breakdown of the mechanism of credit, and reports of falling trade in all districts. Also, though needing capital development more than almost any country, China was being "decapitalized." More capital was leaving the country in respect of past foreign loans and investments than was coming in in the form of new transactions. Instead of capital flowing into the interior, even there the narrow margin of production over consumption was "being drained into the maritime ports for unproductive safety."[56]

In spite of the symptoms of decline, however, Salter advanced the notion that deliberate efforts being made by the Nanking government for "economic reconstruction" would create the fundamental conditions required to encourage the flow of capital to productive enterprise. In his opinion, because of China's natural resources and large, industrious population capable of living and working "under conditions of bare existence," the possibilities of Chinese development "even within the near future" were very great.

The main indicators of China's economic development by which these somewhat heartening views of Salter's could be judged were its financial administration, foreign trade, industrialization, and rural development. The budgets of the central and provincial governments gave an imperfect picture of the country's finances. Some large departments of the government, such as railways and communications, kept their own accounts. There was also manipulation of the accounts by various authorities. In some provinces, such as Yunnan, nothing in the nature of a budget existed and taxpayers had to be content "with items of information used to fill up space in the newspapers."[57] Such informal and irregular practices led to considerable uncertainty about the actual condition of China's financial administration.

Quite apart from the unreliable statistical data, however, there was no mistaking the fact that the Nanking government had a narrow financial

[56]Salter, "China and the Depression," *Economist*, Supplement, 19 May 1834, pp. 2, 16.
[57]Harold I. Harding (Yunnanfu) to Simon, 18 October 1935, FO 19333/File 3928.

base on which to exercise the functions of a central government. It received the maritime customs revenue, part of the salt tax, and the consolidated tax on such items as tobacco, flour, cotton yarn, matches, cement, and wine. About 50 per cent of this income was spent on military requirements. This military expenditure, together with payments for loans and indemnities to foreign countries, accounted for about 80 per cent of the national revenue, leaving a bare 20 per cent for subsidies to the provincial governments and other general civilian expenditures.[58] In view of such circumstances, potential British investors were aware of the strong temptation of the Chinese government to fritter away any loans for daily budgetary rather than constructive purposes.

It was known, of course, that there were a number of items not on any government budget sheets which nevertheless bore on its financial standing. One of these was the cultivation and sale of opium, theoretically illegal but officially permitted, which was a lucrative source of funds. British consuls on the Yangtze River reported that during General Chiang Kai-shek's periodic tours all opium dens, especially those under the control of rival politicians, were "closed in theory" and "a few women and troops were variously reported to have been shot here and there for the sake of appearances."[59] But the transport of opium on the river was "conducted in gunboats" under the Opium Suppression Superintendence Bureau, and the proceeds of the traffic were "remitted direct to General Chiang's Field Headquarters at Nanch'ang."[60]

In spite of these and other distasteful features, British officials did not feel that corruption in government would be fatal to the financial modernization of China. It would only add to the overhead.[61] This confidence was based partly on their belief in the ability of Chiang's brother-in-law, T. V. Soong, and partly on the fact that China obligingly adopted a unified paper currency system based on a sterling standard of exchange and employed Cyril Rogers of the Bank of England to help establish a Currency Control Board.

The most remarkable thing about the external trade of China was its smallness. Although China contained over one-fifth of the world's population, her share of the world's foreign trade was only 2 per cent. With the

[58]Cadogan to Sir Samuel Hoare, 26 July 1935, FO 19243/F4855 (Hoare replaced Simon as foreign secretary in June 1935). See also Salter, "China and the Depression," p. 10; Department of Overseas Trade, *Trade and Economic Conditions in China 1933-1935* (London: H.M.S.O., 1933-37), p. 68.

[59]John W. Davidson (Chungking) to Cadogan, 3 June 1935, FO 19303/F3591.

[60]Sir William M. Hewlett (Hankow) to Simon, 29 November 1934, FO 18084/F7057.

[61]Leith-Ross to Fisher (secret), 4 October 1935, T 160/620.

pre-modern sector of her economy still producing 97.8 per cent of the domestic product in 1933,[62] Frank Ashton-Gwatkin, the economic expert of the Foreign office, noted that China was still a "low organism country" which could survive with a minimum of foreign trade.[63] It was this ability of China to survive without much external trade which had formerly made it impossible for British merchants to convince the government to take a stronger position in China. China had never contributed more than 2 per cent to the total volume of Britain's world trade and only had 5.9 per cent of the overseas investments of British subjects.[64] Although "the China dream, dear to all mercantile hearts of a fabulous market for trade and enterprise" had supposedly faded before World War I,[65] it reappeared very much alive in the 1930's. In some respects the views of large British firms and government officials had come closer together. This convergence of view was born of trade rivalries with Germany, Japan, and the United States in the China market, and it was fostered by the Depression which began in 1929. Britain was gradually lagging behind the others. (See Table 2.) Sir Victor Wellesley, an assistant under-secretary of state, has written that Britain's competitors appreciated the fact that by the close interlocking of finance, industry, and the state, a weapon could be forged that might penetrate British commercial pre-eminence and indeed had succeeded in "capturing many a British market."[66] With the position of the British economy relative to other industrialized countries weaker than ever, it was easier for a strong pressure group offering markets and employment for Englishmen to present its case as being in the general interest. Although China was virtually closed as a market for high-priced British textiles and consumer goods, it was considered to be an enormous potential outlet for heavy industrial and communications equipment and other capital goods which could be sold through local and national Chinese government agencies.

Detailed information on the industrial development in Kuomintang China was almost non-existent. But unofficial studies indicated that industrial capacity was still of modest dimensions and at a relatively primitive stage of organization, with the possible exception of Shanghai. Development of industry was retarded by various factors. Among these were the low purchasing power of the congested peasant population, which limited the

[62]A. Feuerwerker, *The Chinese Economy, 1912-1949* (Ann Arbor: University of Michigan Press, 1968), pp. 16-17.

[63]Ashton-Gwatkin, Minute, 28 May 1934, FO 18047/F3112.

[64]Pratt, Minute, 16 January 1934, FO 18160/F295; also Hoare, Minute, 23 June 1935, FO 19287/F4296.

[65]Pelcovits, *Old China Hands*, p. 300.

[66]Wellesley, *Diplomacy in Fetters* (London: Hutchinson, 1944), p. 23.

size of the domestic market, the anti-dumping legislation which export industries faced in foreign countries, and the scarcity of capital in relation to the scale of China's needs.

Although the outlook for exports of British capital goods to China seemed promising, potential investors had a number of questions: on what terms would foreign capital be attracted to China? Could the foreign investor participate in management and be assured of non-discriminatory taxation? Was the development of heavy industry in China prompted by China's economic needs or mainly by military considerations? Was industrial development to be undertaken by private interests or by organs of government or by both? Undoubtedly in an effort to slow down a developing trend in China, British officials stated quite openly that, except for railways and public utilities, they preferred fewer government projects and greater scope for private enterprise. Private interests, they warned, would "hesitate to compete" in cement works, breweries, sugar refineries, paper mills, oil refineries, chemical works, and general trading organizations where "various official bodies" in China had already begun activity.[67]

The most important problem in China's economy arose from the fact that over 300 million peasants lived "in a state of great distress,"[68] even by the standards of a country the bulk of whose population had always been on a level of bare subsistence. The poverty of China's masses not only retarded much needed industrialization, but it also bred social instability, political unrest, and communist-led rebellion. It was possible to get a highly favourable view of the scope and success of the Nanking government's National Economic Council and its work for peasant welfare from various reports and publications.[69] Occasionally, as papers on rural reconstruction efforts passed through the Far Eastern Department of the Foreign Office, they were minuted to the effect that the Chinese and their League of Nations' experts seemed to be accomplishing some good work. In the main, however, claims made in these reports were seen to be superficial and exaggerated. This negative point of view was forced on British officials by

[67]Department of Overseas Trade, *Report on Economic and Commercial Conditions in China, April 1935–March 1937* (London: H.M.S.O., 1937), p. 42.

[68]Salter, "China and the Depression," p. 2.

[69]For example: National Economic Council of China, *Annual Report*, 1935; Hong Kong and Shanghai Bank, Annual Report, in the *Economist*, 25 April 1936, speaks of the Chinese government paying careful attention to the peasant population; League of Nations (Geneva), *Report of the Secretary of the Council Committee on his Mission to China, January–May 1935*; National Christian Council of China, *Biennial Report 1933-1935*, in Conference of Missionary Societies, papers, Box El(a), gives a report of the Kiangsi Christian Rural Service Union. Thomson, *While China Faced West*, chapters 3 to 5, gives a full critical account of Christian efforts in Kiangsi.

the persistent, if self-interested, complaints of British oil and chemical companies that government monopolies in kerosene and fertilizers were being set up "under the guise of co-operative societies."[70] Confidential reports of League of Nations' experts confirmed these complaints. Government sponsored co-operatives in Kiangsi Province, supposedly a model area, were "a ramp, pure and simple" operated for the benefit of Nanking officials. These officials had made some parks in villages, but had done nothing to improve the basic lot of the peasants in the formerly communist held area: the landlords and their agents were all back again. Chiang Kai-shek had not been able to answer their argument that they wanted some return "for having helped to finance his campaigns."[71] Tenant farmers were once again obliged to pay between 60 and 70 per cent of their produce in rent, and the people were "ripe for rebellion." British diplomatic officers in Nanking endorsed the views from Kiangsi, saying that they were shared by all who "have studied the question at all closely." Distressing as this picture of farming life was, it was "accurate" and would apply equally well "to conditions in almost any of the other provinces in Central China."[72]

By almost any measuring stick, the general prospects for economic progress in Kuomintang China were far from bright, and yet official British observers tended to advance the view that China was already entering a new, formative period of great potentialities. This British attitude was conditioned in the first place by the fact that most foreign interests were situated in the coastal treaty ports, which were relatively more prosperous than the rest of China. The profits which could be generated in the treaty ports, from industry and land speculation, fed illusions about the general state of affairs in the country. Secondly, it was a generally acknowledged, although inexplicable, fact that China's economy had displayed unsuspected vitality throughout her long history. The same vitality was undoubtedly still at work, even if modern statistical data was lacking to prove it. The dynamic factor was the common man of China. In spite of his poverty and misery, the ordinary Chinese made a striking impression on British observers. The "endurance, efficiency and intelligence" of the Chinese worker, wrote Sir Victor Wellesley from second-hand knowledge, made him better fitted than any other to weather economic strain.[73] Finally, a good deal of wishful thinking was undoubtedly related to the desire,

[70]Cadogan to Hoare, 23 December 1935, FO 19327/F7989.
[71]George S. Moss (Hankow) to Sir Anthony Eden, 18 February 1936, FO 20260/F2543 (Eden replaced Hoare as foreign secretary in December 1935).
[72]Robert G. Howe (Peking) to Orde (confidential), 5 May 1936, FO 20260/F2543.
[73]Wellesley, *Diplomacy in Fetters*, pp. 139-40.

reinforced by the great depression in Europe, to find justification for expanding the existing British investment in China.

From the political viewpoint, British observers believed that China's leaders were regaining confidence in themselves and that they acted as if they knew that China could never be permanently beaten or overrun. While the development of Chinese independence inevitably implied the loss of certain British privileges, this trend was not entirely unwelcome, especially as the Nanking leaders were apparently receiving British advisers with the greatest good will. The opinion was held that as long as Chiang Kai-shek personally remained in good health and continued to be amenable to British advice, the prospects for law and order in China would be favourable.

Faith in an individual was a frail reed on which to support British interests and prestige. But if Chiang, who as an octogenarian in the 1970's was still presiding over his rump government in the province of Taiwan, had been left alone by the Japanese, it is possible that British confidence in the survival of his régime, at least for a decade or two, might not have been misplaced. The efforts of the British government to come to an understanding with Japan over China, an important factor in British calculations at the time, are the subject of a later chapter. But in the spring of 1933, progress in direct negotiations between China and Japan to settle their differences over Manchuria gave British observers a comfortable though false sense of optimism that Chiang could safely concentrate his energies on putting down internal discontent and turn to the reconstruction of China's domestic scene.

2

Pressures in the China Market
after the Tangku Truce of 1933

When it became clear in the spring of 1933 that no outside help, from either the League of Nations or the United States, would be forthcoming to save Manchuria, the Chinese government entered into secret negotiations with the Japanese for a settlement. The result was a truce signed in the North China town of Tangku which brought a respite in Sino-Japanese hostilities.

The implications of more relaxed relations between China and Japan soon became the subject of anxious thought in British circles. The new period of "peace" appeared to have as many uncertainties and difficulties as the former condition of war. Prominent nationalist-minded Chinese financiers led by Finance Minister T. V. Soong began pressing Western countries for capital investment and technical assistance in order to check Japan. The Japanese, meanwhile, developed their own pro-Japan faction in Nanking around Premier Wang Ching-wei and enunciated a policy of "White Hands Off China," or an Asiatic Monroe Doctrine as they preferred to call it, in a bid to exclude all Western financial and political influence from China. Faced by these conflicting pressures, interested British observers divided on whether to side with the Chinese nationalists or go along with a Japanese re-ordering of the Chinese market.

When the British Minister, Sir Miles Lampson, learned in a secret meeting at his country cottage near Peking that the Nanking government was going to seek an armistice with Japan, he congratulated the emissaries of the Chinese cabinet for their moral courage. Claiming to be "an impartial friend of China," Lampson assured them that in spite of the humiliation involved and the noisy opposition to be expected from their own country-men, China would not forfeit the moral support of the League of Nations or the Western powers. He advised the Nanking government to drop the question of the Manchurian provinces tacitly for the time being and con-centrate on internal reconstruction. For the moment there was little alterna-tive. He went on to suggest that if China refrained from giving cause for further fighting and consequent encroachments on Chinese soil, time was on her side.[1] This advice not to resist was ambiguous. It was possible that if China acquiesced time might be on the side of the Japanese, who had a growing ambition to co-ordinate the "reconstruction" of China.[2]

The actual terms of the Tangku Truce of 31 May 1933 revealed it to be a purely local military agreement calling for the withdrawal of regular Chinese army forces from a demilitarized zone south of the Great Wall, which included the large Sino-British Kailan coal mining company. With-drawal was to be supervised by Japanese army units who, together with the other powers under the Boxer Protocol of 1901, now had military garrisons in areas of China from which Chinese regular forces were ex-cluded. The published clauses of the truce omitted any reference to political or economic questions.[3] This was an important omission whose long range significance lay in the pattern which it established for further Japanese penetration of China over the next five years. Outbreaks of friction between Chinese and Japanese groups would continue to be treated as local matters, supposedly not involving the authority of the central government in Nan-king. Also, since political matters were not mentioned in the truce, local Japanese army commanders were often able to arrogate to themselves full powers to deal with such questions in the demilitarized zone, while both Nanking and Tokyo could disclaim any responsibility. The "non-political" character of the Tangku Truce allowed Tokyo to pretend that it was not assuming any special position in contravention of the Nine Power Treaty, and at the same time it enabled Nanking to claim to its domestic critics that it had granted no special concessions. Because of the ill-defined and covert nature of the Tangku settlement, foreign diplomats found it more difficult to estimate the true state of Sino-Japanese relationships thereafter.

---

[1]Lampson to Simon, 7 and 19 July 1933, FO 17062/F4566 and FO 17058/F4788.

[2]During the autumn of 1933, the Japanese cabinet decided to promote political de-centralization in North China by organizing local governments which excluded the Kuomintang and using military force if necessary. See J. B. Crowley, *Japan's Quest for Autonomy* (Princeton: Princeton University Press, 1966), pp. 192-95.

[3]Partial terms of the truce appear in the *China Year Book 1934*; see also an item of 19 July 1933, FO 17057/F4788. References to secret negotiations on political and economic matters are in Annual Report, China, 1933, 1 January 1934, FO 18142/F1261. See also T. A. Bisson, *Japan in China* (New York: Macmillan, 1938), pp. 44-51.

The elements of the British commercial community in China which held views on the proper policy which British diplomacy should now adopt toward China were grouped into several organizations. Apart from the traditional Chambers of Commerce, the most important groups were the China Association and the Shanghai British Resident's Association. There was some overlapping of membership in all these organizations, but the latter two in particular tended to represent separate constituencies with definite viewpoints.

The more militant British Resident's Association was organized in 1932 to promote the view that the strong hand of Japan was the best solution to chaos in China.[4] In its meetings and literature, the BRA voiced the frustrations of the great majority of foreign businessmen about the irregularities of life in China. They feared the mass movements, boycotts, labour disturbances, and similar actions by organized or semi-organized bodies, sometimes created at the instigation or with the support of the authorities, which often ended in large sums being paid by whoever was attacked. In the opinion of prominent British merchants, these situations arose from the inability or unwillingness of the Chinese authorities to control their own people or to provide protection to foreign property.[5] Land values were falling in Shanghai in the 1930's, and the BRA was alarmed that Chinese demands for greater participation in the municipal government and the courts within the sanctuary of the International Settlement at Shanghai would aggravate the situation and eventually undermine the great wealth built up under the security of extraterritorial protection. According to the BRA, an "almost ceaseless flow of concessions" by the British Foreign Office to the Chinese Nationalists since the *December Memorandum* of 1926 was "scoffed at" by Chinese and Japanese alike as being the outward and visible sign of lack of power to afford adequate protection to British interests. The ideology of the BRA was: why give up anything we have got before we have to?[6] The proper course for Britain was to resume the lead by joining hands with the Nipponese "whom we all admire as a similar small island Empire."[7] On a visit to Shanghai,

[4]G. W. Swire to N. S. Brown, 5 May 1933, Swire—1082 and S. F. Mayers (British and Chinese Corporation), Memorandum dated 1932, in D. G. M. Bernard (Matheson and Co.) to Foreign Office, 19 July 1935, FO 19243/F4813. For earlier precedents for this kind of militant group, see Pelcovits, *Old China Hands*, chapter 9.

[5]G. E. Mitchell (Shanghai) to Leith-Ross, 19 November 1935, Swire—China and Japan, 1935, no. 55.

[6]J. S. Scott, to G. W. Swire, 14 April 1933, Swire—D.N.O.E. Scott was quoting H. G. Woodhead, described as "the oracle and dictator of British policy" in Shanghai.

[7]Ranald MacDonald, Chairman, BRA, Report to 3rd Annual Meeting, 6 December 1934, encl. in Cadogan to Simon, 6 February 1935, FO 19319/F823.

the British ambassador to Tokyo noticed that H. G. Woodhead, the "ablest British journalist in Shanghai," was really "a Japanese propagandist," and he found that the British community was "anti-Chinese and more inclined to be pro-Japanese" because the Japanese "at least get things done."[8]

The BRA claimed to have signed up almost half of the six thousand British subjects in Shanghai, and it had a small committee in London with a political agent, O. M. Green, former editor of the *North China Daily News*, to keep in touch with members of Parliament. In the course of one parliamentary session, at a time when China had "ceased to be 'front page' news in the British press,"[9] the BRA inspired thirty-seven questions on British policy in China in the House of Commons. The BRA was confirmed in its enthusiasm for this type of action when an official of the British Treasury told a firm of China merchants that the only way to make sure of moving the Foreign Office was to ask "five similar questions in the House of Commons on five consecutive days."[10] The BRA spoke of the China sub-committee of the Foreign Affairs Committee of the Conservative party as its parliamentary group. Through this committee, whose membership was around twenty, the BRA felt it could not only get continuous publicity in the House of Commons but also secure direct access to the foreign secretary without having to go through the permanent officials at the Foreign Office. The BRA reported to its members that when Anthony Eden, the junior minister at the Foreign Office, received a deputation in July 1933, he gave an "unsolicited assurance" that Britain was "certainly not giving up anything in China" and that the government regarded China "as one of their most important problems."[11]

As a ginger group, the BRA irritated the Foreign Office. But the latter was not unduly concerned by this agitation of "irresponsible die-hards"[12] because they represented the moribund, smaller merchant firms whose interests were confined to Shanghai and who wanted to cling blindly to outworn provisions of extraterritoriality. A much more influential group of British interests held that, in spite of its importance, Shanghai was not China. These were the "big *China* firms" who were critical of the narrow

[8]Sir Robert Clive to Vansittart, 1 September 1936, FO 20241/F156.

[9]*Oriental Affairs* (January 1934): 32.

[10]G. E. Mitchell to G. W. Swire, 1 November 1935, quoting E. L. Hall-Patch, Swire—1083.

[11]"Reports and Speeches, 2nd Annual General Meeting, British Residents Association of China," 5 December 1933, Swire—China and Japan, 1933-34, no. 53.

[12]Pratt, Minute, 6 November 1935, FO 18129/F6614.

and short-sighted "treaty-port complex"[13] prevalent in Shanghai. Small merchant venturers might find satisfaction and security within the confines of the treaty ports and appreciate the restraints which the Japanese army placed on Chinese ambitions, but the big firms were determined to expand their operations into the interior where Chinese good will and co-operation were essential. The big China firms consisted of large manufacturing houses, financial institutions, shipping companies, and great selling organizations that had established agencies in the interior with elaborate machinery for the distribution of kerosene oil, cigarettes, dyes, soap, sugar, and other products throughout the country. The five leading firms in this group, in addition to the prosperous Hongkong and Shanghai Banking Corporation,[14] were the Asiatic Petroleum Co. (North and South China) Ltd. (a subsidiary of Shell B.P.), the British-American Tobacco Co. (China) Ltd., Imperial Chemical Industries (China) Ltd., Jardine, Matheson and Co. Ltd., and John Swire and Sons Ltd. These firms were wealthy, politically active in China, and well-connected in London. They had become the inner circle of the China Association, an organization formed in 1889 in order to "represent, express and give effect to the opinion of the British Mercantile Community in their political and commercial relations with the Chinese and Japanese."[15]

Like the BRA, the China Association paid keen attention to party political connections and considered itself fortunate to have the Rt. Hon. Lord Winterton, chairman of the China sub-committee of the Foreign Affairs Committee of the Conservative party, as its president. Lord Winterton was in a position to contact his friend Sir Samuel Hoare and say that when there was "real justification for such action," he would be approaching the foreign secretary personally, since many aspects of "delicate" Sino-British relations could not be discussed by question and answer in the House of Commons without doing harm.[16] Lord Winterton claimed to the China Association that he had managed "to effect and affect certain desirable changes" in the attitude of the Foreign Office to far eastern

---

[13]J. Swire and Sons to Butterfield and Swire (Shanghai), 8 December 1933, Swire— 1082; and G. W. Swire to Captain A. L. Kennedy (*The Times*, Foreign and Imperial Department), 18 July 1933, Swire—1074.

[14]F. C. Mathieson and Sons, *Stock Exchange London and Provincial Ten-Year Record* (London: Mathieson and Sons, 1940) shows that while Barclay's, Midland, and Lloyds Banks were paying 14 to 16 per cent per annum dividends in the 1930's, the Hongkong and Shanghai Bank was paying from 45 to 116 per cent per annum.

[15]China Association, *Objects, Rules and Regulations*, rev. ed. (London, 1958), p. 2; see Pelcovits, *Old China Hands*, chapter 6, for the early history of the China Association.

[16]Winterton to Hoare, 8 July 1935, FO 19300/F4370.

affairs.[17] Evidence to substantiate the claim is lacking, but it is probable that his position gave added prestige to the association. As a matter of tactics, the China Association itself did not indulge in public criticism of the government. It prized its close relationship with the Foreign Office which allowed for the exchange of mutual confidences.

The controlling centre of the China Association was its London committee, which had about 60 firms and 250 individuals as members, as well as branches in Hong Kong and Shanghai. The London committee employed two full-time executive secretaries who provided a variety of services: correspondence with the Foreign Office about commercial grievances in China; quarterly political summaries of Chinese domestic and international affairs for the members; translations of the Chinese press; contact with the Chinese embassy; preparations for semi-annual receptions and dinners in London, at which leading political personages were invited to speak; and occasional tours of China. The China Association responded to criticism that it was out of touch with reality in China by streamlining its executive committee. Although sensitive to charges of being "run by the big interests," a small committee, "uniform in character," was justified on the grounds that the former static situation in China had been replaced by "kaleidoscopic" political and commercial changes and conditions were "very much more competitive than they used to be."[18]

With the preoccupations of the larger companies centred on expansion into the interior of China, the inner circle of the China Association in London was determined to sidetrack the pro-Japanese BRA and smother its "fundamentally foolish and wrong"[19] attitudes to the Chinese and the Nanking government. While it could be shown that many of the big firms later tried individually to come to terms with competing Japanese companies, the China Association as a collective body and its inner councils increasingly condemned Japan's aggressive policy.[20] And since the only barrier to Japanese encroachment was an effective Chinese government

---

[17]Winterton to E. M. Gull, 19 May 1936, G. C. Papers (1936), p. 136.

[18]D. G. M. Bernard to G. W. Swire, 29 October 1935, Swire—1075 and A. W. Burkill, Memorandum, G. C. Papers (1933), p. 384; Bernard, G. C. Papers (1934) pp. 102ff.

[19]J. S. Scott to G. W. Swire, 23 February 1933, Swire—D.N.O.E. and J. W. Swire and Sons to Butterfield and Swire, 2 August 1935, copies to Matheson, British-American Tobacco, Asiatic Petroleum, Imperial Chemical Industries, and Lionel Curtis.

[20]For example: Cadogan to Hoare, 27 January 1936, re ICI, FO 405/275, no. 22; G. E. Mitchell to J. Swire and Sons, 7 October 1938, describing how Jardine, Matheson and Co., by making approaches to the Japanese, were "nailing their colours to the fence" in the Sino-Japanese dispute, Swire—1084; Bernard, Report to Annual General Meeting, 13 May, 1936, G. C. Papers (1936).

and a consequent stiffening of Chinese passive resistance,[21] leading officers of the China Association were increasingly critical of the Foreign Office for its policy of drift and inactivity.

A minority within the Foreign Office agreed with the Shanghai British Resident's Association that it was useless to rely on any Chinese government because the Chinese were constitutionally incapable of governing themselves. If left to themselves, their future lay in the direction of anarchy. This minority believed that it was in the common interest that Japan should intervene and create the kind of order which would mean increased commercial opportunities for all. The prevailing Foreign Office opinion, however, agreed with the China Association that Japan was the main danger. There would be no future for British influence east of Singapore if China came under Japanese control, and British interests would be extinguished in that part of the globe. Judging from the previous forty years, there was little doubt that the "reactionary and military circles" in Japan, as Ambassador Lampson called them,[22] were aiming at the domination of the whole of China.

It was one thing to be clear-eyed about the fate which awaited China and British Far Eastern interests at the hands of Japan, but it was a more difficult matter to propose useful counter measures. Sir Miles Lampson, one of the chief advocates of consessions by the British Foreign Office to the Chinese Nationalists since December 1926, was approaching the end of his tour of duty in China by 1933. He was well satisfied with the cordial relations which he had established with the Nanking government, and his chief, Sir Robert Vansittart, generally concurred that Lampson's record in China was "a long and well filled period."[23] But in the face of the new dark cloud blowing over from Japan, Lampson, in one of his last lengthy despatches, composed while on a leisurely cruise through the gorges of the Upper Yangtse River, could only suggest that suitable means be found to help in "the reconstruction and establishment of a stable and really independent Chinese State" which could not be dominated by any other power.[24] He realized that this remedy was vague and inconclusive, but his argument was that in the long run only the Chinese themselves could save China and prevent such a disaster as her domination by Japan. Based on his long experience in China, Lampson had a shrewd intuition that China would prove too big and tough a morsel for anyone to digest.

---

[21]G. W. Swire to N. S. Brown, 5 May 1933, Swire—1082.
[22]Lampson to Simon, 10 August 1933, FO 17081/F5709.
[23]Vansittart, Minute, 17 December 1933, FO 17064/F6991.
[24]Lampson to Simon, 10 August 1933.

The day to day business of foreign policy, however, could not be run on the basis of speculative intuitions. It fell to C. W. Orde, head of the Far Eastern Department and by nature a cautious man, to draw up some interim guidelines from the discussion which the retiring ambassador's final major despatches had initiated. Orde made two propositions, the first being that Britain should work for China's prosperity. In making this suggestion he was implicitly rejecting the idea that China's progress could only be assured by allowing Japan to take the lead. But his second proposal was that Britain should discourage any Chinese resistance to Japan. Orde elaborated on his contradictory proposals by saying that, since China's economic prosperity depended partly on her political unity and military strength, Britain would have to foster China's strength. But any increase in China's strength was clearly distasteful to Japan, and for this reason Britain would have to be very cautious. Since Japan would suspect a political motive in any British financial aid to China, Orde's solution was that such aid would have to be capable of justification from a sound business point of view. He apparently believed, and he was not alone in this idea, that if a foreign investment was profitable in its own right, it was somehow harder or unreasonable or even illegitimate for third parties to offer objections to its presence. In any case it was obvious that Orde believed the initiative in the Far East lay mainly outside British hands. He, like Lampson, was projecting an essentially passive role for British diplomacy—a policy which clearly presaged further dissatisfaction and conflict with British business interests. There was nothing in all this which was deemed worthy of cabinet discussion, but at least on an interim basis Sir Robert Vansittart considered the conclusions of the Far Eastern Department to be timely.[25]

One of the decisive factors influencing the direction of British commercial policy and practice in China was the nationalistic attitude of the Chinese banker-financiers in Shanghai who stood behind the Nanking government. The precise relationship of business and government in China was itself a matter of some conjecture by British officials, but as they understood the matter, it was not a case of socialistic government involvement adopting national planning or attempting to introduce methods "recommended by intellectuals in Geneva and Washington and . . . practised in Moscow. . . ."[26] It seemed rather a case of having the government guarantee essential trades which in present circumstances offered a risk that the

[25]Orde, Minute, 16 September 1933, and Vansittart, Minute, 20 September 1933, FO 17081/F5709.
[26]F. H. Nixon, Notes for the Advisory Committee ECGD, 19 June 1933, FO 17135/F4223.

private trader, foreign or domestic, would not carry. The "inner 'banking-political' group," or bureaucrat-capitalists as Mao Tse-tung named them, operated what one British official called a spreading network of "private enterprise within the Government."[27] In the semi-official monopolies which marketed such products as tea, tin, wolfram, antimony, and wood-oil, at "a comfortable profit,"[28] it was difficult to discover "how much was Government influence and how much . . . the personal interests of the inner banking group."[29] But apart from the possibilities of personal corruption, the aspect which most impressed British observers was the anti-Japanese sentiment of this group and their determination not to lose their grip on the Chinese market.

Of those Chinese capitalists opposed to any accommodation with Japan the outstanding figure was T. V. Soong, minister of finance and brother-in-law of Chiang Kai-shek, considered along with Chiang and Wang Ching-wei to be one of the three most powerful figures in Chinese politics. Soong was personally well regarded by his British contemporaries. He was described as a natural financier who could grasp the essentials of a complex problem "with uncanny rapidity"[30] and a minister of finance "who could have made his mark in any country of the world."[31] Under conditions in Kuomintang China, his "operations in the large corporations . . . built up for him a powerful fortune."[32] According to W. J. Keswick, head of Jardine, Matheson and Co., who became a close friend of his at this time, Soong was more important for British interests than anyone else in China, not only because of his own outlook and dependability but because he was "the essential link between Nanking warlords and politicians and the Che-kiang moneyed men—between the financial structure here in Shanghai and China proper."[33]

In the summer of 1933, Soong went to Europe and America on behalf of his government to attend the World Economic Conference in London and to seek financial aid and technical assistance for China. As a bar-

---

[27]C. Rogers, 28 December 1935, T 188/35; Mao Tse-tung, *Selected Works* (Peking: Foreign Languages Press, 1961), 4:417; W. Kirkpatrick, 2 November 1937, ECGD 1/19.

[28]Butterfield and Swire to J. Swire and Sons, 13 November 1936, T 188/38.

[29]Kirkpatrick, 2 November 1937. On Chinese monopolies see *inter alia* Beale to Crowe, 28 September 1936 and 14 January 1937, T 188/38.

[30]Salter, *Slave of the Lamp*, p. 113.

[31]Leith-Ross, *Money Talks: Fifty Years of International Finance* (London: Hutchinson, 1968), p. 203.

[32]*The Times*, Obituary, 27 April 1971.

[33]Information from interview with W. J. Keswick in London, June 1971 and letter from Ingram (Nanking) to Lampson, 11 May 1933, quoting Keswick, FO 17062/ F4601.

gaining point, prior to leaving China and at the very time the Tangku Truce with Japan was being negotiated, Soong announced a high provisional tariff indicating that China would pursue a policy of economic nationalism common to most other countries in the world. On many items, especially cotton piece goods, the rates were increased by as much as 50 per cent. Although the tariff hit some British commodities, its main force was clearly directed at thwarting Japan and strengthening Chinese textile and other light industries.[34] At the plenary session of the World Economic Conference, Soong described China's underdevelopment and declared that it was the settled aim of his government to increase the consuming power of China and raise living standards and that to do this China would "welcome Western capital and skill." Surely, he declared on 15 June, in a speech which got a better press in London and New York than in Tokyo, it was not beyond the statesmanship of the world to find a form and a method which would satisfy Dr. Sun Yat-sen's ideal of "political and economic independence [for] China" and still afford "Western capital, industry, and commerce a profitable field for development."[35]

While in London, Soong was feted like a visiting head of state. He was given an audience with the King, a visit with the prime minister at Chequers, and on the latter's urgings[36] individual interviews with the most prominent cabinet ministers, as well as conferences with a host of leading City financiers including Montague Norman, governor of the Bank of England, and Sir Charles Addis. Sir Robert Kindersley of Lazard Brothers investment bankers was pleased to accept Soong's appointment as sole purchasing agent for the Nanking government in England. Soong spoke of placing orders worth £8 million for cotton spindles, rails and rolling stock for a new railway into Szechuan Province, and sixteen river and coastal vessels and of plans to improve the iron and steel industry in China, provided credits could be granted for five to ten years.[37] He also talked of forming an international corporation which would be like the Four Power Banking Consortium, except that the Japanese would be left out and China included.[38]

---

[34]FO 17090/file 62 contains details of the new tariff and British reaction, including the decision not to join with Japan in making a formal protest to the Chinese government.

[35]Maze Papers, 9:31-38.

[36]Ramsay MacDonald to Simon, 23 June 1933, MacDonald Papers, Box 2/7, Public Record Office, London; also MacDonald to Addis, 29 July 1933, ibid. MacDonald was "much concerned" and hoped Britain would find "ways and means of backing up Mr. Soong."

[37]Simon to Lampson, 11 August 1933, FO 17136/F5350.

[38]Pratt, Minute, 17 July 1933, FO 17136/F4753.

In spite of his ability "to tell a possible creditor the sort of thing he might like to hear,"[39] Soong was unable to secure a single farthing in financial aid from the City. One reason was that British financiers could find no acceptable security. The only available source of security—revenue from the Chinese maritime customs—had been mortgaged to the Americans by Soong on his way to Europe for a US $50 million loan to buy surplus American wheat and cotton. The British viewed this as a "disgraceful" breach of the spirit of the China Consortium,[40] an organization of the leading British, French, Japanese, and American banks which had come into existence in 1920 on American initiative to prevent any single power from penetrating China and acquiring a sphere of influence by lending. The consortium was headed by Sir Charles Addis of the Hong Kong and Shanghai Bank, which acted for six British banks that had been promised "the complete but not the exclusive support"[41] of the British government in dealing with China. The consortium as such had never been able to float any loans because the Chinese resented loans subject to international tutelage and considered the consortium an impediment to raising money.

Another reason why Soong could not get British aid at this time was that China was in default of existing loans, mostly for railways, to the extent of £40 million. This would not have been an insuperable obstacle since the Nanking government had given proof of its stability in five difficult years, and for the first time in the history of the republic it had a properly balanced budget. The general manager of the Hongkong and Shanghai Bank, V. Grayburn, wanted to drop out of the consortium and make a loan, but the governor of the Bank of England "vaguely threatened" the bank with loss of status and loss of power to issue any further loans to China if they left the consortium.[42] The main stumbling block was that Soong was impervious to British arguments that it was in the Chinese interest to acquiesce tacitly in the Manchukuo régime. For the City of London, Soong's desire to cut Japan out of a share in the foreign financing of China was an impossible policy. The only result would be to "infuriate Japan," and she was quite capable of backing her annoyance "by the use

[39]Nixon, Notes for Advisory Committee.

[40]Pratt, Minute on Lampson to Simon, 1 November 1933, FO 17108/F6895. See Hull, *Memoirs*, 1:274, for the U.S. rejection of a similar Japanese complaint.

[41]Treasury Memorandum 1935, "The China Consortium," T 188/48.

[42]Orde, Minute of conversation with Addis, 30 October 1933, FO 17135/F6845. See also H. Clang (Bank of England) to Leith-Ross, 1 August 1935, T 188/48, for a reiteration of the need for British far eastern banks to keep in step with their potentially more powerful American counterparts.

of force."[43] British capital was "notoriously nervous of such entanglements,"[44] and the Foreign Office supported those who controlled the
money markets in accepting the Japanese veto and in refusing to abandon
the consortium.

Soong was more successful in evading British obstruction over his bid
for technical assistance from the League of Nations. The Chinese government currently had fourteen League experts in China giving advice on
diverse subjects, and Soong requested that someone be sent out to co-
ordinate and give direction to this work. The person he had in mind was
a Pole, Dr. Ludwig Rajchman, Director of the Health Section of the
League of Nations Secretariat, who had already made several visits to
China. Rajchman was admitted by everyone to be a man of prodigious
capacity, enthusiasm, and intelligence. The only difficulty in the eyes of
the British government was that he had aroused the opposition of the
Japanese because of his undoubted sympathy for the Chinese point of
view. Such a man was bound to be a thorn in the side, but since the
Chinese had sent for Rajchman to be "their chief political adviser" and
because he wielded such great influence in China, the Foreign Office wired
to Geneva its concurrence with Rajchman's appointment.[45]

Following British approval, Dr. Rajchman called at the Far Eastern
Department of the Foreign Office and talked with Sir John Pratt. In
response to Pratt's question as to what advice he planned to give the
Chinese government, Rajchman replied that they "ought to tighten up the
boycott as much as possible . . . keep up the strongest possible resistance
to Japanese aggression in North China . . . and encourage a sense of national unity." Unless resistance to Japan were kept up, he said, Chinese
unity would disintegrate. The only two alternatives in China were the
present "camp" or communism. If the latter prevailed, China would break
up in chaos and confusion; this would be a disaster to the whole world
and everything possible should be done to avert it. The powers, according
to Rajchman, would have to strengthen China in her struggle against
Japan, not by money and munitions but by internal strengthening, reform,
and administrative modernization.[46]

Anthony Eden was filled "with alarm" when he heard of Rajchman's
views about Chinese resistance to Japan in the spring of 1933. He

---

[43]Pratt, Minute on Addis to Wellesley, 17 July 1933, FO 17136/F4779. For
Japanese veto of Soong plan for an International Corporation minus Japan, see D.
Nohara (Yokohama Specie Bank Ltd.) to Addis, 31 July 1933, ibid.
[44]Pratt, Minute, 11 August 1933, FO 17128/F5376.
[45]Pratt, Minute, 22 March 1933, FO 17127/file 1842.
[46]Pratt, Minute, 25 March 1933, ibid.

considered it an improper attitude for a League official and would "give a lot" to stop Rajchman from going to China.[47] Fear of heavy trouble in Parliament and from Dr. Soong made it impossible for the British government to withdraw its approval of the Rajchman appointment, but Eden and Vansittart asked Sir Eric Drummond, secretary-general of the League, to give Rajchman a categorical warning to keep out of politics once and for all and to stipulate that his appointment would be for one year alone and only as an experiment.[48]

T. V. Soong eventually returned to China with his adviser, the American Wheat and Cotton Loan, and arrangements for barter trade with Germany. But these results of his overseas tour were insufficient to sustain his views on a Western oriented policy within the Chinese cabinet. Chiang Kai-shek and Premier-Foreign Minister Wang Ching-wei decided instead to meet Japan's wishes by consolidating the Tangku Truce with a political and economic rapprochement. Provided loss of face could be avoided, Chiang and Wang held that only such a policy would free them to deal with the Communists and other internal enemies of the Nanking régime. Soong was forced to resign as minister of finance in October 1933. Even after his political defeat, however, Soong remained in a position to control the levers of China's economic policy. While his brother-in-law H. H. Kung took over as finance minister, Soong kept his grip on economic affairs by virtue of his positions as chairman of the National Economic Council (see Table 3), head of the Bank of China, and, perhaps most important, as the moving spirit and controller of the China Development Finance Corporation.

The CDFC was an organization of Chinese banks for "finance as opposed to banking,"[49] with whom all foreign banks could deal. It was officially launched from the Shanghai Banker's Club on 2 June 1934, with Soong's younger brother, T. L. Soong, as general manager. Regular dividends of 12 per cent plus bonuses were promised on an original capital subscription of 10 million in Chinese National currency. The CDFC was the creation of the French financier, Jean Monnet (later famous as the pioneer of the European Common Market in the 1960's), who was in China on T. V. Soong's invitation to devise some method of circumventing

[47]Eden, Minute, 30 March 1933, ibid.

[48]Vansittart, Memorandum, 12 July 1933, ibid. During the discussion in the Foreign Office of the Rajchman affair, Vansittart gave vent to his anger and frustration in a racist outburst: ". . . nothing will stop this intriguing Jew from being an intriguing Jew. He has politics in his blood," 14 July 1933, ibid.

[49]Ingram (Shanghai) to Simon, "Minutes of a Conversation with M. Monnet," 6 April 1934, FO 18078/F1933.

the Four Power Banking Consortium's control of the flow of foreign capital into China. In London Monnet was regarded with suspicion as narrowly removed from an "adventurer pure and simple,"[50] and the British Treasury tried to do "anything possible . . . to sabotage Monnet"[51] because he represented antagonism to Japan. But many British and other foreign concession hunters who were currently having a thin time in China found Monnet's talk "extremely clear and convincing."[52]

The previous British aloofness in China demonstrates the significance of the CDFC as a fundamentally new channel for foreign business. "Up to quite recent times," as Sir John Pratt explained it,

> British merchants in China have had a sheltered and artificial existence. The Treaties and the timidity of the Chinese placed them in a privileged position in which by trading through a comprador they made easy profits without much effort or risk. In effect the comprador traded under the protection of the foreign merchants and the more the latter, with the help of the Consul and the gunboat, asserted his privileges and rode rough-shod over Chinese rights and aspirations the better for his business. The pent up resentment of the Chinese exploded in 1925.

In fact, as far back as the 1925-26 boycott of British trade the British government had publicly recognized that the Chinese were entitled "to be masters in their own House"[53] and that, pending revision, the treaties should receive a more liberal interpretation. Among the more politically alert sections of the British business community there was a commercial counterpart to the British government's *December Memorandum* of 1926. It was a recognition that the comprador would have to be dropped as the connecting link with the Chinese community because the Chinese nationalist movement had denounced such people as "running dogs of imperial-

---

[50]Christopher Chancellor (Reuters) to Simon Harcourt-Smith, 31 July 1935, FO 19243/F4955.

[51]S. D. Waley (Treasury) to Leonard Browett (Board of Trade), 10 December 1935, FO 19252/F7782. Pratt also reported a conversation with Li Ming, a prominent Chinese banker who headed a syndicate of Shanghai banks opposed to Soong and who was believed to be in close touch with the Japanese. Li Ming said the CDFC was "a political and not a financial scheme" which would fail because it lacked Japanese good will, 23 June 1934, FO 18078/F3834 and Cadogan to Simon, 21 December 1934, FO 18079/F7566.

[52]H. C. Wilcox to Orde, encl. from E. M. Gull, 10 July 1935, FO 19307/F4445.

[53]Pratt, Minute on "Notes by Sir F. Leith-Ross on his Mission to China," 6 August 1936, FO 20218/F4498.

ism."[54] Faced with the political necessity of going on to "direct touch between the foreigner and the Chinese rank and file,"[55] the foreign firms began recruiting western university-educated Chinese staff to act as Chinese managers and political go-betweens. Typical of the firms taking this approach were the Kailan Mining Administration and Butterfield and Swire. As assistant general manager of the North China mining company in which £10 million of British capital was invested, C. Ku received the same unprecedented £7,500 annual salary as did the British general manager, E. J. Nathan; and as a member of Chiang Kai-shek's National Defence Commission, Ku was the connection with "the inner circle" in Nanking.[56] In the case of Butterfield and Swire, T. K. Tseng (a Cambridge graduate) avoided the "risk of becoming 'a running dog' "[57] by his outside connections as vice-minister of railways and treasurer of the Boxer Indemnity Fund.

The "Chinese manager," however, was only a temporary palliative. Such a fragile link was not strong enough to shield foreign firms from the strikes and boycotts organized by labour unions and potential Chinese competitors. Some of the bigger British firms, such as British-American Tobacco Ltd., which had 27,000 employees (of whom 600 were European) and "a vast investment of British capital," were able to enlist the support of the British ambassador in making direct representation to Chiang Kai-shek on these problems.[58] But in spite of his good will to foreign capital, Chiang Kai-shek was unable and could not be expected "to intervene personally every time a tang-pu [party bureau] or a labour union upsets

[54]Hao Yen-p'ing, *The Comprador in Nineteenth Century China* (Cambridge, Mass.: Harvard University Press, 1970) p. 223, describes the comprador as the "middleman between East and West." The characteristic of all Chinese negotiations was the indirect approach through a third party who in trade matters was called for convenience the comprador (Portuguese, "buyer"). Under the system, a Chinese introduced Chinese business to his foreign principal; he and not the principal took the risk. The comprador was generally a proprietor or part proprietor in a Chinese firm. Formerly the subservience of the Chinese "permitted them to accept positions such as compradores which cloaked the extent of their authority and influence." H. A. Ottewill (DOT), Minute, 10 September 1934, FO 18101/F5438.

[55]J. Swire and Sons to G. M. Young (Shanghai), 17 December 1926, Swire—1079.

[56]Nathan to Turner (Chinese Engineering and Mining Corporation, London). 22 September 1934, Nathan Papers, C.426, Bodleian Library, Oxford.

[57]J. K. Swire, 1 March 1935, and G. W. Swire, 13 April 1934, Swire—D.N.O.E.

[58]Sir Hugo Cunliffe-Owen (B.A. Tobacco) to Hoare, 9 July 1935, FO 19237/F4407; Cadogan to Chiang Kai-shek, 1 June and 30 August 1935, FO 19320/F4472 and FO 19321/F6420. See also files on affairs of the Peking syndicate in 1934 and 1935, FO 18127 and FO 19291.

industry."[59] In order to facilitate the flow of foreign capital and guarantee its safety, a new formula would have to be found.

The new formula was contained in Jean Monnet's simple but, for those times, unusual argument in favour of partnership with the China Development Finance Corporation. If foreign companies wished to continue to operate in China, they would have to include Chinese capital in a genuine partnership. As real partners, the Chinese would have everything to gain through a proper conduct of business. On the other hand any foreign enterprise which tried to operate alone was "open to every kind of reproach of exploitation, imperialism, etc."[60] Without the "Chinese façade," all the fulminations of their respective embassies would be unable to protect foreign companies. When there was a representative and organized body of native financiers, such as the CDFC, there was no safe or effective way to deny them participation in major economic developments. Monnet's thesis, which has become familiar in the modern era of the multi-national corporation, was supported by Sir Arthur Salter. In a much-quoted part of his report to the Chinese government, Salter said that the best basis for the investment of foreign capital in China in the future would be in "association on equal conditions (not necessarily in equal proportions)" with Chinese capital. In the earlier period when the railways were being built, there had been no way to gather and mobilize Chinese capital. But now the Chinese banks fulfilled this function, and the best security for the foreign investor would be the "close association with Chinese investors whose fortunes are linked with his and who will bear the controlling share of responsibility."[61]

In considering the advice of those professional economists, the heads of the big British firms found that the difficulty lay in "arranging satisfactory cartels, as Chinese enterprisers are still prone to seek irregular benefits," which made them unsatisfactory partners.[62] However, whether or not British firms were convinced by the Monnet-Salter line of reasoning, it became increasingly plain that the Chinese were sufficiently well organized to demand a share in any major industrial undertaking in their country. And with the formation of the CDFC, the initiative in financing Chinese development passed from foreign to Chinese hands and allowed the Chi-

[59]Sir Frederick Whyte, Memorandum for British American Tobacco Co., encl. in Cadogan to Wellesley, 2 November 1934, FO 18048/F6507.

[60]Ingram to Simon, "Minutes of a Conversation with M. Monnet."

[61]*Economist*, 19 May 1934, p. 9; see also G. C. Papers (1934-35), pp. 161-62; Pratt, Minute, 28 May 1934, FO 18047/F3112; Department of Overseas Trade, *Trade and Economic Conditions in China 1931-33* (London: H.M.S.O., 1933), p. 11.

[62]Brown to J. Swire and Sons, 20 July 1934, Swire—1082.

nese banks to invite piece-meal co-operation of such foreign financial institutions as they desired. The first British entrepreneurs to form a partnership with T. V. Soong's CDFC were the Matheson-Hong Kong and Shanghai Bank group. Apparently in defiance of the wishes of the City and oblivious to the "political implications" for British relations with Japan,[63] a syndicate was formed on equal terms between the British and Chinese Corporation and the CDFC to float a CN$16 million loan on the Shanghai market to rehabilitate the Shanghai-Hangchow-Ningpo Railway.[64] Other firms soon followed suit to make contact with the CDFC. Pending negotiations for CDFC partnership in the China Navigation Co., a Butterfield and Swire subsidiary which operated the largest British merchant fleet in Chinese waters (eighty river and coastal vessels), T. V. Soong was allotted and paid for shares in the Oriental Paint, Colour and Varnish Co. Ltd., a smaller Swire subsidiary.[65] Interviewed in London in May, 1971, W. J. Keswick said: "In the 1930's Jardine, Matheson & Co. had considered taking in Chinese capital, but drew back for two reasons: (1) where Jardines were satisfied with making 5 per cent profit, the Chinese wanted 15 per cent, and (2) where Jardines thought in the long term—say ten years ahead—the Chinese thought of today only; they wanted to get their money out before some misfortune could intervene."

In addition to the power of the Shanghai bankers, there were other reasons compelling British enterprise to seek closer relations with the Chinese capitalists. These reasons included the changing character of trade from consumer to capital goods, the rise of German competition, and the need to find protection from Japanese military encroachments into North and Central China. The dramatic decline in United Kingdom cotton textile exports to China (from £7,250,000 in 1929 to a mere £300,000 in 1936) in the face of the Chinese protective tariff and the growth of domestic industry had led the British Commercial-Diplomatic service to conclude, as early as 1933, that British exports in the future would be in iron and steel products, electrical apparatus, power plants, water works and other public utilities, railway and road transportation equipment instead of in consumer goods. But sales of this type were more difficult to secure than con-

[63]Pratt, Minute, 29 August 1934, FO 18079/F5280.

[64]Copies of the loan contracts are in Cadogan to Simon, 17 October 1934, and Howe to Simon, 3 December 1934, FO 18079/ file 68. Compared to previous railway contracts, the terms of the Shanghai-Hangchow-Ningpo Loan, the size of commissions, and stipulations about the purchase of materials were "not at all favourable to the British & Chinese Corporation or to British industry generally"; Pratt, Minute, 1 September 1934, FO 18078/F5154.

[65]Butterfield and Swire to J. Swire and Sons, 2 November 1934, Swire—1082; also Crowe to Orde (secret), 12 September 1935, FO 19326/F5873.

sumer goods, because they depended on close contact with Chinese government purchasing departments and facilities for guaranteed long-term credits in a situation where all of China's disposable assets were mortgaged to the hilt.[66]

The Germans, by their close touch with the buyer, by state subsidized export prices, liberal credit terms, and barter arrangements, had overtaken Great Britain as a supplier of metals and machinery to the China market by the early 1930's.[67] The British commercial counsellor in Shanghai, Louis Beale, pointed to German successes and argued tirelessly that, in spite of the present comparative unimportance of the China market to British manufacturers, China was in a formative period and that the policy followed by British business now would determine the course of future trade with China to a much greater extent than was possible in the case of more mature and settled countries. Over the years Beale favoured more "collaboration and less competition" among British manufacturers, bankers, and merchants engaged in the China market and encouraged a select group of large-scale manufacturers and financial interests to adopt a "bolder policy of co-operation with Chinese interests, individual and governmental." He urged stronger backing for this policy of partnership with Chinese interests to avoid at least a "partial disappearance from the field of China."[68]

In addition to meeting the German competition, the big China firms saw partnership with the capitalists gathered around Chiang Kai-shek and T. V. Soong as the means of enlisting the Chinese, "actuated by self-interest, to fight our battles for us,"[69] in repelling a Japanese assault on British interests south of the Great Wall. With this thought uppermost in their minds, Butterfield and Swire, Jardine, Matheson and Co., British-Ameri-

[66]Beale to DOT, 13 July 1933, FO 17091/F4679. DOT to A. G. N. Ogden (Chefoo), 11 December 1935, FO 19288/F7789; Knatchbull-Hugessen to Eden, 20 August 1937, encl. from Beale, "Respecting Economic Trends in China," 10 June 1937, FO 21002/F5483; Harcourt-Smith, Memorandum, "The Industrial and Economic Position in China," 18 December 1933, FO 18052/F7761; Barber (Board of Trade) to Foreign Office, 11 May 1935, FO 20995/2718; all these documents provide evidence of the changing British commercial policy towards the China market.

[67]*DGFP*, Series C, 1933, 1:811, 867; 1934, 3:761; 1936, 5: 348, 411, 502, provide details of German revolving credit and barter arrangements. Agreements provided for China to supply raw materials at 10 per cent below world market prices. See also Beale to Eden, "Respecting German competition with Great Britain in the China Market," 25 March 1936, FO 20271/F1649.

[68]Knatchbull-Hugessen to Eden, 12 July 1937, encl. from Beale, "Future of Britain and Japan in China," 6 April 1937, FO 20965/F3975/14, and Beale, "Respecting Economic Trends in China" (see n. 66).

[69]J. Swire and Sons to Brown, 9 November, 1934, Swire—1082; also Brown to J. Swire and Sons, 20 July 1934, ibid.

can Tobacco (China) Ltd., Imperial Chemical Industries (China) Ltd., and probably others all made efforts to interest T. V. Soong and his friends in taking up partnership offers. But Soong was a hard bargainer with a shrewd understanding of international politics. He saw the potential security which a partnership with Chinese interests offered the British investor as a bargaining lever. When the British government showed reluctance to question Japanese claims to sole leadership in East Asia or to challenge Japanese infringements of the "open door" in North China, Soong stalled indefinitely on negotiations with the British firms. It was clear, he told one British firm late in 1935, that the Japanese were trying to push the British out of the Far East; so far it was not shown that the British government was not going to "pull up stakes" and leave, in which case there was no value in investing in British firms as they would be a target for Japanese aggression.[70] T. V. Soong's price for large-scale Sino-British economic co-operation was an engagement by the British government, by word or action, to resist Japanese encroachments on China.

If one of the decisive factors influencing the direction of British policy in China which lay outside British hands was the nationalistic attitude of Chinese capitalists, another was the attitude of the Japanese government. The pace of Japanese encroachments on China had temporarily slowed in the period following the Tangku Truce as the Japanese minister to Nanking advised his government to pursue a "duck" policy. In explanation of his term, Akira Ariyoshi said that a duck was an aquatic bird greatly to be admired because it always displayed a serene and stately mood above water while busily paddling beneath the surface.[71] For many months Japanese progress had been slow because the Chinese kept to discussion of technical matters about rail, postal, and customs services between China and Manchukuo. But after T. V. Soong's dismissal from office in October 1933, Japanese pressure began to show more substantial results. A significant move on Chiang Kai-shek's part was the appointment of Japanese-educated Tang Yu-jen, general secretary of the Central Political Council of the Kuomintang, to be administrative vice-minister of foreign affairs in charge of Sino-Japanese questions, a post which he held until he was assassinated in December 1935. In this position Tang was in constant communication with Yakichiro Suma, the Japanese consul-general in Nanking, who of all the Japanese officials in China was regarded by

---

[70]J. K. Swire to Beale, 31 October 1935, Swire—1075; also in Crowe to Orde, 7 November 1935, FO 19330/F6968; J. K. Swire, "Minute of Interview with Dr. T. V. Soong," 9 May 1935, Swire—D.N.O.E.

[71]Colonial Office to Foreign Office, "Review of Chinese Affairs" June 1934, FO 18122/F5368.

British diplomats concerned with the Far East as "the real Japanese power" in China. Suma used his position to make it abundantly clear that he resented American and European financial and technical assistance to China and regarded it as some "deep laid plot"[72] to develop China to the exclusion of Japan. Because of Japan's propinquity to China, the Japanese claimed that "in any and every future development loan Japan should have the right to the *dominant* share."[73] Suma also demanded the acceptance of Manchukuo as a *fait accompli* and a reduction in the Chinese customs tariff against Japanese imports. He told the British Legation that 30 per cent of China's political leaders, headed by Premier Wang Ching-wei, favoured a rapprochement with Japan, while only 20 per cent were relentlessly opposed and about 50 per cent were apathetic. Suma was working with Premier Wang on ways to win over the apathetic group within the next two years. In order to make the acceptance of the Manchukuo issue more palatable, Wang needed a "fresh slogan on which to rally Chinese opinion," and he and Wang were examining the possibility of "creating a bogey out of the menace of communism and Soviet designs which would justify China and Japan in joining forces so to speak."[74]

Japanese desires in China were the subject of the Wang-Ariyoshi conversations in March-April, 1934. During this time the Japanese felt that "amicable progress" was being made. Wang had said that as the Manchurian question was difficult—like a reef in the sea—it would be reserved as it was, but he would let the ship go through, and he intended to lead the people and "open the road for friendship" with Japan.[75] The Chinese government was understandably reticent about publicizing its dealings with the Japanese, but the British Foreign office was well informed on the trend of the Wang-Ariyoshi conversations, partly because of Suma's volubility and also because the British Secret Intelligence Service was intercepting Suma's secret reports to Tokyo. In the midst of the Wang-Ariyoshi talks, an official spokesman of the Japanese Foreign Ministry, Eiji Amau, gave what was termed an "unofficial" press conference in Tokyo in which he stated publicly what Suma had been talking about in private. Amau

[72]Sir Eric Drummond (Rome) to A. W. G. Randall, 1 June 1934, FO 18098/ F3252; see also Cadogan to Wellesley, 17 May 1934, encl. from Holman (Nanking), 3 April 1934, FO 18047/F2892. Suma was described as "a powerfully made man . . . with a swivel eye and a pronounced Oxford accent," who was head of Japanese Intelligence and one of the "outstanding personalities in Far Eastern affairs." G. W. Swire to Orde, encl. from E. M. Gull, 19 July 1935, FO 19313/F5752.

[73]Cadogan to Simon, 26 June 1934, encl. from Beale, Report on talk with Y. Suma, 9 April 1934. FO 18078/F3858.

[74]Cadogan to Simon, 9 March 1934, FO 18096/F13339.

[75]Suma (Nanking) to Koki Hirota (Tokyo) from Ariyoshi, 20 April 1934, IMTFE, Exhibit 3243, T 29570-77.

warned the powers of any "undesirable assistance to China." He cited the American Wheat and Cotton Loan, sales of aircraft, and the supply of military and technical advisers to China by America and European nations as being contrary to the peace of the Orient. He stated flatly that no "reconstruction scheme" for China could succeed without Japanese co-operation.

The Amau statement created a flash of excitement which was reflected in newspapers of the day. In London, for example, *The Times* interpreted Amau's statement as an epoch-making departure, a Japanese "Monroe Doctrine" for East Asia which spelled an end to the "open door" and "equal opportunity" of the Nine Power Treaty of 1922.[76] Chinese papers seized the occasion to stir up the interest of Japan's rivals. The Shanghai *Shih Shih Hsin Pao* stated on 21 April 1934 that the situation was in-finitely more dangerous than when Japan had made her Twenty-One Demands on China in 1915 and suggested that if the three friendly powers—Great Britain, America, and Russia—had any vision, they would stop their compromising with Japan and "at once arise" to safeguard their own interests and be faithful to their undertaking to preserve the peace of the world.[77]

Except for the tiresome questions which newspaper clippings might arouse in Parliament, the Foreign Office of course was not unduly troubled by such comment. The British government was, however, concerned to know why the Japanese statement had been made at this time and to what extent Japan's anger was directed at Great Britain. Furthermore, the government had to consider how to react, if at all, to Japan's claim to be the sole judge as to when the peace of East Asia was threatened and to her apparent disregard of the Nine Power Treaty which called for mutual consultations in such circumstances.

From the messages which flooded into the Foreign Office following Amau's statement, a slightly reassuring picture was pieced together for the British Cabinet. Sir John Simon told his colleagues that the motive for Japanese action derived from events not connected with Great Britain but elsewhere.[78] The Japanese did not like the German military mission under

---

[76]*The Times*, 20 April 1934. See also Reuters despatch from Tokyo, 18 April 1934, on "hands off China" warning, FO 18097/F2204. The Amau Declaration is in R.I.I.A.—Documents, 1934, Chatham House, London.

[77]Translation by Sir Herbert Goffe, G. C. Papers (1934), pp. 137-40.

[78]Cab 17(34), 25 April 1934, CAB 23/79.

von Seeckt now visiting China;[79] they considered the American Wheat and Cotton Loan a breach of the consortium agreement; they feared exclusion from an international loan which the French financier, M. Monnet, was reportedly negotiating; they objected to a report on technical assistance to China about to be issued by Rajchman on behalf of the League of Nations; but there was no specific criticism of Great Britain. The foreign secretary had also taken particular notice of intelligence reports on a Chinese conference supposed to have been held during the first half of April 1934 at Nanchang and attended by Chiang Kai-shek and the chief politicians in the Nanking government. At this meeting Chiang had insisted on the need to consolidate the government's position in the central Yangtse provinces from Shanghai to Hankow. Material and money for this, Chiang had said, could not be expected from the United States and Great Britain but only from Japan. Therefore, he had ordered that a full and formal settlement should be made over Manchuria and that the League of Nations advisers should finish their work quickly and go home. The Japanese knew that the pro-Japanese faction in Nanking had won. It was in a "moment of exuberance"[80] that the Japanese Foreign Ministry spokesman had made his press statement to drive home the point that no large scale enterprise in China could hope to succeed unless it had the blessing of Japan. Amau had spoken somewhat tactlessly, and the effect on public opinion in China would make it all the more difficult for Chiang Kai-shek to proceed with his policy of reliance upon Japan. But Amau's views were undoubtedly those of the Japanese government, who had not disavowed him, and reflected Chiang Kai-shek's decision to make an accommodation with Japan.[81]

Even though Simon felt reassured that Japan was aiming her words

[79]The famous German general visited China in 1933 and 1934 at Chiang Kai-shek's request to train the Chinese Army, *DGFP*, Series C, 1933, 1:773; Liu Chih-pu, *Military History of Modern China* (Princeton: Princeton University Press, 1956) is the standard account. Seeckt was followed by von Falkenhausen, who stayed with a mission of sixty military advisers until 1938.

[80]Memorandum, "Japanese Declaration Concerning China," 26 April 1934, FO 18097/F2339. Simon minuted: "This explains a lot," 29 April 1934, ibid.

[81]The Tokyo embassy reported the Amau statement reflected accurately a policy known "to be behind Japanese action" for the previous two years. Sir Francis O. Lindley (Tokyo) to Simon, 19 April 1934, FO 18096/F2193. See also Grew, *Ten Years* (New York: Simon and Schuster, 1944), pp. 130, 137. The American ambassador knew that Amau's statement was taken almost verbatim from one of Foreign Minister Hirota's instructions to the legation in Nanking, a fact confirmed in *Taiheiyo senso e no michi* [*The Road to the Pacific War*] (Tokyo, 1962-63), as cited in E. M. Robertson, *The Origins of the Second World War* (London: Macmillan, 1971), p. 251.

"at others rather than ourselves," he told the cabinet that it was impossible to avoid noticing that the tenor of the Amau statement was "a challenge to the principle of equal rights for all Powers in China."[82] Japan, in fact, "appeared to be acting in breach of the Nine Power Treaty."[83] Simon, who according to his chief adviser always looked "as if he had just got out of a cold bath,"[84] found the situation most disturbing. Japan appeared to be following the German model of ignoring treaties. But in saying that the Japanese statement was both a challenge and an *action* in breach of the Nine Power Treaty, he was clearly exaggerating. Perhaps he was storing up debating points to counter the insistent pressure coming from Neville Chamberlain for a definite Anglo-Japanese rapprochement. In any case, with the necessity of making a statement in Parliament in the back of his mind, Simon instructed his ambassador in Tokyo to speak "in a most friendly spirit" to the Japanese foreign minister and point out that the principle of equal rights in China was guaranteed very explicitly by the Nine Power Treaty to which Japan was a party and that the British government "therefore assume" that the Amau statement was not intended in any way to abridge the common rights of other powers in China. The cabinet approved Simon's velvet approach to Japan and also his avowed decision not to communicate with the United States or any other power on the subject in order not to give the impression of creating an anti-Japanese bloc.[85] The reluctance of the Foreign Office to challenge Japan over the Amau statement is emphasized by Sir Robert Vansittart's Minute of 20 April that

> . . . up till last night I was endeavouring to prevent enquirers from making too much of this incident. But it is evident . . . that that line cannot be held. . . . It is a question of considerable gravity. . . . The nature of our representation to Japan will ultimately have to be made public in the House.[86]

When Ambassador Lindley (on Simon's instructions) called on the foreign minister, Hirota complained about the "ulterior motives" of rumoured loans, of the activities of League of Nations personnel, and of Chinese tariffs which closed the "open door" to Japan, but he gave assurances that Japan did not intend to violate the Nine Power Treaty. Hirota advanced the suggestion that since Japan had not denounced the Nine Power Treaty, she

---

[82]Simon to Lindley, 27 April 1934, FO 18097/F2351.
[83]Cab 17(34), 25 April 1934, CAB 23/79.
[84]Vansittart, *The Mist Procession* (London: Hutchinson, 1958), p. 437.
[85]Cab 17(34), 25 April 1934, CAB 23/79. Also Simon to Lindley (Outfile), 23 April 1934, FO 18097/F2211.
[86]Ibid.

could not therefore be claiming any rights over and above the common rights of the signatory powers. Lindley "nodded agreement"[87] with Hirota's dubious thesis and wired home that Hirota's assurances should be accepted and the incident considered closed. In Lindley's opinion it was folly to ignore the vital interests of Japan in China. Japan's attitude might be considered to be "as unreasonable as it is unpleasant," but all Britain could do was "to try to reconcile it with our own interests."[88]

As far as the British government was concerned, the incident might have ended there had not the Americans also been seeking clarification of the Amau statement. A potential Anglo-American misunderstanding over the Amau statement arose when in the course of casual remarks to U.S. Ambassador Bingham, Sir John Simon, who together with Prime Minister MacDonald placed greater emphasis on Anglo-American co-operation than other members of the cabinet, was understood to have proposed that the two powers co-operate to resist Japanese pretensions. Bingham cabled Washington to this effect on 21 April 1934.[89] Simon, however, had made no note of this point in his report of the conversation with Bingham. Therefore when an American embassy official called back on 24 April to say that the United States would prefer to limit matters to an exchange of views with Great Britain, the Foreign Office was mystified that there had been any suggestion of co-operation "since we always try to avoid giving unnecessary umbrage to Japan by taking joint action with America."[90] When the matter was drawn to Simon's attention he denied responsibility and stated that no such idea as co-operation with America had ever been mentioned. Meanwhile Hirota gave the American Ambassador, Joseph Grew, a three paragraph "official statement" and sent a copy of it to Lindley with the notation that this declaration was for publication, a fact which Lindley made explicit in his message of transmittal to the Foreign Office.[91] The first two paragraphs of Hirota's document affirmed what was not so, namely the Japanese government's desire to uphold the "open door" and "equal opportunity" in China,[92] while the last paragraph

[87]Hirota to Japanese embassies in the United States, Britain, China, and Manchukuo, 26 April 1934, IMTFE, Exhibit 3244, T 29579-85.

[88]Lindley to Simon, 26 April 1934, FO 18097/F2350, F2351; see also FO 18098/F3008.

[89]See Borg, *Far Eastern Crisis*, pp. 78-79; *FRUS*, 1934, 3:121-22, 125, 131.

[90]Wellesley, Minute, 24 April 1934, FO 18097/F2430.

[91]Lindley to Simon, 27 April 1934, 7 May 1934, FO 18097/F2375, F2606. Hirota's note of 27 April is in R.I.I.A. Documents—1934.

[92]See Crowley, *Japan's Quest*, pp. 195-96; Hull, *Memoirs*, 1:280, and *FRUS*, 1934, 3:654, for Ambassador Saito's request in May 1934 for a joint U.S.–Japan communiqué to signal a bilateral detente which would replace, in effect, the Nine-Power Treaty.

contained a qualification which stated that Japan was opposed to any foreign activity in China prejudicial to the peace and order of East Asia. Subsequently there was a heated controversy in Britain over the fact that Sir John Simon used only the first part of Hirota's official document in his statement to the House of Commons on 30 April 1934 and left out the part which had "a sting in its tail."[93] With the press in Japan still harping on Japan's special mission in East Asia, the British cabinet was challenged for its "cap-in-hand attitude" to Japan[94] and questioned why it was trying to cover up Hirota's third principle. Simon tried to defend himself by saying that it was unnecessary to mention the last part of Hirota's statement because opposition to what was prejudicial to peace and order in East Asia was the common object of all the signatories of the Nine Power Treaty. Furthermore, Hirota's statement had been officially communicated to the United States ambassador, and His Majesty's ambassador had only received a copy—suggesting by inference, and quite erroneously according to Lindley's message of 27 April, that it was up to the United States government to be the first to make it public.[95]

The British government was reluctant to draw any new conclusions from the Amau incident and tried hard to pretend that nothing had happened. The government had been following the Wang-Ariyoshi political conversations and viewed them as a welcome sequel to the Tangku Truce. It had hoped that these conversations would lead to a normalization of Sino-Japanese relations on the basis of the *status quo* on both sides of the Great Wall. As a result of pressure from Parliament and in the press about the Amau declaration, the foreign secretary had initiated polite enquiries in Tokyo. The resulting official assurances from Tokyo, however, did nothing to abate the suspicions, both among the public and in the Foreign Office, that Japan was aiming to establish a protectorate not just in Manchuria but over the whole of China. The Tangku Truce did not appear to be leading to tranquility in the Far East after all. As the *Sunday Observer* warned its readers on 6 May 1934, Japan was pursuing a policy definitely aimed at securing paramountcy in China to the detriment of the interests of other powers, "more particularly the British" whose investments in China were larger than those of any other country.

The confusions and complications which arose over the Amau affair make it obvious that the policy of the British cabinet toward British rights and interests in China following the Tangku Truce cannot be properly

---

[93]R. Allen, Minute, FO 18097/F2500. Simon's statement of 30 April 1934 is in R.I.I.A.—Documents, 1934.
[94]Lord Ponsonby, 92 *H. L. Deb.*, 7 May 1934.
[95]Simon, 289 *H. C. Deb.*, 7 May 1934.

understood in isolation from events and forces operating in other parts of the world. By this time there were certain disturbing influences at work in Europe, too, which forced the government to reconsider its whole global policy, of which the Far East was but one component.

3

Discord over High Policy, 1933-34:
Search for Far Eastern Allies

In 1933 the chiefs of staff told the cabinet that the British armed forces, with their existing strength, could no longer be responsible for both national and imperial defence. Confronted with this information, the British cabinet faced what has been described as a new and terrible dilemma in the formulation of their foreign policy.[1] In face of the German menace, Britain had to decide whether to concentrate her defence resources on national safety with an expanded air force or on Japan and imperial defence with an efficient and mobile navy.

The confidential documents of the British Foreign Office emphasize that Britain had no expansionist aims between the two world wars. She wanted to keep what she had and live in peace. The guiding lights of her policy therefore were to maintain the balance of power and preserve the *status quo*.[2] But in the unsettled times at the end of the 1920's these objectives were becoming increasingly difficult to achieve. In the aftermath of World War I, Britain had been trying to rebuild her domestic economic and financial position in face of the war debts and reparations problems, and now, in the 1930's, she found herself in the midst of an unprecedented world-wide depression. She had attempted to pacify Europe by adjusting the Versailles peace settlement to re-admit Germany into the ranks of the great powers, only to find that Nazi Germany walked out of both the

---

[1]C.I.D. paper 1112-B, 19 May 1933, CAB 4/22 and S. W. Kirby, *The War in the Far East* (London: H.M.S.O. 1957), 1:12; D. C. Watt, *Personalities and Policies* (London: Longmans, 1965), p. 83.

[2]*DBFP*, Series 1a, 1:846-81.

League of Nations and the World Disarmament Conference. In the Far East, Britain had dropped her alliance with Japan and accepted the Washington treaties as the price of good Anglo-American and Commonwealth relationships, only to be confronted with Japan's seizure of Manchuria and withdrawal from the League of Nations. After the Mukden Incident in 1931, it became painfully obvious to the cabinet that both the balance of power and the *status quo* in East Asia were threatened by Japan. And because Germany was beginning to play a similarly disturbing role in Europe, there was no escaping the fact that in 1933 the world, in the words of Sir Robert Vansittart, was going "steadily downhill."[3]

The cabinet soon took a decision for rearmament in principle, but their dilemma remained one of priorities. A special Defence Requirements Committee of the Committee of Imperial Defence, composed of the chiefs of staff, Sir Warren Fisher (Treasury), Sir Robert Vansittart (Foreign Office), and Sir Maurice Hankey (Cabinet Secretariat) as chairman, was therefore established in October, 1933, and given the task of recommending defence priorities. From this time on British government leaders and their advisers spent many months debating possible lines of high policy for the coming years. Some of the warmly contested decisions made in this period cast a long shadow over the events of the later 1930's. One question facing the historian is why the British cabinet made virtually no effort to develop contact with the Soviet Union or the United States in order to check Japan, since both these countries favoured the *status quo* and felt their interests threatened by Japan's growing military power and penetration into China. Another, hitherto even more baffling, topic has been why leading personalities of the cabinet tried to pursue a balance of power in the Pacific and stability in China by seeking closer ties with Japan—the only nation whose declared intentions and every action since September, 1931, were aimed at achieving an exclusive predominance in East Asia. In the discussion which follows, the early stages of the British attempt to achieve a friendly, bilateral understanding with Japan are considered against the background of official attitudes toward the Soviet Union and the United States and assessments of their policies relative to the developing crisis in the Far East.

The British government was well aware that the Soviet Union was having her own problems with Japan in the 1930's. By constant harassment, the Japanese were forcing the Russians to sell out their interest in the Chinese Eastern Railway which ran across northern Manchuria to Vladivostok. And, according to British intelligence reports, the Japanese army

[3]C.I.D. paper 1112-B.

was continuously threatening Russian frontiers in Siberia by constructing a network of strategic railways and roads in Manchuria.[4] Incident had followed upon incident along the Soviet-Manchurian border with a regularity which was "wearisome to record."[5] From these and other facts it was obvious that the British were not alone among the European nations in their fears of Japanese expansionism and aggression. The question was whether the Soviet Union could prove to be of assistance in alleviating British fears.

An answer to this question was provided by the chiefs of the imperial general staff in their semi-annual reviews of imperial defence. Until these reviews were opened to the public in 1968, it was often assumed, following memoirs of Anthony Eden and other cabinet ministers, that it was "an almost universal opinion" in Britain that the military power of the Soviets was "in disarray and of poor quality."[6] But, in fact, from 1933 through to February 1937, at least (the great purge of Soviet generals took place on June 11, 1937), the chiefs of staff reported a growing respect for the military power and potential of the Soviet Union.[7] In their opinion, by 1935 the Soviet army and air force were already in many ways "the most powerful military machine in the world." The chiefs of staff were aware of the internal discontent and economic dislocations which existed in Stalin's régime. In spite of this, however, they considered that the Soviet military machine was backed by a civil and military industry which in a comparatively short space of time would render that huge state practically self-supporting in war.[8] In defence, the Soviet armed forces were already a power to be reckoned with; in attack, they would "probably be less effective."[9] The strength of the Soviet army, according to these reports, rose from 81 divisions in 1931 to 108 in 1937, and it was calculated that in 1937 the Russians were in a position to put at least 75 divisions into the field on their western front within one month of mobilization, together with 2,000 aircraft.

In the Far East the Soviet position was relatively stronger than in Europe. After the Soviets had built a large army on a war footing in

---

[4]Memos no. 1 and 6, 21 March 1934, C.P. 77a, CAB 24/248; Pratt, Minute, 14 May 1934, FO 18090/F2811; Manchukuo Annual Report, 18 March 1935, FO 19326/F1774.

[5]Cadogan to Simon, 18 March 1935, FO 19326/F1774.

[6]Anthony Eden (Lord Avon), *Facing the Dictators: The Eden Memoirs* (London: Houghton, 1962), p. 162.

[7]The Review of Imperial Defence for 1937 was dated 25 February. See C.I.D. paper 1305-B, CAB 4/25.

[8]C.I.D. paper 1181-B, 29 April 1935, para. 27, CAB 4/23.

[9]C.I.D. paper 1305-B, para. 32.

Siberia, the British observed that the Russian recipe was "when the Japanese hit, hit them back harder."[10] Soviet preparations in the Far East included a large force of long-distance bombing aircraft in the maritime province, "which constitutes a serious threat to Japan," and a submarine force that was "a factor which cannot be disregarded." From these facts the chiefs of staff concluded, without being too precise, that in the event of war between the United Kingdom and Japan "the assistance of the U.S.S.R. might be of considerable value." Although the military advisers of the cabinet did not venture to discuss the question in terms of a political bargain, they indicated that in return for such assistance the Soviets would want evidence of Anglo-French solidarity against Germany and would probably wish to induce the British government to make a pronouncement "in favour of the defence of the *status quo* in every part of Europe."[11]

From the political point of view, the turbulent history of Anglo-Russian relations in the fifteen years or so since the Bolshevik Revolution made an understanding with the Soviet Union seem unlikely. Although there was a gradual rise in trade, diplomatic relations between the two countries had been fitful. The British wanted payments made to expropriated British bondholders, while the Soviets demanded compensation for claims arising out of the British intervention in Russia after the revolution. The British resented hostile and subversive propaganda directed at the British Empire, while the Soviets charged that the British were engaging in counter-revolutionary activities in Russia. The difficulties, basically, had arisen out of British fears that the successful communist revolution presented a permanent threat to the whole political and social structure of Western Europe. The British had no reason to suppose that the Soviets had abandoned the ultimate hope of world revolution or that if the German and Japanese menaces were removed, they might not revert to their policy of hostility towards the British Empire. But in the meantime the facts of the matter were that the Soviet Union was fearful of German and Japanese aggression and recognized a similar preoccupation on the part of the British government.

On this basis, Laurence Collier, head of the Northern Department of the Foreign Office, who was more responsible than anyone for supervising day-to-day political relations with the U.S.S.R., advocated a reappraisal of the deep freeze which characterized Anglo-Soviet relations. The old idea that the Soviet Union was the avowed enemy of Great Britain was out of date. A grandson of Sir Thomas Huxley and reared in the aristocratic tradition, Collier was no political radical. But it was obvious that such

[10]Clive to Eden, 12 April 1937, FO 410/98, no. 63.
[11]C.I.D. paper 1305-B.

important developments as President Roosevelt's diplomatic recognition of
the U.S.S.R. in 1933 and the latter's membership in the League of Nations
in 1934 made some revision of British attitudes in order. *Pravda* articles
might still be irritating and M. Litvinov "a mischievous monkey,"[12] but
by damping down the activity of the Communist International, the Soviet
Union was no longer a menace which constituted a bar to Anglo-Russian
collaboration in matters of foreign policy toward third parties. In 1933,
the Northern Department of the Foreign Office showed its sensitivity to
changes in the political weather by predicting that some day Soviet Russia
and Great Britain would have a common enemy, though they might not
fight him at the same time. This might sound strange to the Committee of
Imperial Defence, Collier remarked, but after all, Palmerston had once
said that "we have no eternal friends nor eternal enemies. Our interests
only are eternal."

Collier, who had served in the Tokyo embassy and in the Far Eastern
Department of the Foreign Office (and later became ambassador to Nor-
way), consistently pursued his argument in favour of balance of power
politics regardless of past friendships or ideological considerations. In his
mind the ultimate policy of Japan was to dictate to the other powers a
final settlement of all Far Eastern problems which would give Japan a
monopoly of trade and political influence in China and the Far East
generally. Collier's views were not unique in the Foreign Office, but he
went further than many in his certainty that among Japanese leaders, as
in Hitler's Germany, the sentiments of "imperialism and militarism" were
quite as strong as any held by the advisers of Kaiser Wilhelm II.[13] On
every possible occasion, and in terms not dissimilar to those used by the
Soviet ambassador, Ivan Maisky, Collier argued that Great Britain should
co-operate with the Soviet Union to keep her away from Germany and in
the Anglo-French orbit "where she now is" and should make more effort
to bring the Americans and Russians "into an anti-Japanese front with
us."[14] In a restatement of the classic balance of power doctrine, he argued
in 1934:

> A Power vitally interested in the maintenance of the "status quo," as
> we are, can keep on tolerable day to day terms with Japan, as with

---

[12]Simon to MacDonald, 3 October 1934, Simon Papers, FO 800/291.

[13]Collier, Minute, 21 October 1933, FO 17338/W11987.

[14]Collier, Minute, October 1934, January 1935, and June 1936, FO 18169/F5943,
FO 19238/F192, and FO 20250/F3715. A rare gesture was made by Britain in March
1935 when Anthony Eden, then without cabinet rank, accepted an invitation to go to
Moscow. See C.P. 41(35), 22 February 1935, CAB 24/253; FO 19343/F2391; Eden,
Facing the Dictators, Chapter 9.

Germany, but cannot hope to do more than that, in the long run, and ought not to want to do so. For any closer friendship would involve the betrayal of the "status quo."

... the idea that we could buy security for ourselves by acquiescing in Japanese control of China or a Japanese attack on Russia [was] a dangerous fallacy, comparable with the idea that we should divert German attention from ourselves by encouraging the Germans to swallow Austria, or the Baltic States. In either case the "aggressive" Power having increased its strength, would in the long run become an even greater danger than it is now. . . .[15]

Collier's comments on the Foreign Office minute papers were ignored rather than answered. There is little evidence in the context of the far eastern crisis that the permanent head of the Foreign Office or the cabinet ministers themselves ever spent much time considering the possibility of contacting the Soviet Union with the aim of exchanging views about Japanese policy. The most obvious and perhaps the main reason for this complacency was that British leaders hoped the mutual antagonisms of the two far eastern neighbours could be taken for granted. Such a defence strategy had the virtue of not putting any burden on the British taxpayer. The expectation of the cabinet, apparently, was that the "reciprocal anti-pathies of the two races," to use a phrase of Sir George A. Mounsey, deputy under-secretary of state for foreign affairs, would restrain both from doing any actual harm to British interests and would prevent the development of any one-sided predominance.[16] A further possible explanation for keeping the Soviet Union at arm's length in the Far East might have been that such a policy corresponded to Britain's developing strategy in Europe. Anthony Eden complained that during his visit to Moscow in 1935 the Russians attributed an "almost Machiavellian subtlety" to British leaders in encouraging Hitler to satisfy his appetites in the East at Russia's expense.[17] But the idea of doing nothing to thwart Hitler's ambitions in Eastern Europe, which became apparent in 1938, was hinted at by Laurence Collier and was already clearly in the minds of the highest officials by 1936.[18] British security presumably would be maintained at the expense of sleepless nights for the men in the Kremlin.

In addition to these considerations, there is, as one might expect, evidence to suggest a continuing reticence toward the Soviet Union because

[15]Collier, Minute, 20 April 1934, FO 18184/File 591/23.
[16]Mounsey to Cadogan, 31 May 1934, Cadogan Papers, FO 800/293.
[17]Eden, *Facing the Dictators*, p. 162.
[18]See Hankey to Eden, copy to Baldwin, 8 June 1936, CAB 63/51.

of the revolutionary propaganda and postures of Soviet foreign policy, especially before that country joined the League of Nations and became an opponent of the revisionist powers. Sir Samuel Hoare, for example, continued to raise complaints from the India Office, perhaps with good reason, that Comintern agents directed by Moscow were actively trying to destroy British rule in India by violence.[19] Also, on one occasion when a junior minister suggested in cabinet that Britain should call Japan's bluff by going some distance towards an accommodation with Russia, Stanley Baldwin, lord president and leader of the Conservative party, headed off the discussion with a curt interjection that an alliance with Russia against Japan would be "a complete change of policy."[20] On another occasion, Neville Chamberlain, chancellor of the Exchequer, expressed his anxiety lest Britain, under the League of Nation's Covenant, might be called upon to help Russia repulse an attack from Japan whereas it was "beyond question" that Britain would maintain a neutral attitude in such a conflict.[21]

The same reluctance for contact with Russia can be found in the writings of Sir Robert Vansittart, head of the permanent officials at the Foreign Office, who as late as 1936 worried about the Soviet Union as a "merchant of 'dangerous thoughts.' "[22] Ideological considerations, openly stated as such, seldom appear in Sir Maurice Hankey's minutes or other papers of cabinet discussion, and Keith Feiling says that with respect to the Soviet Union "not a trace" of an ideological motive can be found in Chamberlain's as-yet-unavailable correspondence.[23] But from the examples cited above and the remark of Sir John Simon during the last weeks of his term of office as foreign secretary—that it would be "a curious spectacle" to see "British Tories collaborating with Russian Communists"[24]—a role for ideological factors in decisions of the British cabinet about the Soviet Union must be assumed.

To a man like Laurence Collier, who had no admiration for Soviet economic doctrines or political practices, but who tried to model his approach to Britain's foreign policy needs after the fashion of a political realist such as Palmerston was reputed to have been, the prevailing opinion about the Soviet Union in the higher echelons of British policy making was one of narrow-minded, unreasoning doubt and unexamined suspi-

[19]Hoare to Simon, 17 March 1934, Simon Papers, FO 800/289.
[20]26 June 1934, CAB 27/507.
[21]C.P. 223(34), 16 October 1934, CAB 24/250.
[22]Vansittart, Memorandum, 16 December 1936, FO 20278/F7781g.
[23]Keith Feiling, *The Life of Neville Chamberlain* (London: Macmillan, 1946), p. 407.
[24]27 March 1935, Simon Papers—Diary.

cion.[25] There was no guarantee, even if Britain had made an approach to Russia to check Japan (instead of seeking Japanese friendship), that Stalin, who was also preoccupied with Germany, would have been willing to make a commitment. But the fact remains that the cabinet, for whatever reasons, did not seize upon its military advisers' appraisal of the Soviet Union's powerful military position as a basis for making an approach to that country. Nor did the cabinet ever consider the favourable estimates of the Foreign Office about the political attitudes of Stalin and Litvinov toward British desiderata as positive and plausible elements on which to shape a far eastern strategy.

Compared to relations with the Soviets, contacts between the British Conservative government and the American government were relatively smooth. But below the surface of diplomatic courtesies, Anglo-American rivalries were sharp and relations were often tense and difficult in the 1930's. This was not surprising because on a whole range of economic, political, and military affairs—repayment of war debts, parity in naval armaments, American isolationism and disassociation from the affairs of the League of Nations (legacies of World War I)—relationships were aggravated. Furthermore, at the level of social and political contacts, highly placed British officials resented condescending American attitudes. These men were offended by the way their counterparts in America seemed to be politely tolerating a Great Britain "shackled by remnants of mediaevalism," weakened by war, and "distracted by the preoccupations of a disintegrating empire";[26] meanwhile America herself had fifteen million unemployed and a national income reduced by 50 per cent. This does not mean to say that America lacked friends in Britain. At the cabinet level both Prime Minister MacDonald and Foreign Secretary Simon displayed a noticeable desire for Anglo-American friendship and co-operation. But the predominant opinion at the upper levels of the government was best summed up by Sir Robert Vansittart when he said that existing British relations with the United States were about as good as "that unreliable country will or can allow them to be."[27]

A graphic insight into some Anglo-American irritations was contained in a letter by the secretary of the cabinet to a colleague in 1933. This colleague had complained of the "insensate folly" of alienating Japan to placate America by breaking off the Anglo-Japanese Alliance in 1921.

---

[25]Interview with Sir Laurence Collier, 12 May 1971, in London. During this discussion Collier quoted Winston Churchill to the effect that Neville Chamberlain would have been a good mayor for Birmingham in an off year.

[26]C.I.D. paper 1112-B.

[27]Vansittart, Minute, 21 December 1934, FO 16612/A9235.

According to the letter, which was given wider circulation at the request of Chamberlain, this action had been necessary because the United States had come out of World War I almost unscathed, immensely wealthy, but in a truculent, anti-British frame of mind. The Americans did not conceal their intention of using their wealth to deprive Britain of her position as the leading sea power. Owing to the terms on which British war debts to America had been contracted, they were in a position to "make tremendous and immediate demands." These demands could have shattered Britain's credit just at a time when London was beginning to recover from New York the position as "financial centre of the world" which appeared to have been lost forever. On all sorts of questions "the Americans were adopting a nasty and menacing attitude," and Britain agreed to the Washington treaties on the Far East in order to "gain time on the financial question." The termination of the Anglo-Japanese Alliance had been "absolutely indispensable" if Britain were to avoid difficulties with America and regain her financial power.[28]

American attitudes on naval armaments were also condemned as unreasonable. According to Sir Warren Fisher, permanent under-secretary at the Treasury, Britain and Japan were both willing to accept "vulnerability" as the test of naval needs, but the United States rejected it. As key British officials viewed the matter, the United States was impregnable, and therefore her demands for parity with Great Britain and superiority over Japan were based either "on *amour propre* or a desire for aggressive power or on both."[29] If it were not for the attitude of the United States government in the negotiations for a new naval agreement in 1934-35, Britain and Japan, in Fisher's opinion, could have reached a mutually satisfactory arrangement without any difficulty. As it was, America was blamed for the failure of the London Naval Conference of 1935.

In the political arena also the Conservative government was reluctant to tie itself to the United States. The American government had shown itself to be unreliable and unable to know or make up its own mind. American policy, not only with respect to Europe and the League of Nations, but toward China as well, had been erratic and, according to Sir Victor Wellesley, inconsiderate in the recent past.[30] Even more crucial in creating strains in the Anglo-American relationship in the context of the Far Eastern crisis

[28]Hankey to General Sir Archibald Montgomery-Massingbred (Chief of the Imperial General Staff), copies to Chamberlain, Baldwin, and Simon, 22 September 1933, CAB 21/369.

[29]Fisher, Memorandum for Chamberlain, copy to Admiral Sir Ernle Chatfield (Chief of Naval Staff), 7 November 1934, Chatfield Papers.

[30]Wellesley, 1 February 1932, *DBFP*, Series 2, 9, no. 239.

was the wish of the British government to be on friendly relations with Japan, a power universally regarded as America's "principal enemy."[31]

The most controversial episodes of the 1930's, revealing Britain's dilemma over the choice between Japan and America, occurred during the Manchurian crisis of 1931-32. The British and American governments both played a game of "diplomatic hide and seek"[32] during these events, and it later transpired that neither government was prepared to take any overt measures, beyond words, to stop Japanese aggression. But their diplomatic manoeuvrings during the crisis were conducted in a way that poisoned relations between them throughout the 1930's.[33] The crux of this complicated matter, as it affected the Anglo-American relationship, lay in the several occasions when the United States Secretary of State, Henry Stimson, invited the British government to join him in issuing statements which were directed primarily and unmistakably at Japan. The first occasion was early in January 1932 when Stimson proposed a declaration of "non-recognition" of any situation, treaty, or agreement brought about by means contrary to the covenants and obligations of the Pact of Paris. And later in the same month, after Japanese naval marines had attacked and occupied part of Shanghai, inflicting thousands of casualties, Stimson urged the British government to join the American government at once in formal and categorical representations to Japan that the International Settlement in Shanghai was sacrosanct and to consider sending additional naval units to Shanghai.[34]

The British government, which wanted to keep on good terms with both Japan and the United States, was embarrassed by Stimson's initiative and tried to avoid making any bilateral statements or actions with the Americans. The first approach by Stimson was rebuffed when the Foreign Office stated that it had already received the necessary assurances from the Japanese government that the latter intended to respect the "open door" in

[31]Simon, C. P. 80(34), 16 March 1934, CAB 24/248.

[32]Viscount Cecil to E. Colby, 7 January 1933, Cecil Papers—51168, British Museum, London.

[33]Memorandum, 1 October 1936, FO 20275/F6358. These episodes have provided grist for controversy ever since: H. Stimson, *The Far Eastern Crisis* (New York: Harper, 1936), presents the American case, while J. T. Pratt, *War and Politics in China* (London: J. Cape, 1943) defends the Foreign Office. C. Thorne, *The Limits of Foreign Policy* (London: Hamilton, 1972) is the most comprehensive scholarly treatment of the 1931-33 crisis.

[34]*FRUS*, Japan 1931-1941, 1: 76; *DBFP*, Series 2, 9, no. 53, 5 January 1932, no. 114, 25 January 1932, no. 128, 27 January 1932, and Simon to MacDonald, 29 January, 1932, Simon Papers, FO 800/291.

Manchuria.[35] The Foreign Office later acknowledged that this was a tacti-
cal mistake,[36] but in the meantime it had served the other British preoccupation of pleasing the Japanese.[37] Later approaches by Stimson were
declined or rather postponed by Sir John Simon on the technicality that
Britain could not appear to be deserting the League of Nations where the
matter would be coming up for consideration.

In a letter to the prime minister (which for some unexplained reason
was not included in the archives until 1962), Simon reveals more clearly
than elsewhere his reasons for not wanting to get too closely involved with
the Americans. Britain had to remember, he said, that "though America
expresses great surprise if we do not act with them on these occasions, if
we do they will leave us with the brunt of the work and of the blame."[38]
Another reason for eschewing American initiatives in the Far East was
that pressure to stop Japanese expansion on the Chinese littoral was a
hopeless and perhaps misplaced effort. In holding this view, Simon was
reflecting a die-hard current of opinion in the Foreign Office which, in the
early stages, favoured a Japanese victory to drive Chinese troops away
from Shanghai because, as the consul-general in Shanghai put it, of all that
the foreigners, especially the British, had suffered in recent years from the
"unjustified pretensions of Chinese nationalism."[39] In sum, Simon was
telling the prime minister that the Americans, as partners, were unreliable
for a project that was unsuitable.

All the various factors which contributed to the difficulties of Anglo-
American co-operation, whether they were differences over naval requirements, economic rivalries, or divergent political approaches, led the Foreign
Office to conclude that while promoting friendly relations with the United
States did not call for the sacrifice of any essential interests, the Americans
would have to be handled with much patience, for progress would inevitably be slow.[40] After the American attempt to put pressure on Japan
in the "Stimson episode," referred to above, it became almost a standing
instruction in the Foreign Office to be very careful, "almost abstemious

---

[35]Ibid., no. 61, 8 January 1932, no. 66, 9 January 1932; Foreign Office press
communiqué, *The Times*, 11 January 1932.

[36]Pratt, *War and Politics*, pp. 218 ff and appendix; Minutes, 3 to 24 June 1935,
FO 20275/file 2412.

[37]*DBFP*, Series 2, 9, no. 84, 15 January 1932. Sadako Ogata, *Defiance in
Manchuria* (Berkeley: University of California Press, 1964), pp. 164-65, says
Japanese cabinet records show that Simon's rejection of Stimson's request for a joint
Anglo-American "non-recognition" declaration was regarded as an outstanding pro-
Japanese gesture.

[38]Simon to MacDonald, 29 January 1932, Simon Papers, FO 800/291.

[39]*DBFP*, Series 2, 9, no. 395, 9 February 1932, no. 404, 10 February 1932.

[40]C.I.D. paper 1112-B.

in fact," in co-operating with the United States in East Asia. The Americans, having "thrust us forward to our cost" would "let us down or stab us in the back."[41] This was extreme language. In part it reflected an accurate British assessment of the current of isolationism which was running strongly in American politics. But it also tended to obscure the fact that neither country, for obvious military reasons following the Four Power Pacific Treaty of 1921, was prepared to offer a direct challenge to Japan in that country's proclaimed sphere of influence. In any case by 1934 the contemplation of Anglo-American collaboration against Japan became irrelevant. The American government, as Professor Dorothy Borg has shown in her detailed study, was anxious to avoid antagonizing Japan, at least until American naval strength increased. And the British cabinet, for reasons which must now be examined, took a decision in 1934 to seek a permanent friendship with Japan.

The decision to seek Japan's friendship arose out of the study which the Defence Requirements Committee was making on priorities for British defence spending. After several months of deliberation the DRC had reported its main assumption, that Britain should be ready for trouble with Germany within five years. The other potentially hostile country was Japan, and the greatest danger would be a simultaneous conflict against Germany and Japan. With this in mind, the first recommendation of the DRC was that Britain should try to get back to her old terms of cordiality and mutual respect with Japan. However, in view of the current difficulties, arising mainly from trade rivalry, the DRC proposed a provisional policy of "showing a tooth" by completing the Singapore naval base in order to regain the standing which had been lost in recent years, and then returning to the ultimate policy of accommodation and friendship.[42] The qualification of "showing a tooth" represented a compromise within the DRC which still left the balance between national safety and imperial defence to be decided. The main attention, apparently under Sir Warren Fisher's insistence, should be devoted to national safety and the German menace. This implied concentration on the air force. But the formula for "showing a tooth" to Japan allowed the navy-orientated chiefs of staff to save face and retain their preference of major commitments for defence in the following order of importance: "(1) the defence of our possessions and interests in the Far East (2) European commitments and (3) the defence of India

[41]Vansittart, Minutes, 14 and 21 December 1933, FO 17375/W14129, FO 16612/W9235.

[42]C.P. 64(34), 7 March 1934, CAB 24/248. Cab 8(34) CAB 23/78; also C.P. 70(34), Memorandum by Prime Minister on C.P. 64(34), CAB 24/248.

against Soviet aggression."[43] The cabinet would have to make the final decision.

The cabinet received the report of the DRC early in March 1934 and immediately began a discussion of its contents. It soon became obvious that there was a wide divergence of opinions within the cabinet and the matter was transferred to a standing ministerial sub-committee on disarmament. This sub-committee, which included fifteen of the eighteen full cabinet ministers and Anthony Eden, met to debate the DRC report on two widely separated occasions in early May and late June 1934. On the last day of July 1934 the full cabinet finally gave its approval to the recommendations of the sub-committee.

At the first meeting of the cabinet to discuss the DRC report there was little difference of opinion about the seriousness of the potential threat arising from Germany and the focus of cabinet discussion therefore turned to the DRC recommendation for improving relations with Japan. Prime Minister MacDonald began by raising certain doubts. How could a commercial policy which was aimed against Japan be reconciled with improved relations? Also what bearing would such a policy have on Anglo-American relations? He thought the Americans would regard any agreement with Japan as an alliance against themselves and therefore "the more quietly we could improve our relations with Japan the better."[44]

The chancellor of the Exchequer, Neville Chamberlain, quickly emerged as the most ardent and consistent supporter of the DRC recommendations on Japan. Only friendship with Japan would allow Britain to concentrate on Germany. In getting around the problem of difficulties with Japan, Chamberlain's self-confidence was sometimes more evident than the clarity of his arguments. The Japanese had been ruffled by the termination of the Anglo-Japanese Alliance but since they "now realised that they were coming up against western standards of civilisation,"[45] whatever that may have meant, Chamberlain thought their hostility could be overcome by frank discussion which would lead to a bilateral non-aggression pact. British trade rivalries with Japan were admittedly difficult, but Chamberlain did not dwell on this topic. Japan's ambitions in China were also a problem. Any pact with Japan would have to be subject to certain assurances about China, but only south of the Great Wall where "our interests at once become common."[46] Chamberlain, in common with many of the political

[43]C.P. 264(33), CAB 24/244. This priority was confirmed again in 1935.
[44]Cab 9(34), 14 March 1934, CAB 23/78; also C.P. 70(34), 12 March 1934, CAB 24/248.
[45]Cab 9(34), 14 March 1934.
[46]Minutes, ministerial sub-committee, 1 May 1934, CAB 27/506.

élite and officer class in Britain as debates in the House of Lords in April 1934 and commentary in the newspapers show, was prepared to offer recognition of Japan's conquest of Manchuria. As to America, "what were we going to lose?" He proposed to make it clear to America that Britain "could not pull the chestnuts out of the fire for them" in respect of the coming naval conference with Japan. Britain should not oppose Japan's desire to alter the ratio of capital ships in her own favour. And Britain should tell America that she was not prepared to submit herself to the limitation of a naval treaty.[47]

As the discussion developed, several ministers, such as Lord Londonderry (Air), Sir Philip Cunliffe-Lister (Colonies), and Lord Halifax (Privy Seal) sided readily with Chamberlain. Others, notably J. R. Thomas (Dominions), Lord Hailsham (War), and Anthony Eden (without portfolio) were opposed to placing any trust in the good behaviour or pledged word of the Japanese government. But the two ministers principally involved, Sir John Simon (foreign secretary) and Sir Bolton Eyres-Monsell (First Lord of the Admiralty), took a vascillating position. Their changing stands reflect intensive behind-the-scenes pressures, of which only scraps of evidence are available. A good deal of the pressure apparently had less to do with the politics of the situation than with the pride and place of the navy as the senior branch of the services.

At first they both supported Chamberlain. Eyres-Monsell thought a non-aggression pact with Japan might please America because it would show her "that we could exert influence on Japan." At this first meeting Simon was also inclined to agree with Chamberlain that a non-aggression pact with Japan would be of advantage. There was something to be said for the view that if Japan was to expand, "such expansion was preferable on the Continent of Asia rather than southward."[48] In view of the doubts of the prime minister and others, the cabinet commissioned Simon and Eyres-Monsell jointly to prepare a definite recommendation for improving relations with Japan. Almost overnight Simon reversed the ill-considered opinion he had expressed in cabinet and, without consulting Eyres-Monsell, produced a paper which condemned the idea of an Anglo-Japanese pact as a "flash in the pan."[49] It would shock America, create difficulties with Canada, be taken by British public opinion and by members of the League of Nations as a condonation of Japanese proceedings in Manchukuo, and be a demonstration to China that, as far as Britain was concerned, Japan

[47]Cab 9(34), 14 March 1934.
[48]Ibid.
[49]C.P. 80(34), 16 March 1934, CAB 24/248.

"might have a free hand against her." Confronted with the fact that the foreign secretary now disagreed radically with the DRC report, the cabinet decided to postpone a decision and refer the whole question to the ministerial sub-committee on disarmament.

Before the sub-committee could hold its first meeting on the DRC report, two important diplomatic exchanges involving Britain and Japan took place in April. On April 17 the Japanese Foreign Office spokesman, Eiji Amau, issued the famous "white hands off China" statement. The British cabinet, as we have seen in the previous chapter, tried, not too successfully, to reassure itself that Japan's anger was directed at others.

The second exchange came after the cabinet took a decision on 18 April to curb Japanese textile imports into the British Empire. In this case there was no possibility that the Japanese government could avoid seeing itself as the target of British action. During the previous twelve months, as Japanese exports increased rapidly, prolonged discussions between government and business representatives of the two countries trying to arrange a division of world textile markets had proved to be unsuccessful.[50] Japanese exporters, blocked by a Chinese boycott which began in 1931, were making deep inroads into traditional British markets. The export of Japanese bleached cottons to British India, for example, had increased four times, and Japan was now buying almost half of India's raw cotton exports.[51] Under strong pressure from the Lancashire manufacturers,[52] the cabinet decided to act, by coincidence, on the day after the Amau declaration. Sir John Simon was instructed by the cabinet to inform the Japanese ambassador, "with the accompaniment of every expression of goodwill," that the British government felt it impossible to delay any longer in protecting its interests and was imposing quotas to restrict Japanese imports into the colonies.[53] These two developments served as a warning to the ministerial sub-committee considering the DRC report that the difficulties of reaching a political understanding with Japan were increasing rather than diminishing because of commercial rivalry.

When the sub-committee convened there were several days of rambling discussion. The prime minister announced that the sub-committee was assembled to "try and start peace with Japan"[54] and to draft a document

[50]"Notes" of March 1936, BT 11/516, summarizes talks which took place at Simla, Tokyo, and London in previous years.

[51]Sir Horace Wilson to Hon. Walter Runciman, 28 November 1933, BT 11/219, Pt. 1.

[52]Minutes of meeting with Clare Lees, 13 November 1933, ibid.

[53]Cab 16(34), 18 April 1934, CAB 23/79; also C.P. 81 and 106, CAB 24/278.

[54]Minutes, 1 May 1934.

which could be a statement of policy. MacDonald, who had come to the conclusion that the Disarmament Conference of the League of Nations would fail, was apparently won over to the idea that Britain should seek security by trying to get a Pacific agreement through separate talks with Japan—although he added the rider that the United States should be brought in if possible. Neville Chamberlain took an active part in the discussion and returned to themes he had expressed at earlier meetings of the cabinet. His main point was that friendship with Japan was of utmost importance because Germany was the most serious potential enemy. It would not be possible to fight both Germany and Japan at the same time. In addition, he felt that there was "no immediate evidence of an aggressive spirit" on the part of Japan.[55]

Eyres-Monsell agreed with Chamberlain's idea of doing something to give Japan satisfaction, but continued to insist that, since Germany had no navy, Japan was the greatest security risk. Therefore, Britain needed a fully equipped navy and a properly defended base at Singapore. Without these "our Empire in the East" would fall, whereas if Singapore were properly defended it would make war less likely.[56]

Simon and Eden saw great difficulties in Chamberlain's line and feared that a wide political approach might encourage Japan to stake out bigger claims than she would otherwise and that as a result Britain would find herself in an uncomfortable position. These ministers, and others who shared their viewpoint, were impressed by the conclusions of a voluminous study prepared over a period of six months in 1933 and 1934 by the Far Eastern Department of the Foreign Office.[57] This special study of the far eastern situation concluded with a unanimity on a political question which was "most unusual,"[58] that an alliance with Japan—either political or commercial—would be fatal to British interests. Sir Robert Vansittart, in commending the study to the cabinet, had concluded that while Britain should not antagonize Japan, it was Chinese good will which should be cultivated by Great Britain, bearing in mind "our extensive trade and large vested interests."[59] Fundamental Japanese expansionist aims in China, not to mention cotton trade rivalries and naval difficulties, made it inadvisable if not impossible to tie Britain's far eastern policy to Japan.

Sir John Simon, however, did not have the courage of the Foreign Office's convictions. Nor did he have the willpower to match Neville Cham-

---

[55]Minutes, 3 and 5 May 1934, CAB 27/507.
[56]Ibid.
[57]C.P. 77(34), 21 March 1934, CAB 24/248; also in FO 18160/F295.
[58]Pratt, Minute, 2 November 1934, FO 18048/F6507.
[59]Vansittart, letter of transmittal, 12 March 1934, FO 18160/F295.

berlain's determination. Therefore he accepted the idea that in principle an agreement with Japan would contribute to possibilities for peace. However, for the moment Chamberlain was forced to agree to the proviso that this principle would not be used as a directive as it stood without some elaboration.

After this inconclusive and, for Chamberlain, disappointing discussion on the political and security implications of the DRC report, Chamberlain directed the attention of his colleagues to what he called the financial and domestic implications of the report at the June meeting of the ministerial sub-committee. As the person responsible for finances, he told his cabinet colleagues bluntly that the whole range of the DRC's proposals were impossible to carry out. The cabinet would have to choose the salient questions. The starting point, he said, was that the anxieties of the British people were concentrated on Europe rather than on the Far East. And since, in addition, Germany was the greatest potential threat to Britain, Chamberlain insisted that the cabinet would have to postpone the idea of sending to Singapore "a fleet of capital ships capable of containing the Japanese Fleet or meeting it in battle."[60] With his priorities in mind, Chamberlain proposed to cut £8 million (40 per cent) off the navy's requests for new construction, reduce the army's increases by £20 million (50 per cent), and give the air force £3 million (20 per cent) more than it expected for air defence squadrons. The strategic corollary of Chamberlain's financial allocations was, of course, the improvement of relations with Japan and a defensive posture towards Germany and Europe.

When the full meaning of the chancellor of the Exchequer's proposals became evident, vociferous opposition came from various quarters within and without the cabinet. Senior civil servants and high military officers managed to inject their views into the debate either by direct contact with ministers or by writing letters to each other and sending carbon copies to ministers they wished to bolster or influence. Their influence is attested to by the subsequent appearance of their arguments in the minutes of cabinet discussion.

Some of these highly articulate men raised arguments in an attempt to counter the proposed cuts in the navy's estimates. Chamberlain's proposals, it was pointed out, would spell the end of the empire which gave Britain its great voice in the world. The fundamental principles of the system of imperial defence—a strong and mobile navy, despatch of the capital fleet to Singapore and the Far East, and the safeguarding of maritime communications—were being thrown overboard by Chamberlain.

---

[60]Minutes, ministerial sub-committee, 25 and 26 June 1934, CAB 27/507.

If Britain were in so rotten a condition that she was not willing to maintain the empire, then she would "become once more nothing but an insignificant island in the North Sea."[61] Precedents were cited to remind the cabinet that an empire can crumble as rapidly from the circumference as from the centre.[62] A further criticism was that Chamberlain was rearranging the priorities of the DRC not in view of the real state of world affairs, but "in the order in which uninformed public opinion has casually placed them."[63] This appeared to introduce a new principle into calculations of defence strategy. Did not the government, which had at its disposal "great masses of information and a well-ordered machine for digesting it," have a responsibility to lead, not follow, public opinion which was necessarily ill-informed and guided largely by scare headlines in the daily press?[64] As to the main danger, the admirals argued that the fear of Germany was "a fear of what Germany *may* do." In the meantime Britain had France "at our elbow." In the Far East "we stand alone."[65] The admirals also challenged Sir Warren Fisher's suggestion that it was worth the risk of slighting the United States in favour of Japan. If the choice were between Japan and the U.S.A., the latter could be a far greater menace if antagonized, and Britain therefore should work for a naval agreement. If unable to get it, she should "agree to differ, but without quarrelling."[66]

Within the ministerial sub-committee the First Lord of the Admiralty made an emotional appeal that the end of the seapower of the British Empire was a shameful policy which was not advocated "even by the Communists in this country."[67] With Japan going through an Elizabethan period of expansion, the danger in the Far East was an hourly one, whereas no one claimed that an attack on the British Isles could mature before five years. For strategic as well as sentimental reasons, the Admiralty had made clear that it favoured a political rapprochement with Japan. But there was nothing in the history of the most recent twenty years to show that Britain could rely on the good will of Japan unless Britain was in a position to oppose unreasonable action on her part.

[61]Chatfield to Fisher, 16 July 1934, Baldwin Papers, vol. 132, Cambridge University Library, Cambridge.
[62]Hankey to MacDonald, Baldwin, Simon, Eyres-Monsell, and Eden, 22 June 1934, CAB 63/49.
[63]Little to Chatfield and Eyres-Monsell, 21 June 1934, ADM 116/3436.
[64]Hankey, 22 June 1934.
[65]Little, 21 June 1934.
[66]Chatfield to Fisher, 16 July 1934.
[67]Minutes, 25 and 26 June 1934.

After Eyres-Monsell spoke, important cabinet members rallied to his cause. The Minister of War, Lord Hailsham, condemned Chamberlain's attitude as one of "despair and defeatism." On the question of where the main danger lay, the prime minister sided with the Admiralty and against Chamberlain. MacDonald was particularly impressed by the position of the Dominions, who saw Japan as a menace. Japan, he thought, was very troublesome, whereas so far he was not "particularly carried away by the potential menace from Germany." The situation in Germany "was very fluid," and there might be a "greater menace" in the aggressive nature of French policy: the visits of Monsieur Barthou to Roumania and other Eastern European countries might force Germany's hand. Russia would not help Britain unless she got "a very large *quid pro quo*." In one of the rare occasions when Baldwin participated in these foreign policy discussions, he said he found himself in general agreement with the prime minister. He believed that both Germany and Japan were political mad dogs "but the scope for a mad dog was wider in the Far East than it was in Europe." He was alarmed at Chamberlain's naval proposals, particularly from the Dominions' point of view, and at the "rather acute trade rivalry" between Britain and Japan which was coming to a head. Baldwin suggested an Imperial Defence Loan campaign among the public as a possible way to raise money.[68]

In spite of their sympathy for the position of the navy, both MacDonald and Baldwin qualified their criticisms of Chamberlain's programme in important respects. Because of the uncertainties in Europe, Baldwin thought it was necessary to go ahead without any delay in the air rearmament programme. And the prime minister agreed with Chamberlain on the necessity for financial prudence—the pay cuts to the civil service of 1931 would have to be reversed, and, in addition, the promised reduction in income tax would have to be delivered; it was essential to find a "political solution" to some of Britain's difficulties. These comments by the titular leaders of the government, taken together, reveal a substantial measure of agreement with Chamberlain's programme. Perhaps for this reason, although his proposals had received scant support during the prolonged discussion, Chamberlain's opinions and self-confidence remained unshaken as he answered his critics in reply to the debate.

Chamberlain spoke with the air of a man who had already won his point when he told his colleagues in the ministerial sub-committee that he had not expected general assent in the first instance. With respect to domestic public opinion, he reiterated that increasing service estimates

[68]Ibid.

could not be carried without public support, and while the public might be ignorant, they were not stupid. Therefore to educate the public that security in the Far East constituted as great an issue as the air defence of Britain would be an extremely difficult task. After the promises which had been made about restoring the pay cuts, could the government now go to the public and say that they had had a reduction in income tax and half the pay cuts had been restored, but now it was found impossible to go further because of defence necessities? He thought this might be necessary, but it would be difficult. Some ministers had suggested floating a defence loan. This, said Chamberlain, was a broad road which led to destruction and future generations would have the onus of repaying it. The question was whether the government was in a position to spend £100 million in the next five years and, if so, how to spend the amount decided.

The crux of Chamberlain's proposals was not sending the battle fleet to the Far East. He had been surprised by the reactions of Simon and Eden as they seemed to reflect more anxiety about Japan than he had expected. In the absence of any evidence, Chamberlain found it difficult to believe that Japan wanted to fight Britain. The only danger he visualized at the moment was Japanese aggression in China, and, if that occurred, Britain might want to be able to tell Japan to keep her hands off China. Admittedly that would not be possible under his proposals. Chamberlain, who was evidently apt to ignore facts and advice which he found inconvenient, thought the risk in the Far East "was only of a moderate character." He did not think any public announcement should be made regarding the change of policy in the Far East, although under questioning he agreed that the Dominions would have to be informed. In the meantime, the cruisers would be able to protect British trade—that was not the job of a battle fleet anyway—and if the situation in the Far East changed for the worse, his programme could be modified.

Chamberlain's performance was impressive. He was right in insisting that political problems and strategic dangers should determine the technical necessities of rearmament and not vice versa. Since the top political and military advisers of the cabinet had been unanimous in the DRC report in singling out Germany as the greatest potential threat, Chamberlain was on solid ground for rejecting the DRC priorities and demanding that greater attention be given to defence against a threat which would likely be airborne. The DRC, however, had not been categorical in their views about Japan—advocating both friendship and the showing of a tooth—and the weakness of Chamberlain's case was his singularly positive attitude to Japan. He was, of course, as unwilling as any of his colleagues to contemplate the abandonment of the empire to Japan. But his refusal to see any immediate evidence of an aggressive spirit on the part of Japan lent an air of unreality to his programme and weakened the credibility of his argument. He would have done better to admit the obvious—that Japan was a dangerous aggressor—but say that some solution other than building battleships would have to be found. Instead, he argued that Japan's activities were not incompatible with British foreign policy objectives and that an Anglo-Japanese friendship should be consummated. Sir John Simon's lack of political courage or temperamental inability to make up his mind when faced with a difficult situation meant that Chamberlain's error in political judgment was not squarely or forcefully challenged by the person chiefly responsible for foreign policy. As a result the ministerial sub-committee discussion on Japan was inconclusive and tended to become confused with service rivalries over budget allocations. The sub-committee was unable to draft for the cabinet the reasoned statement of policy toward Japan that the prime minister had originally requested.

The situation was somewhat anti-climactic when the full cabinet met at the end of July, 1934, to approve the recommendations of the ministerial sub-committee on the DRC report. The defence of the empire in the Far East was still affirmed as the highest military priority.[69] But this was pure face-saving for the chiefs of staff, because the cabinet had already decided to start rearmament a step nearer home. In the Commons on 19 July, Acting Prime Minister Baldwin had announced a programme of air rearmament for home defence. On the financial side, in spite of Eyres-Monsell's continuing protests, the navy's estimates, which would have been the basis for the defence of the far eastern empire, were pigeon-holed. Chamberlain's proposals prevailed unamended, and the Admiralty had to be content with the vague promise that "so far as financial exigencies allow" steps should be taken to remedy the very serious weakness of the defensive position in the Far East. There were many other recommendations, but only one bearing directly on the Far East. Slighting the advice of the Foreign Office not to tie Britain's far eastern policy to Japan, since that country had fundamental aims to which Britain could not give support, the cabinet approved Chamberlain's demand that Britain should seek to secure "a permanent friendship with Japan."[70]

Chamberlain, who maintained his own private contacts with Japanese government representatives, lost no time in seeking to promote a political alliance with Japan. His budget had taken the problem of Japan out of the hands of the navy and he was definitely unwilling to leave the matter in the procrastinating hands of the Foreign Office. From his holiday retreat in

---

[69]Cab 31(34), 31 July, 1934, CAB 23/79.
[70]Ibid.

Scotland, Chamberlain wrote to Sir John Simon proposing British recognition of Manchukuo (the Japanese name for the puppet régime they had established in 1931) in return for a Japanese guarantee not to pass the Great Wall and invade or monopolize China proper:

> ... the more I have turned it over the more convinced I have become that this is one of those crucial points in history which test the statesman's capacity and foresight. ... Moreover I can't help reflecting that if you could bring off an agreement with Japan such as I have suggested, it would stamp your tenure of office with the special distinction that is attached to memorable historical events. ... I hope ... that you will some day be remembered (inter alia) as the author of the "Simon-Hirota Pact."[71]

Although not insensible to the flattering suggestions contained in Chamberlain's letter, Simon, with the advice of Vansittart, was still doubtful as to what the political effect of a pact with Japan would be. Answering his own question, with emphasis and in a negative sense, he replied by saying it would be *"to give Japan a free hand in the Far East so long as she respects British possessions there."*[72]

In the meantime, the organization of a high level delegation from the Federation of British Industries to Japan and Manchukuo in the autumn of 1934 provided Chamberlain with an opportunity to test public opinion and perhaps create support for a renewal of Anglo-Japanese political friendship. Ostensibly the FBI mission's purpose was to study industrial conditions, but its members' public speeches had strong political overtones suggesting a weakening of the pledge of non-recognition of Manchukuo which Britain had made at the League of Nations.[73] The mission was received by the Emperor with such publicity that it became the subject of debate and criticism in Parliament and the British press because of the official support which it was assumed to have. When the FBI mission returned from Japan,

[71]Chamberlain to Simon, 1 September 1934, Simon Papers. Chamberlain's draft eventually became C.P. 223(34), "The Future of Anglo-Japanese Relations," 16 October 1934, CAB 24/250, which Chamberlain persuaded Simon to submit jointly to the cabinet but which was never formally considered by the full cabinet. Cab 26(34), 24 October 1934, CAB 23/80.

[72]Simon to Chamberlain, 7 September 1934, Simon Papers.

[73]Sir Charles Seligman, a prominent London banker, member of the Board of Trade's Export Credits Guarantee Department since 1921, and a member of the FBI delegation, was quoted as saying: "I am a great advocate of British recognition of Manchukuo. Most of the businessmen I associate with hold the same view." 4 October 1934, *Osaka Mainichi and Tokyo Nichi Nichi*. Information on origins and official involvement in the delegation is in files 164/10 and 591/23, FO 18114 and FO 18184.

it published its favourable impressions of Japanese rule in Manchukuo and also sent a private letter to the cabinet which strongly reflected Chamberlain's point of view.[74] The central point of the letter was that British trade relations with China, the security of British possessions, and the solution of Anglo-Japanese trade rivalries made "an understanding between the two countries . . . essential." Japan, it reported, wanted specially friendly relations with Britain in order to follow a common policy of co-operation in China. While the FBI mission was still in Japan, stories inspired by the Japanese "Foreign Office spokesman" began to appear in the Japanese and British press about the possibility of an Anglo-Japanese non-aggression pact.[75] One Japanese paper understood that "views have recently been secretly exchanged" and that negotiations had made progress.[76] The British Foreign Office was mystified by these reports, suspecting a "gross prevarication," and Prime Minister MacDonald asked if anything could be done to "stop this game."[77]

The astonishing fact was that the improbable rumours of secret negotiations between British and Japanese principals in Tokyo on matters of high policy, unknown apparently even to the British prime minister or the Foreign Office, were well founded. Neville Chamberlain and Sir Warren Fisher had given secret instructions to an ex-officio member of the FBI delegation, A. H. F. Edwardes, adviser to the Japanese embassy in London,[78] to contact the Japanese cabinet and raise "a certain proposal" which

---

[74]G. Lucock to Sir Horace Wilson, C.P. 9(35), 4 January 1935, CAB 24/253.

[75]*Morning Post*, from "a special correspondent," 24 August 1934.

[76]Sir Robert Clive to Simon, telegrams 255, 258, 19 and 20 October 1934, FO 18184/F6221, F6258.

[77]Minutes, ibid.

[78]Francis Piggott, *Broken Thread* (London: Gale and Polden, 1950), p. 245, identifies Edwardes's position. Edwardes had been a member of the Chinese Maritime Customs Administration for many years and in 1929 became acting inspector-general after the dismissal of Aglen. Edwardes was in turn dismissed by the Nanking government after the Chinese press accused him of displaying imperialistic attitudes, taking instructions from the British consul, and financing the enemies of the Kuomintang (*Shih Shih Hsin Pao* [Shanghai], 3 August 1928, Maze Papers, 2:126). His successor as inspector general, Sir Frederick Maze, tended to confirm the Chinese accusations and furthermore charged that Edwardes had carried on shady financial manipulations to overpay himself and inflate his lifetime pension from the Chinese government (Maze Papers, 9: 135-42). The Far Eastern Department of the Foreign Office considered Edwardes to be "neither competent nor trustworthy" (Pratt, Memorandum, 10 August 1936, FO 20253/F4902). A favourite of the Japanese, Edwardes had become financial adviser to Manchukuo after 1931 and subsequently adviser to the Japanese embassy in London. In this position he apparently had easy access to Fisher and Wilson and was the source on which Chamberlain and Fisher relied for briefing on China. It was Edwardes who first talked to the head of the FBI about sending a mission to Japan and Manchukuo (Crowe to Orde, 25 June 1934, FO 18114/F3841.

had been discussed "at a purely private luncheon party" at "Gwynne's place."[79] After his return to London, Edwardes sent a "personal and confidential" report on his conversations with the Japanese cabinet ministers to Sir Warren Fisher.[80] This report was read by Chamberlain, but a search of the Foreign Office and cabinet files has failed to reveal that these secret meetings in Tokyo were ever known or reported to the Foreign Office or to the prime minister. This omission appears to have been deliberate because on one occasion Chamberlain's private secretary, Mr. J. D. Fergusson, reminded him that in discussion with his cabinet colleagues Edwardes "cannot of course be referred to."[81] It was an early indication of the leadership style which Chamberlain was to exhibit as prime minister when he continued to handle issues of national importance outside the accepted constitutional procedures.

Edwardes reported to Fisher that on arrival in Tokyo he had informed the Vice-Minister of Foreign Affairs, Mamoru Shigemitsu, that he was carrying personal letters to certain members of the Japanese government from Ambassador Matsudaira which he thought referred to "the conversation at a purely private luncheon party at which a certain proposal had been discussed." Shigemitsu had replied that Matsudaira had written a "very guarded hint of the matter and saying I would amplify this on arrival." Edwardes then proceeded to give Fisher a précis of the conversations which he held with Mr. Shigemitsu (28 September and 24 October), Mr. Hirota, foreign minister (1 October), Admiral Osumi, minister of the navy (22 October), General Hayashi, minister of war, and General Araki, late minister of war (24 October).

According to Edwardes, he had told his Japanese listeners of the friendly feeling of "the man on the street" in England towards Japan and that a few isolated incidents—the breaking off of the Anglo-Japanese Alliance, the Manchurian Resolution of the League of Nations, and the restriction of Japanese imports into Great Britain and the colonies—should not be allowed to affect the judgment of the Japanese people about this "essential" fact. Many Englishmen regarded the breaking of the alliance as a great mistake which had ushered in an era of disorder in the Far East; similarly, it had been regrettable that the "West had ever interfered with matters

---

[79]Edwardes to Fisher, 26 November 1934, T 172/1831. H. A. Gwynne was editor-in-chief of the *Morning Post* from 1910 to 1937 when it merged with the *Daily Telegraph*. A former editor of the paper described it "generally recognized as a champion of Conservatism for over a century" (Wilfred Hindle, *The Morning Post 1772-1937: Portrait of a Newspaper* [London: G. T. Foulis, 1962], pp. 4, 235) which in the post-war years backed lost causes.

[80]Edwardes to Fisher, 26 November 1934, T 172/1831.

[81]Briefing papers, 16 and 23 January 1935, T 172/1831.

concerning the East" with reference to Manchukuo, and it was hoped that the friendly spirit of the Federation of British Industries' mission would lead to amicable discussion between industrialists of the two countries. What might appear to be public antagonism to Japan in Britain "emanated entirely from pacifist sources," although Edwardes admitted, in response to Hirota's questioning, that America might possibly disapprove of Anglo-Japanese co-operation. Edwardes told Admiral Osumi that he hoped Japanese naval demands would not be extreme, since that would "give a bad impression," but that it should never be forgotten that whatever difficulties the Japanese navy might get into, "the sympathy of the British Navy would always be with them." Osumi had replied that he was "much interested in my saying this" as it was exactly what Admiral Dreyer, British commander-in-chief, China Station, had said to him recently, but it must be remembered that "Japan had her difficulties in 1935." Edwardes asked if Osumi was referring to the question of the League of Nations taking away the islands mandated to Japan, and he took the opportunity of passing on Sir Warren Fisher's "personal private message that we were 'not interested and would not play' "; to which Osumi replied that he only wished that his young officers could hear that. Edwardes reported to the head of the British civil service that he had closed all his interviews by saying his remarks were made "in an entirely private capacity" and in no sense was he an "official spokesman" for anyone.

On the eve of his departure from Tokyo, the vice-minister of foreign affairs had given Edwardes "the following private statement" for Sir Warren Fisher which Edwardes thought it advisable to record in writing:

(1) The Japanese Government would greatly welcome a gesture of friendship from this country.

(2) A non-aggression pact is considered too formal an instrument in view of the friendly feelings of the Japanese people, but that if this was desired there would of course be no objection.

(3) A proposal for a "Gentleman's Agreement" would be warmly received and it was suggested that such an agreement could be put forward as follows:

Documents could be exchanged between the two countries recording our past friendship and reiterating its continuance in the future, this part of the document to be available for publication if desired and agreed upon. In addition, there could be a private agreement that if either country had its own difficulties, or if there were mutual questions between the two countries, in any part of the World, such matters could be frankly and fully discussed between the two countries without, of course, binding either party.

It was also suggested that if the machinery for industrial discussion evolved by the British mission developed satisfactorily the two Governments should assist if and when any points discussed by the Industrial Committees proved difficult of solution.[82]

From Edwardes' report several things were apparent. The attention which he had received showed that the Japanese government was anxious for British friendship. But it was also clear that they were more interested in a gesture of British good will and moral support than in any binding agreement to assist each other in the case of difficulties with third parties. The absence of any direct reference to Manchukuo or China showed the strict limits within which Japan wished any British involvement in East Asia. From the British side Edwardes was unable to give the Japanese much information about the possible intent of an understanding and the extent of its commitments. He indicated only that in return for Japanese reasonableness in naval and other demands, his friends advocated that Britain should recognize Japan's sphere of influence and agree not to interfere with matters concerning the East. Through normal diplomatic channels the British had already learned that Japan wanted a political entente.[83] Through the Edwardes-Shigemitsu conversations, the Japanese, on the other hand, learned more about the political thought and methods of Neville Chamberlain and Sir Warren Fisher than they did about the possibilities for consummating a "Simon-Hirota Pact."

Chamberlain's hopes for such a pact suffered a setback toward the end of 1934 as a result of opposition from several quarters. This opposition stemmed from those concerned with the state of Anglo-American relations as well as from those who were familiar with the trend of Japanese politics and aims in China. Public figures who could be classified as "pro-American" at this time, including Lord Lothian, J. L. Garvin (editor of the *Observer*), and others connected with Chatham House, were apparently aware that some members of the cabinet were pushing for an understanding with Japan. Since they felt that this would harm the more important relationship with America, they stirred up a publicity campaign. Taking advantage of the visit of General Smuts, the elder statesman from South Africa, to England in November 1934, they were successful in organizing a flurry of activities to expose and denounce the idea of any agreement with Japan

---

[82]Edwardes to Fisher, 26 November 1934.

[83]Naval Conference Meetings, 35(24) and 35(31), CAB 29/149, contained a message to this effect from Ambassador Matsudaira.

which excluded the United States.[84] It also happened that within the cabinet itself those ministers concerned about co-operation with the Americans were worried by the possibility that Japan would denounce the London Naval Treaty, which was up for renewal in 1935. The American government was known to be anxious to keep the battleship ratio of America, Britain, and Japan at 5:5:3, respectively. Japanese negotiators, on the other hand, had announced that they were determined to walk out unless the two great Anglo-Saxon powers would agree to battleship parity. With the prospect of Japan forcing unrestricted naval construction, the cabinet was not inclined to consider other matters which might give the appearance of siding with the Japanese government.[85]

But perhaps most serious for Chamberlain's plans for friendship with Japan were the scathing reports on current Japanese aims and activities being sent home by G. B. Sansom, commercial counsellor in Tokyo and expert on Japanese affairs. Sansom wrote that the Federation of British Industries' mission had given rise to "an extraordinary crop of rumours" in Japan: Britain was going to recognize Manchukuo, lend Japan money to buy the Chinese Eastern Railway, renew the alliance, "tell the United States to go to the devil, split up China, desert the League of Nations, and ... ensure the peace of the Far East by encouraging Japan to have a whack at Russia." Sansom had never seen anything like "the present attempt to *fabricate* an Anglo-Japanese understanding," and he held that their latest professions of friendship were false. Talk of all kinds of commercial favours "if only we will be friends" was "a trap," and if Britain accepted Japan's overtures now, she would be "making a first-class political blunder, of which the consequences may be terribly serious." Japan's ambition at the moment was "colossal," and the Japanese were feeling a cold wind blowing from somewhere and did not wish to face their enemies without one sympathizer and possible supporter. Sansom said that he was not "anti-Japanese"; his feeling, as always, was the same mixture of "admiration for their great qualities and despair at their silliness." But the same people were not in charge as formerly. No doubt the pendulum would swing back, he concluded, but until it was more or less at rest, this was not a country to make bargains with "unless they were very favourable, very explicit and very easily enforced."

---

[84]See Watt, *Personalities and Policies*, pp. 96-99. Lothian thought these meetings and press articles had "completely defeated" the element which was "working for renewal of the Japanese Alliance." Lothian to G. Shaw (Antung), 21 November 1934, Lothian Papers, GD 40/17/34.

[85]Cab 36(34), 24 October 1934, and Cab 38(34), 29 October 1934, CAB 23/80. See also entry for 20 October 1934, Simon Papers—Diary.

Sir John Simon was pleased to receive Sansom's reports. They contained material he needed to offset the letter from the FBI mission which Chamberlain and his friends had circulated to the cabinet. In introducing Sansom's reports to the cabinet, Simon said that he had no hesitation in considering that Sansom's opinion "must be the authoritative one in this matter" because he was on the spot in Japan, had thirty years experience there, and was generally acknowledged to be "the greatest living authority on that country." In addition, to back up Sansom, who, after all, was only a commercial counsellor in the Tokyo embassy, Simon had the Foreign Office draw up a memorandum on the "Political Aspects of Trade Rivalry or Co-operation with Japan in China," which was also circulated to the cabinet.[86]

According to this memorandum, which was signed by C. W. Orde, head of the Far Eastern Department, the fundamental questions to consider were "the nature of Japanese ambitions in China" and the extent to which Britain could "afford to become identified with them in the minds of the Chinese." There could be no doubt, he said, about the generally aggressive spirit of Japanese policy in its attempt to dominate China and seize control of the Chinese market. There would be constant friction between the Chinese and the Japanese, and "the subtlety and quicker intelligence" of the Chinese in obstruction would likely exasperate the energetic and efficient Japanese into trying to solve difficulties by force. In "the present day world," His Majesty's government could not "morally afford" to put herself in the same camp with exponents of such policies. And besides, it was difficult to do good trade with a hostile people. For British economic interests, the first policy consideration must be to "remain on good terms with the Chinese themselves." Orde concluded with the main proposition which animated Foreign Office thinking on China: Britain should refrain from endeavouring to introduce a general coherence into the somewhat chaotic situation in China; the rehabilitation of China would proceed for a long time to come in a piecemeal manner because the necessary administrative and political unity for comprehensive measures did not exist. The Treasury, with obvious justification, called this a policy of drift. But, citing various experts, Orde affirmed that his conclusion was one with which "no good judge" would disagree. Britain's policy would have to be of an opportunist nature, even though he knew that "minds naturally ardent, or by predilection systematic" would dislike this view.

[86]C.P. 8(35), 7 January 1935, and encl. from Samson, 10 November 1934 and 12 October 1934, CAB 24/253; also in T 172/1831.

The documents which the Foreign Office circulated to the cabinet, showing Japanese policy in an unfavourable light, were not well received at the Treasury. If such ideas were left unchallenged, Chamberlain's whole effort to create a permanent friendship with Japan would be undermined. It is not surprising therefore that from the ardent mind of Sir Warren Fisher there came some biting comments. Fisher, who was responsible for civil service appointments and promotions, described his one-time protegé as "singularly unpromising material," a "pedantic ass, admirably suited to join the eclectic brotherhood of Oxford or Cambridge." Orde's pedantry, according to Fisher, was only equalled by his "quite obvious ignorance of human nature, and at the same time he is obsessed with the fixed idea that original sin is monopolized by Japan, and our only proper attitude is, therefore, never to soil ourselves by contact with such impiety."[87] Fisher capped his ridicule of the head of the Far Eastern Department by calling Orde's memorandum a "revised version of the Book of Lamentations." Sansom's opinions were also denigrated by innuendo, and he was called "slightly hysterical." Even though Sansom had thirty years of experience in Japan, for the past year or two, he had supposedly been "disgruntled and labouring under a sense of grievance against the Japanese."[88]

It was easier to cast aspersions on the British foreign service officers than to answer their arguments. Would Neville Chamberlain accept vituperation, innuendo, and sarcasm as an answer to the sometimes vigorous but reasoned presentations of the Foreign Office? His terse comment on the Sansom document was simply, "I am not impressed by this letter and agree that it is not worth circulating to the Cabinet."[89] Fisher requested the opinion of A. H. F. Edwardes on Sansom's document. In what must have been, at least technically, a breach of the Official Secrets Act, the adviser to the Japanese embassy was shown Sansom's report. In due course Edwardes submitted a memorandum which, predictably, maintained that Sansom's view was "unnecessarily distorted." According to Edwardes, Japan was sincere.[90] Such reassurances from the agent of the Japanese government, whatever they may have been worth, were not of much help to Chamberlain since he could not use them in any way. Meanwhile, the course of events and the combination of forces both outside and within the cabinet were all tending to create an unfavourable climate in which to pursue his plan for a friendship pact with Japan.

[87]Fisher to Chamberlain, 21 January 1935, T 172/1831.
[88]Fergusson to Chamberlain, 15 January 1935, ibid.
[89]Chamberlain, Minute, 19 November 1934, ibid.
[90]Undated, ibid.

In spite of disappointments, as the year 1934 drew to a close Chamberlain could take considerable satisfaction from the cabinet debates on high policy. His financial proposals and the political considerations which motivated them had been accepted by his colleagues. British strategy, in the Far East at any rate, had taken definite shape. In the north, Britain would rely on the mutual antagonisms of Russia and Japan to hold each other in check and prevent any one-sided preponderance from developing. The Americans were an entirely unreliable but non-hostile element from whom nothing could be expected but words. However, it would not cost Britain much to keep the Americans non-antagonistic. The defences of the Singapore naval base would be strengthened gradually. But to relieve some of the burden upon the navy and the British taxpayer for the defence of British possessions and interests south of the Great Wall of China, as well as for communications to the Dominions, the cabinet had agreed to seek the permanent friendship of Japan. If rearmament against German air attack was the key to saving the British Isles from disaster, the understanding with Japan was to be the vital political instrument saving the British Empire from Japan. The great remaining difficulty was to locate suitable raw materials with which to construct this political keystone of British high policy in the Far East and then to find the occasion to put the keystone into place.

4

Neville Chamberlain and the China Market Lobby in 1935

A new and unexpected opening for Chamberlain to seek to establish British co-operation with Japan in China arose early in 1935. This opening came as a result of a Chinese silver currency crisis which led the Chinese government to appeal to British and American sources for help in the form of an exchange stabilization loan. British financiers wanted to respond because, as they put it, "the pot was boiling over in China."[1] They believed that unless steps were taken, a very serious crisis was imminent, not only for the stability of the Nanking government but also for the exchange position of the British banks in the Chinese treaty ports.

Sir Warren Fisher was quick to seize upon the political possibilities which a loan to China might offer. He was not interested in a small loan to support the Chinese exchange because that would be throwing money away. But a "constructive loan" for the rehabilitation of China was another question, and, perhaps most important, it was a policy which Britain "might pursue in agreement with Japan."[2] Since Fisher believed that the Foreign Office would not approve such a policy "owing to their distrust of the Japanese," he personally contacted Ambassador Matsudaira who agreed that "this was an occasion not to be lost."[3] The Chinese leader, Chiang Kai-shek, was meanwhile also approaching the Japanese directly to negotiate a Sino-Japanese Friendship Treaty which would include the abolition of all the unequal treaties.[4]

[1]Montague Norman, Governor, Bank of England, 2 January 1935, FO 19238/F50.
[2]Ashton-Gwatkin, Minute of conversation with Fisher, ibid.
[3]Fisher to Chamberlain, 21 January 1935, T 172/1831.
[4]Crowley, *Japan's Quest*, pp. 211-12.

The Chinese silver crisis was raised in the cabinet, and after it had been discussed inconclusively at two or three meetings in January and February 1935, Chamberlain initiated the formation of a five-man cabinet committee called Political and Economic Relations with Japan.[5] The committee, composed of the prime minister, foreign secretary, chancellor of the Exchequer, president of the Board of Trade, and minister of war, met three times in the spring of 1935. Its discussions dealt almost entirely with China.

The first business to come before the committee was a dubious proposal by the Treasury for a four-power conference in London, including Japan, America, France, and Britain, but without China, to set the affairs of China in order.[6] The purpose of the proposed conference was to rehabilitate China through a large "reconstruction loan." The suggested loan, which would be subject to China's acceptance of budget reforms and supervision by an international board of control, clearly had all the earmarks of previous stratagems by which Western powers sought to impose their will on undeveloped areas of the world. The difficulties in the way of getting Chinese agreement to such a plan were admittedly formidable, especially since the control of Chiang Kai-shek's "so-called Central Government"[7] was actually over only three of twenty-four provinces. However, the spectre of possible negative consequences to British investments of "at least £300,000,000 on a conservative estimate" and to "vast trading interests and our employment at home"[8] unless something was done to avert economic collapse in China seemed to require some kind of action.

The optimism, even enthusiasm, which Chamberlain and Fisher had for the possibility of rehabilitating China was apparently based on a private briefing which they had received from A. H. F. Edwardes. According to Edwardes, the ills of China could be cured if General Chiang Kai-shek was "openly supported by the interested World Powers and . . . financially backed by them." Chiang would then be in a stronger position than any other Chinese leader. Some Chinese, especially the student class, would protest any form of foreign control as derogatory of China's sovereign rights and national pride, but Edwardes dismissed such considerations as negative thinking. It would be more constructive, he argued, to say that the banking classes in China would welcome the opportunity of "having China's house put in order"; and as that class had "much to say" in

[5]Cab 4(35), 16 January 1935, Cab 9(35), 13 February 1935, CAB 23/80.

[6]C.P. 35(35), 8 February 1935, CAB 24/253, and Minutes of Meeting, P.E.J. (35), 18 February 1935, CAB 27/596.

[7]C.P. 35(35), 8 February 1935.

[8]Fergusson to Chamberlain, 15 January 1935, T 172/1831.

Chinese politics, there were strong grounds for believing that "the voice of opposition to foreign participation in the reconstruction programme can be silenced." He had no hesitation in suggesting that the governors of the independent provinces could be won over to the central government by a money grant. This would also stop the spread of communism in China, since communism was entirely due to civil war and was "foreign to Chinese mentality, especially of the peasant classes."[9] As if to leave no doubt about the attitude of his Japanese masters, Edwardes slyly concluded that England would not be "entirely guiltless" if she allowed chaos in China proper to drift along, forcing Japan, already in control of Manchuria, to take military action south of the Great Wall.

This was not the kind of rationale which could be used to justify a policy in Parliament, nor apparently did the Treasury chiefs deem it politic to place the full meaning of Edwardes's proposals before their cabinet colleagues. Again, it was the awkward fact that the advice which Chamberlain and Fisher were secretly accepting from the employee of the Japanese government was exactly contrary to the counsel being given to Foreign Secretary Simon by the British foreign service.

The far eastern adviser for the Foreign Office, Sir John Pratt, drew on his profound knowledge of Chinese history to hammer home the truth that any government of China selected by foreign powers and bolstered with loans, instead of developing into a strong government, inevitably crumbled in the face of jealous or scornful domestic adversaries.[10] The Reorganization Loan of 1912, to which Chamberlain and Fisher had referred in their presentation to the cabinet,[11] did not fail, as claimed, because Yuan Shih-kai had died. On the contrary, according to Pratt, the loan was "the direct cause of his fall and untimely death." The Japanese had had a similar experience with their Nishihara Loan to the Anfu government at Peking during World War I. Pratt was convinced that no good could come from the Treasury plan. If an international conference were held in London without China's participation, he was certain that the Chinese would take alarm and fear that they were about to be handed over "bound hand and

[9]Edwardes, "Notes-Confidential," 14 January 1935, ibid.

[10]Pratt, who was beyond doubt the intellectual heavyweight in the Far Eastern Department, had first gone to China as a student interpreter in 1898. He became the outstanding member of the China Consular Service and should have become consul-general at Shanghai, but the British community there would not have a half-caste. Pratt's mother was West Indian, and one brother was the actor, Boris Karloff. Pratt was transferred to the Foreign Office as adviser on far eastern affairs in 1925, a post which he held until his retirement in 1938. Information from interview with Sir Laurence Collier, 12 May 1971.

[11]C.P. 35(35), 8 February 1935.

foot to Japan."[12] Furthermore, he predicted that the United States and France would not work loyally to make the scheme succeed. After an international conference had approved foreign control in principle, Japan would regard herself as having a free hand to take any measures she saw fit. Pratt thus opposed any grandiose plans to rehabilitate that vast and amorphous mass of humanity which existed within China. He advised, and the foreign secretary and prime minister eagerly seized his suggestion, that Britain should take one step at a time. Since the crux of the present financial difficulty in China was an inflationary American silver purchasing policy, that was obviously the place to begin.

With these arguments, the Treasury's ambitious plan was temporarily checked in the cabinet committee by the prime minister and foreign secretary.[13] Unfortunately, however, the question of the American silver policy could not be raised directly for fear of American complaints that Britain was trying to interfere in their domestic politics. Since American susceptibilities could not be ignored with impunity, the cabinet committee worked out a carefully worded telegram to Nanking, with copies to Washington, Tokyo, and Paris, turning down the Chinese request for the small loan referred to earlier, but expressing Britain's concern about the financial crisis in Shanghai and inviting the Chinese government to make suggestions for assistance which might involve "the friendly agreement of the other Powers."[14] The cabinet committee stressed, in its circular telegram, that a détente between China and Japan was "of supreme importance" to the general interest of the countries mainly concerned, since without it there could be "no satisfactory solution of any of the particular problems with which these countries were faced." In addition to the telegram, MacDonald and Simon agreed to Chamberlain's apparently innocuous proposal to add a financial attaché to the diplomatic staff in Peking and to request the other powers to do likewise so that the financial situation could be investigated more closely.

As it turned out, the reaction of China and the others to the British government's low-key initiative over the Chinese financial crisis was not enthusiastic. After some British prompting, the Chinese ministers, who feared that they were being asked to stroke the back of the Japanese tiger, publicly welcomed the suggestion for consultations with other powers,

[12]Pratt, Memorandum on C.P. 35(35), 9 February 1935, FO 19239/F975.

[13]Minutes, P.E.J. (35), 18 February 1935.

[14]Simon to Cadogan, 22 March 1935, Outfile, FO 19239/F1017, and Aide Memoire to the Chinese government, 8 March 1935, FO 405/274, no. 79.

but privately expressed a desire to exclude Japan from any loan discussions.[15] The Japanese reaction was also tepid. The Japanese foreign minister formally expressed "warm appreciation" of the British message[16] but the suggestion for sending a financial expert to China was ignored. More disturbing, the semi-official Japanese press charged that the American and British governments were preparing a loan to China "in order to checkmate a Chinese and Japanese entente."[17] The United States government also declined to send any expert and told the British ambassador, Sir Ronald Lindsay, that it was anxious to avoid any course of action which might put pressure on China to come to terms with Japan.[18] Clearly, a friendly agreement over China was not in the offing.

Officials at the Foreign Office were not disappointed at the check given to the overactive minds at the Treasury. The Far Eastern Department of the Foreign Office was content to allow the so-called financial crisis in China to solve itself. It had become obvious, as they suspected all along, that the crisis was almost entirely in Shanghai, with the interior affected scarcely at all. Moreover, it was noted that the well-respected Bank of China showed a very sound appreciation of the measures that should be adopted to restore China's economy. In the bank's annual report there was "not a hint" that a foreign loan was one of the things which China required to make her an attractive field for foreign investment.[19] There was no need for panic measures. As for the larger questions of high policy in the Far East which the Treasury had raised, the officials in the Foreign Office could envisage no alternative to the rather unheroic and opportunistic tactics of keeping in touch with the United States, seeking to minimize Sino-Japanese frictions, and, without antagonizing Japan, quietly cultivating Chinese good will.

But for Sir Warren Fisher and Neville Chamberlain, the Chinese financial crisis was still "an occasion not to be lost." For them, the loan project remained as much a political device to establish an understanding with Japan over China as a remedy for China's economic ills. Unlike the Foreign Office, the Treasury, for political reasons, was determined to pursue an active policy in the Far East. Was there not some way in which a

[15]Waley to Orde, encl. from H. H. Kung to Rajchman (Geneva) via Salter, 14 March 1935, FO 19240/F1683; Cadogan to Simon, 13 and 20 March 1935, ibid., F1666, F1834; Appendix P.E.J. (35), 3 May 1935, CAB 27/596.

[16]Clive to Simon, 26 February 1935, FO 19240/F1291.

[17]*The Times*, 5 March 1935 (from Tokyo correspondent).

[18]Lindsay to Simon, 2 March 1935, FO 19240/F1443; *FRUS*, 1935, 3: 545, 568, 575, 593; Borg, *Far Eastern Crisis*, p. 128; John B. Blum, *From the Morgenthau Diaries* (Boston, 1959), pp. 204-28.

[19]Pratt, Minute, 14 May 1935, FO 19240/F3058, quoting Chang Kia-ngau, Chairman, Bank of China, in *North China Daily News*, 1 April 1935.

City-backed loan to China could be arranged which could also win Japanese favour? This was the persistent question on Treasury minds.

Fortunately for Chamberlain and Fisher, a new source of energy and political strength came to the surface at this moment, in the form of an *ad hoc* pressure group of business leaders who had interests in the China market. Representing prominent companies and endowed with strong personalities, these men could command attention in almost any circle. By their political connections, these people (from now on referred to as the China market lobby) were destined to have a powerful influence on the direction of British policy in the Far East.

British businessmen had been slow to take any political initiative in the developing crisis. At the time of the Amau statement almost a year earlier, in April 1934, British entrepreneurs in the Far East had been understandably reluctant to be openly critical of Japan. When the President of the Board of Trade, Walter Runciman, had called the heads of a number of the big firms together for an informal conference on the subject of Japan's policy on 7 May 1934, they had been unable to make any definite suggestions.[20] The venerable China Association had tried to sound a neutral note by saying that it opposed any attempt to close the "open door" by Japan or against Japan. But it had added that helping China to become a modern state was a perfectly legitimate activity for all who felt friendly towards her and that it was an object which should be "steadfastly pursued."[21]

In the months following the Board of Trade conference on the implications of the Amau doctrine, however, and as Japan continued to make gains in China, it had become an urgent matter for the "big five" British firms who were active in the interior of China to know what policy the British cabinet would pursue, in order that they could determine their own corporate tactics in the Far East. As Warren Swire, who had refineries, factories, and a fleet of eighty merchant ships plying the China seas, put it: if the government intended to co-operate with Japan in keeping China in a "treaty position," then British companies could afford to remain purely British and work with Japan as much as with the Chinese. But if, on the other hand, the cabinet planned to renew the Anglo-Japanese alliance in some form "without any care for British interests in China," then, left to fend for themselves "under a purely Japanese domination of China," the

---

[20]"Notes on an Informal Discussion Relating to Trade with China," (strictly confidential), FO 18100/F2806.

[21]G.C. Papers—1934, pp. 102ff, 155-57; also Gull to Foreign Office, 9 May 1934, urging support to a League of Nations technical agent in spite of opposition which might come from Japan, ibid., p. 111.

British companies would have to respond to T. V. Soong's overtures and make a timely effort to get into partnership with China and win Chinese support against the "inevitable Japanese attempt to oust all western influence."[22] In this presentation of alternatives it was already possible to detect a potential conflict between the interests of the big British China firms and the decision of the cabinet to seek a permanent friendship with Japan.

The most energetic and determined efforts to force the cabinet to come to an early and definite decision on China policy originated with the young W. J. Keswick,[23] who, with his younger brother John, was heir to the great Jardine, Matheson and Co. fortune. Keswick had written from China to Walter Runciman complaining that of recent years British policy had been weak. He contrasted British with Japanese policy: "Briefly, they [Japan] slap the Chinese in the face and then successfully shake hands afterwards. We do neither." There may have been good reason for it, the brash, thirty-two-year-old Keswick continued, but if this "laisser faire attitude" was allowed to continue, there would be grave dangers. Runciman had sent this letter over to the Foreign Office asking that "a comforting reply" be sent to show that the government was alive to the importance of support to British houses in China.[24] However, with Shanghai slipping into an acute business depression, bringing about the "complete stagnation of trade,"[25] as well as definite signs of increasing Japanese influence, Keswick was in no mood to be comforted, and he proceeded to Peking to interview the British minister. Keswick issued a thinly veiled threat to Cadogan that, unless His Majesty's government could give assurance of a "stronger policy," Jardine, Matheson and Co. would very soon have to decide whether they were going to "get out." They had not, for instance, replaced any of their vessels for about eight years. Cadogan listened attentively but said he could give no assurances such as were being requested.[26]

After further discussion, Keswick and his brother set off across the

[22]G.W. Swire to Crowe (DOT), 14 August 1934, Swire—1074.

[23]W. J. (Tony) Keswick was born in 1903. He was educated at Cambridge, returned to China to take a position in the family firm of Jardine, Matheson and Co. in the 1920's, married the daughter of F. O. Lindley, former ambassador to Japan, in 1937; later he became Chairman of the Shanghai Municipal Council (International Settlement), and then Director of the Bank of England, Hudson Bay Co., British Petroleum, and other companies. Keswick was described as "the best British representative out in China and he knows what he is talking about" (Leith-Ross to Nixon [ECGD], T 188/68).

[24]Runciman to Simon, 28 November 1934, encl. from W. J. Keswick, 7 September 1934, FO 18102/F7043.

[25]Brenan (Shanghai), Intelligence Report for half year ending 31 March 1935, FO 19303/F3327.

[26]Howe (Peking) to Orde, 21 January 1935, FO 19287/F465.

trans-Siberian railway bearing a letter of introduction from the British minister to Sir Robert Vansittart, permanent under-secretary at the Foreign Office.[27] In this letter, Cadogan summarized for Vansittart the three alternatives which the Keswicks had placed before him. The first was to go on as they were at present, which they were reluctant to do unless assured of a return to the "gunboat policy." The second was to go in with the Japanese by bringing in a large firm such as Mitsui and then rapidly selling out to them. They had not yet approached the Japanese but claimed that the way "was open." The third alternative was to take the Chinese, specifically T. V. Soong, into partnership. They had been negotiating with Soong for some time, and he would bring in with him "some of the Soong millions, including some of the Chiang Kai-shek money of course— £5,000,000 was the figure mentioned." The Keswicks estimated the capital of their family firm to be around £20 million. Cadogan gathered that partnership with the Chinese was the favoured alternative, but before making such a move the Keswicks wanted to know if they would have the support of His Majesty's government which they had "hitherto enjoyed." Cadogan told Vansittart that he personally favoured the third alternative from the general point of view of British relations with the Nanking government. He thought it should be encouraged despite the dangers of jealousy from other Chinese and possible difficulties for other British firms less favourably placed with Chinese contacts.

Possibly inspired by the impending return of the Keswick brothers from China, the *ad hoc* group of men referred to earlier got together in London in late February and early March, 1935. Although the minutes of their meetings do not identify the participants, later developments indicate that among their number were Sir Harry McGowan (Imperial Chemical Industries Ltd.), Archibald Rose (British-American Tobacco and Chartered Bank), Lt. Gen. Sir George Macdonogh (Asiatic Petroleum Co., Shell— B. P.), Warren Swire (John Swire and Sons), and the Keswicks (Jardine, Matheson and Co.) on the business side, and Sir Arthur Salter, Lord Lothian, Lionel Curtis, and perhaps others on the academic and political side.[28] In a personal interview many years later, W. J. Keswick confirmed

[27]Cadogan to Vansittart, 11 March 1935 (21 February 1935), FO 19287/F1623. Copies went to Crowe, Runciman, and Chamberlain, who later received the Keswicks personally.

[28]See G. W. Swire to Curtis, 1 November 1935, and Curtis to Lothian, 28 October 1935, Lothian Papers, GD 40/17/307. Curtis wrote that "when these City people come for advice on a major question like this," it was up to people "like us to give them the best that we have at our disposal," and that he was arranging a meeting at Chatham House or a dinner party for the purpose of bringing the interested parties together.

that in placing their views before the official world in London, the British China Houses were assisted by people like Judge Richard Feetham and Mr. Lionel Curtis who were associated with *The Round Table* journal. Mr. Keswick recalled that through their personal contacts and educational background "these very able men smoothed the way and put the merchant in touch with the higher circles in politics and diplomacy."[29]

The China market lobby decided "to prove" to the Foreign Office, the Treasury, the Board of Trade, and the Department of Overseas Trade that there was "an impressive coalition of interests," commercial, shipping, banking, and political, "all urgently resolved" to impress on His Majesty's government the need for some speedy action on the "present plight of China and the active diplomacy of Japan." It was agreed that direct representations to all four departments were needed to reinforce the pleas already made by individuals. In addition, a debate in the House of Lords under the initiative of Lord Peel would provide an opportunity to mobilize "representative Peers" drawn from "many spheres of public life and commercial interests" to show the importance of the whole issue and make the required impression. The key political-economic demand of the lobby was framed by men attuned to the growing anti-imperialism in Asia. It would be for "equality of treatment," a slogan which would replace the out-of-date phrase, "open door" in China, which represented "a principle applicable by Imperialist powers to exploitable countries." Presumably, however, it was equality of treatment with the advancing Japanese imperialists and not with the disorganized Chinese which was being demanded. The main point was that the government should not be allowed to forget that the Chinese market was valuable. Nor should it be supposed that Chinese good will was valueless. China might be weak today, "but not forever," and the very nature of her weakness was perhaps Britain's opportunity. The source from which assistance came now would have a "far-reaching influence on the character of Chinese policy, and therefore on foriegn interests." The politicians in the lobby concluded that only action on a broad international basis could meet Chinese requirements and legitimate Japanese aims and at the same time protect foreign interests. Translated into practical terms by Lord Lothian, this meant an open conference to clear the matter up, involving the agreement of the five nations most closely involved: Japan, China, the United States, Russia, and Great Britain.[30]

[29]Interview, 17 May 1971.

[30]All this information comes from two anonymous documents entitled "Far Eastern Crisis, Memorandum on Discussion of February 27th 1935," and "A Note on Far Eastern Crisis, with special reference to Chinese Currency Problem after

Meanwhile, as individuals of the China market lobby began probing government intentions, it became evident to them that there were two widely divergent attitudes in the Foreign Office and the Treasury.

The Foreign Office was largely unresponsive. Sir John Pratt had been given the task of commenting on the problems raised by the owners of Jardine, Matheson and Co. He developed a powerful argument rejecting the demand for a stronger policy. "The short answer about the gunboat policy," Pratt thundered,

> is that gunboats are very convenient and effective aids to policy so long as you are not driven to using them, but the moment you are, then the spell is broken and either you have to abandon the gunboat policy altogether or you have to continue on an ever increasing scale until you are driven to such actions as Japan's seizure of Manuchuria.[31]

Even if the Foreign Office were so short-sighted as to want to try it, Pratt was undoubtedly on the mark in commenting that public opinion in Britain would never permit such a policy. Threats did not now frighten the Chinese but merely aroused their ill will. If the British aim was not to secure the good will of the Chinese but to compel compliance by force, then His Majesty's government would have to be prepared to use force on the same increasing scale as the Japanese had. Where would it all end?

What alarmed the Keswicks, in Pratt's opinion, was that British policy might lead to the surrender of extraterritoriality. What they did not realize was that a new and better system would replace the treaty system which bore no relation to modern conditions and had ceased to afford satisfactory protection to British merchants. The Chinese were "quite rightly" determined to keep the economic development of their country under their own control, and the best chance of preventing this reasonable aspiration from developing into one of the more rabid forms of economic nationalism rampant elsewhere in the world lay in China's need for the capital, energy, and ability that foreigners could best supply. Pratt thought that the Keswicks should be encouraged to admit Chinese capital into their firm because those firms that continued in the old ways, relying on their treaty rights and sighing for an imaginary golden era of the past, were likely to go to the wall. Pratt placed little credence in the threat of selling

---

Discussion of March 26th, 1935." Lothian Papers GD 40/17/291. The debate, in which ten peers spoke, was monopolized by a pro-Japanese faction. 96 *H.L. Deb.*, 3 April 1935.

[31]Minute, 14 March 1935, FO 19287/F1623.

out to Japan. This would be a difficult transaction if only because the net worth which Jardines claimed was equal to one-sixth of Japan's annual budget. Provided the admission of Chiang Kai-shek and T. V. Soong into the partnership was not given the appearance of a move to checkmate the ambitions of Japan, a possibility which Pratt rightly assumed might be in Soong's mind, there seemed no reason to fear any Japanese reaction. As for the danger of Chiang Kai-shek falling from power, "the Chinese genius for compromise," Pratt thought, would prevent any very tragic results.

Pratt's argument was a solid defence of the record of the Foreign Office in handling affairs in China in recent years. Special privileges based on unequal treaties and force could no longer be upheld easily or justified publicly by the British government. After a nationalist and revolutionary upsurge in 1925-27, China was becoming a nation like other independent, sovereign nations. From now on British traders would increasingly have to rely on their own initiative and enterprise in China, as they did in most other parts of the world outside the British Empire. While British China Houses were couching their demands under the fine-sounding heading of "equality of treatment," they were in fact demanding maintenance of the special rights and privileges which had accrued to British entrepreneurs over the years by virtue of Britain's former unquestioned and dominant position in the foreign trade and finances of China. Such conditions appeared to have disappeared forever.

The highest officials of the Foreign Office agreed entirely with Pratt's critical presentation and found Keswick's suggestions to be "neither very helpful nor constructive."[32] Their response therefore, was limited to an assurance that if Keswick took the Soong family into partnership there would be no difficulty about the continuance of that elusive but valued possession—official support by His Majesty's government, provided only that Jardines retained a predominant British interest.

The reception of the China market lobby by the Treasury may be summarized more briefly. Treasury officials were so impressed by Keswick's forceful remarks about the need for a stronger policy that they encouraged him to prepare a memorandum for the chancellor of the Exchequer.[33] Later, in an appointment arranged personally by the governor of the Bank of England,[34] Keswick and three other members of the

---

[32]Mounsey, Minute, 15 May 1935, FO 19287/F3444; also Minutes by Orde and Vansittart, 15 March 1935, FO 19287/F1623.

[33]"A Note on China Policy," 3 April 1935, T 172/1831; also in FO 19287/F2600. Authorship of the document is attributed to Keswick in J. Swire and Sons to Butterfield and Swire, 18 October 1935, Swire—1083.

[34]Norman to Fergusson, 29 March 1935, T 172/1831; also Crowe to Orde, 23 April 1935, FO 19287/F2600.

China Association presented their case directly to Chamberlain. They painted a picture of the economic development of China, especially in the field of heavy capital goods, now offering a splendid opportunity which they were eager to seize. Success, they stressed, would assist in the revival of manufacturing in England. They affirmed that the companies engaged in the China trade realized that "a forward policy of their own" was necessary. But since a forward policy in China required new capital expenditures and long term commitments, they would be willing to go ahead only if they had a firm assurance that they would be "actively supported by His Majesty's Government both in Whitehall and on the spot." The threat to their situation, they told the chancellor, came from two sources: Japanese policy and a silent war of attrition against the British treaty position by the Chinese.

Keswick and his associates spent some time complaining about erosions of the treaties. The difficulties in this regard they attributed as much to the weakness and fatalism of every branch of the British foreign service as to the growth of Chinese nationalism. With notable exceptions, Keswick told Chamberlain, all that these officials asked for was "peace in our time." They contemplated the eventual evacuation of the Far East as the accepted end of British policy. Against this interpretation of policy the firms engaged in the China trade wished to enter "their emphatic protest." But they knew from constant experience that this negative attitude of their own officials in East Asia would persist and deepen unless His Majesty's government took up the challenge of the present crisis and proved that they were "resolved to keep the flag flying in the Far East."

The major attention of the deputation, however, was devoted to the "critical position" of British interests owing to the increasing predominance of Japan in China. Through persuasion or coercion, Japan was getting China to give Japanese interests "a position of special privilege." The special privileges were achieved by Japanese advisers who were penetrating into all the administrative departments of the Chinese government at Nanking—hitherto a happy hunting ground for British advisers.[35] This development would mean "persistent discrimination against British interests." Japan's rapidly increasing power called for a "realistic review of the political and commercial position of Great Britain." For the British firms, a realistic policy entailed a mixture of co-operation and competition with Japan, but the emphasis was on competition. They considered it unrealistic for Britain to continue an aloof policy. The leading businesses

---

[35]See an untitled three-page memorandum (confidential) dated 20 March 1935, probably by Chamberlain's private secretary, T 172/1831.

believed that unless a concerted policy was adopted in which they and the government co-operated on active lines, they would be driven from the Far Eastern market. They urged that an "intimation" be given to both Chinese and Japanese governments that the British government would defend existing British interests against any further encroachments. They urged the government to recognize that unless Britain used all her available weapons, "her prestige, her financial resources, her control of raw materials and markets," which, although short on military power, were not inconsiderable, Japanese domination was "inevitable and the liquidation of British interests a mere matter of time."

In spite of its militant tone, the China market lobby disclaimed any desire for a reversion to the "gunboat" policy, nor did it advocate an openly hostile attitude towards Japan. At one point a suggestion was made that co-operation with Japan, a theme of special interest to Chamberlain, was essential and that "useful bargaining points exist on both sides." This possibility, however, was given no elaboration. Recollecting many years later, W. J. Keswick said that it was impossible to meet Japan's demands and still stay in China. The main aim at that time, he felt, was to keep them engaged in a prolonged dialogue, to raise questions and doubts in their minds about the advisability of their action and its possible effect on world opinion. The British approach "was based on a strong element of bluff.[36]

The China market lobby made several specific suggestions to the government. The first was that Great Britain take the initiative in the Chinese currency problem by inviting any powers prepared to co-operate to take part in a discussion to find a basis for financial assistance to China. This would prove His Majesty's government's positive attitude towards the internal problems of China and in defence of British interests. (This proposal was strikingly similar to the one which Fisher and Chamberlain were advocating in the cabinet committee. From some of the confidential information contained in this proposal, it is possible to infer that the Treasury may have assisted Keswick in its formulation.) The second proposal was that the British minister to China be raised to the status of ambassador—as had been done by Russia and Italy. The third suggestion was that the British headquarters be transferred to Nanking, the capital of China. It was to this question that the China market lobby attached the greatest importance. Such a move would enable the British representative to be in closer contact with the foreign commercial community in

[36]Interview with W. J. Keswick.

Shanghai. Even more important, it would allow him to influence those controlling events in China. The British China firms stressed again and again that in the "peculiar condition of Chinese public life," the British minister could only discharge his function effectively if he had continuous personal relations with the leaders of the Chinese government. His influence depended on the ease with which he could secure access to the real head of the government, General Chiang Kai-shek, and the senior officials of such ministries as Finance, Railways, and Communications as well as the Foreign Ministry. If it were objected that this programme of personal relations with various government departments was unusual for the head of a diplomatic mission in a foreign capital, the objection fell to the ground "in face of the realities of Chinese politics."[37] Already Japanese infiltration of advisers was threatening the paramount influence which the British minister had always held with the Chinese government.

Neville Chamberlain was greatly impressed by the presentation of the China market lobby. As prime minister two years later—at the Imperial Conference in 1937—he was still talking about the deputation from firms in Britain with interests in China which he had received in connection with the government's policy in China. At the time he must have had some reservations over some of their unfavourable views about Japanese policy. But the main result of their representations was that he decided to join forces, in May 1935, with the president of the Board of Trade, Walter Runciman, to convince cabinet colleagues that something must be done to stop the "marked decline of British influence and prestige" in East Asia.[38]

In preparation for a long delayed second meeting of the Cabinet Committee on Political and Economic Relations with Japan, the two ministers circulated several documents. In a review of events since the first meeting of the committee in February 1935, they quietly indicated to their colleagues that the Chinese currency situation had stabilized itself and that there was no fear of an immediate breakdown. However, new developments brought out by the China market lobby indicated an even more serious situation which threatened to undermine the position of British trade in China. Twenty prominent businessmen, headed by Sir Harry

[37]"A Note on China Policy," T 172/1831.

[38]Minutes, Eleventh Meeting of the Principal Delegates held at 10 Downing St., 2 June 1937, CAB 32/128, 5; "Further Note on the Financial and Economic Position of China," by the chancellor of Exchequer and the president of the Board of Trade, 3 May 1935, CAB 27/596. For an earlier draft of this document see Fergusson, T 172/1831.

McGowan,[39] had signed an edited version of the Keswick memorandum and submitted it to the government. This version was slightly less militant in its attitude about Japan—a compromise which may have been necessary in order to get the larger sponsorship or, perhaps more likely, out of deference to Chamberlain's wishes. The final document, embodied in a "Further Note on the Financial and Economic Position of China" by Chamberlain and Runciman, was a position paper of fundamental importance.

Chamberlain and Runciman reported on the representations from the China market lobby in vigorous tones. The leading British firms, they said, had confronted the government with a basic question: whether future policy was to "remain one of *laissez-faire*" or whether the trading interests in China would be regarded as "continuing and expanding ones." The businessmen had contrasted the forward policy of Japan with the acquiescent policy of Britain. There had been a "marked decline" of British influence and prestige which was creating a serious situation. If the difficulties confronting British trade arose solely from the present Chinese currency crisis or the competition of cheap Japanese goods, they would be solvable with patience and enterprise. But the problem was of another and greater dimension. Japan was engaged in "steady and persistent pene-

---

[39]The names of the others are listed in W. R. Louis, *British Strategy in the Far East 1919-1939* (Oxford: Clarendon Press, 1971), pp. 228-29. Basing himself on an isolated slogan in the edited version, Louis gives the misleading impression that the plea of the British China Houses did not go beyond or "boiled down to an effective affirmation of the traditional policy of Free Trade." The traditional "free trade" régime, beyond having the government provide commercial intelligence and advice to traders, was to ensure that British merchants received equal treatment with the traders of other nations and suffered no unwarranted discrimination at the hands of local authorities. Such a *laissez faire* condition had never existed vis-à-vis the Chinese after the privileges granted by the treaties of Nanking and Tientsin. The British China firms were demanding the maintenance of treaty rights which had little in common with "free trade." With respect to foreign competitors, the main demand of the lobby was that Britain's *paramount* position in influencing the internal affairs of China by strategically placed advisers should be vigorously defended by the British government "at Whitehall and on the spot."

McGowan was chairman and, for a time, sole managing director of Imperial Chemical Industries Ltd., Britain's largest industrial firm, in which, incidentally, Chamberlain's son was employed. According to I.C.I.'s 1932 annual returns, Chamberlain owned 11,747 shares (see items of 6 and 13 July 1939) FO 22830/A4160, A4671. Perhaps the possibility of conflict of interest explains why McGowan was not part of the delegation which presented the brief to Chamberlain. McGowan was apparently the cartoonist's dream of an industrial tycoon. During his twenty-five year domination of I.C.I., he moved around as if he were the head of a great empire, revelling in contact with important people. He was one of a group of businessmen, mainly Scots, who had a reputation for bridging the gap between industry and politicians. Information from interview with W. J. Reader, historian, Imperial Chemical Industries Ltd., April 1971.

tration" of China, including a process of infiltrating Japanese "advisers" into the various departments of the Nanking government and thus "undermining the British position," with the result that British investments, which were "still the largest foreign investments in China," and British trade were both threatened. It was not merely a question of safeguarding investments amounting to £300 million or of protecting the interests of particular British companies operating in China; but for the sake of trade and employment in Britain, it was "clearly out of the question" to contemplate being pushed out of Britain's existing market in China or being deprived of a fair share in the potential market, especially for capital goods. In view of this situation the two ministers felt that it was not enough to make statements or declarations: there was a critical turning point in China, and if Britain was to maintain her trade there, "as we are bound to make a supreme effort to do," the government ought to act quickly as well as decisively.

Did these urgent sounding words mean that Chamberlain had lost sight of his hopes for friendship with Japan? Chamberlain himself was aware that an unqualified stand about British China interests could jeopardize his other ambition, and he did not, in fact, go as far as the China market lobby demanded. His proposals for action, in contrast to his argument, were cast in temperate tones. Where the China market lobby had asked for "equality of treatment" with Japan, he spoke only of Britain's right to have "a fair share" of the Chinese market. He also watered down some of the sharpest statements about Japan which his secretary had proposed in a first draft. In addition, he included some reassurances about the attitude of the Japanese government of the type which Sir Warren Fisher's contact, A. H. F. Edwardes, was supplying to the Treasury. Thus Chamberlain and his shadow, Walter Runciman, professed to be impressed by "the fact" that "all those engaged in trade and commerce in China and even in Manchukuo" took the view that Japan would not be averse to co-operation with Britain and that in fact "she is anxious for co-operation." In spite of the reports which the British foreign service and the China market lobby itself had presented about the unbounded nature of Japan's ambition to be the sole controlling influence in China, Chamberlain preferred to believe, without stating any facts, that "the balance of the evidence" showed that, from the Japanese as well as the British viewpoint, there was "in fact room for us both in the Chinese market." If the British were prepared to accept tough Japanese conditions for participating in the Chinese market, Chamberlain was undoubtedly right in his contention. He hinted, but only in the vaguest terms, at the price which he thought Japan would ask and which he probably considered to be reasonable: some help "in the sphere of finances," some co-operation "*vis-à-vis* the Chinese" and relief from "a growing feeling of isolation" in the international community. But these were questions for consideration at some future occasion.

In the meantime, some definite move was required to demonstrate Britain's intention in China, and the cabinet committee was invited to examine the proposals of the China market lobby for (1) moving the Legation to Nanking, (2) raising the minister to the status of ambassador, and (3) any other measures to make clear both to China and Japan that Britain had no intention of allowing herself to be ousted from "our position in China" and "our fair share of the Chinese market."

When the cabinet committee gathered at 10 Downing Street on the morning of 14 May 1935, its attention turned immediately to the three proposals at the end of the Chamberlain-Runciman note. The prime minister emphasized the importance and special character of the post in China while Chamberlain pointed out that the position of the British minister in Peking had been affected by a Japanese decision, communicated a few days previously, to raise the status of their representative in China to an ambassador. Chamberlain had the satisfaction of citing as an example of Japan's desire for friendship with Britain the fact that they had deferred publication of the decision to allow Britain to take similar action and have the news announced simultaneously. There was little to discuss. The foreign secretary grudgingly agreed, in view of the Japanese action and because the Treasury favoured the change, to seek His Majesty's pleasure that same afternoon and inform the cabinet the following day, but he doubted whether the proposed change of status would materially alter the position.[40]

The proposal to move the Legation to Nanking was the more substantial item, and it took up most of the time of the committee. Runciman opened the discussion by saying that the expenditure of £150 thousand or more to move from Peking to Nanking would be "a very cheap investment as compared with the enormous value of our China trade and interests." Lord Hailsham favoured the transfer for daily contact with the central government but mentioned certain losses involved. The Peking Legation quarter was compact for defence purposes, and following the Boxer disturbances in 1901 Britain had the right to have her own armed guards in Peking. This would not be available in Nanking. Also, the Peking building was the largest and finest in the whole Legation quarter, and it would be a shame to give it up. Sir John Simon, always looking for the middle ground, said he wished to keep both quarters, but Chamberlain insisted that definite action

---

[40]The Japanese were acceding to a Chinese request for an exchange of ambassadors. Crowley, *Japan's Quest*, p. 212; Minutes, P.E.J. (35), 14 May 1935, CAB 27/596.

was needed as a "clear demonstration" that Britain did not intend to be pushed out of China. A definite move was needed in order to bring an end to present feelings of uncertainty. A decisive act by the government would be an inducement to British enterprise "to embark on further capital investments in that country." The political effect of raising the British representative to the status of ambassador would be greatly diminished because Japan had anticipated Britain doing this. However, an announcement that the embassy was being moved to Nanking, Chamberlain concluded, would have considerable influence. It would be "an indication to China and to the world that we intended to maintain our prestige in that country." Ramsay MacDonald gave his approval to the move and added that the "moral effect of a large and important site" would be of great value. Since other countries would likely follow Britain's example, the prime minister predicted a competition for good sites. Consequently, Britain, he said, should not start on a small and niggardly basis.

The discussion concluded with an agreement in principle to move the embassy to Nanking. The cabinet's subsequent approval of the committee's recommendation marked a signal victory for the China market lobby as well as for the Chinese government. For reasons which had been explained in their memorandum to the cabinet committee, the physical location of the embassy was not a superficial question for the British China companies. They had been demanding this move ever since the Kuomintang régime was established in Nanking in 1928. After a visit to China on their behalf in 1931, Lionel Curtis had written a book called *The Capital Question of China* to promote this idea, but the Foreign Office had always resisted and found cogent reasons for not making any move.

Finally, with respect to the third proposal in the Chamberlain-Runciman note, the cabinet committee approved a suggestion by Runciman, that the staff of Louis Beale, commercial counsellor, who had exceptionally valuable contacts with the leading figures in the Chinese government, should be increased. After the cabinet committee had concluded its deliberations, it only remained for the China market lobby to be informed of the government's response to their representations. On May 28, 1935, a small deputation led by Sir Harry McGowan and representing the twenty signatories of the brief to the cabinet was received by the foreign secretary. Sir John Simon assured these gentlemen that they need entertain no doubt whatever of the fact that "His Majesty's Government were in China and meant to stay there."[41] The government was alive to the difficulties and possibilities of

---

[41]Minutes of Meeting, 28 May 1935, Cadogan Papers, FO 800/293.

British trade in China and "would give British businessmen in China their fullest diplomatic support."

The foreign secretary elaborated on the limits and possibilities of diplomacy. His listeners appreciated the fact that opposition to Japan on major issues was ultimately impossible. The wisest course "as far as practicable" was to work with Japan, or at least to avoid working against her. However, to their keen appreciation, Simon told the group in strictest confidence of the impending cabinet approval for a decision to establish the headquarters of the British ambassador in Nanking.[42] This was what they had most desired and was considered the key link to strengthen British prestige and win Chinese good will. As a further practical step, to show British interest in China, Simon pointed out that a financial attaché was to be appointed to the embassy to help resolve the simmering Chinese currency crisis.

The China market lobby had obviously scored something of a triumph. The leading core of business concerns had gathered together an influential group of people who had worked out a series of political propositions and several practical proposals. These in turn had been taken around in various forms to the major departments of state. Thereafter, the ministers concerned had come together formally to make their decisions and get cabinet approval. The decision of the cabinet in May 1935 was to strengthen British diplomatic representation in dramatic fashion and thereby raise British prestige and influence in China.

In the context of British global strategy, the decision of May 1935 was an unexpected move. It was clearly accepted as such, without enthusiasm, by the Foreign Office. The previous relevant cabinet decision, in July 1934, had been to accept Britain's weak military position in the area relative to Japan. At that time it was expected that this strategic weakness would be offset by a political friendship. But such an entente had so far made little progress. Unless the present initiative could be bent to serve that purpose also, it would inevitably lead to greater friction with Japan and add to, rather than lessen, British worries in the Far East. Under Chamberlain's inspiration the British government was now embarked on potentially conflicting policies in the Far East. But Chamberlain appeared to be unruffled by this prospect. He was looking ahead, and he placed great faith in the ingenuity and power of British finance to resolve the potential conflicts. He hoped that the financial brains in London could approach both Japan and China through the sphere of finances and provide a lever to remove

---

[42]Actual approval was not given until 4 June, Minutes, P.E.J. (35), 4 June 1935, CAB 27/596.

the grievances of British trading and investment houses in the China market. Over in the Foreign Office, frustrated and weakly led by Sir John Simon, officials had half-resigned themselves to China policy being formulated "in the minds of high circles . . . outside . . . the Foreign Office."[43] They found that trying to follow the Treasury was like "walking along a rather dimly lit path towards a goal which is not very clearly defined." And the Foreign Office, which had no match for the powerful Chamberlain-Fisher combination, faced further surprises. In order to prepare the ground for increased activity in the Far East, Chamberlain had not only successfully prodded Simon into upgrading British diplomatic arrangements in China, but then, to the astonishment of everyone, the Treasury appointed its highest ranking economic adviser, Sir Frederick Leith-Ross, to China to stay, as it turned out, for almost a year.

[43]Wellesley to Lindsay (secret), 12 March 1935, FO 19287/F1659; also Orde, Minute, 17 April 1935, FO 19240/F2504.

5

The Leith-Ross Mission Phase One: in the Far East

The Leith-Ross mission had its origin in a Treasury proposal to name Sir Frederick Leith-Ross as British financial expert to China and E. L. Hall-Patch as financial adviser to the British embassy. This proposal was made and approved at the meeting of the Cabinet Committee on Political and Economic Relations with Japan early in June, 1935. A decision to send a financial adviser to the embassy had already been taken in principle in March. The minutes of the June meeting fail to explain, however, why a financial expert of such high standing was being added or the purpose of his mission. The announcement of the mission to the Chinese government, to Parliament on 17 June, and in the press was also not very revealing. It merely stated that the British government desired the most authoritative advice which it had at its command to be made available in connection with the current currency and financial crisis in China and that Leith-Ross was going to discuss with the Chinese and other governments concerned "the problem to which the present situation gives rise."[1] But because of Neville Chamberlain's preoccupations with the Far East, it was beyond question that Leith-Ross would have broader objectives than those publicly admitted. These objectives turned out to be a simultaneous search for co-operation with Japan, the promotion of a détente between China and Japan, and the bolstering of British economic interests in China. This was asking a great deal in a complex situation, and the instructions which Leith-Ross took with him were inadequate to encompass all three desiderata.

[1]Waley to Foreign Office, 6 June 1935, FO 19241/F3666.

As the economic interests came to predominate, the other two objectives inevitably faded into the background.

Sir Frederick Leith-Ross was a man of considerable standing in Britain. He had been chief economic adviser to the prime minister and chancellor of the Exchequer on financial relations with foreign countries since 1924. His rank in the civil service was equal to that of the permanent heads of the great departments of state. He had conducted negotiations with the United States and Germany in 1933-34, and in 1935 he was also vice-chairman of the economic committee of the League of Nations. It was for these reasons that Sir Robert Vansittart commented, "we are indeed sending a big gun," when Leith-Ross's mission to China was approved.[2]

The Leith-Ross mission passed through various stages from June 1935 to July 1937. At first there was a time of preparation in London, from 4 June to 10 August 1935. Then Leith-Ross went to the Far East where he spent about ten months. He stayed in Tokyo for three weeks and arrived in China in late September, where he worked for nine months. After an attempted fence-mending trip to Japan in June 1936, he returned to London while the other members of his mission, Hall-Patch (Treasury) and Cyril Rogers (Bank of England), stayed on in Shanghai and were joined there by William Kirkpatrick (Export Credit Guarantee Department). The second part of the mission consisted of Leith-Ross's report to the cabinet and his continuous direction thereafter of many aspects of British far eastern policy from his London base through the year July 1936 to July 1937.

The press communiqué from the Foreign Office announcing the Leith-Ross mission to China appeared in *The Times* on 10 June 1935, just three days after the Cabinet reshuffle in London which brought a *duumvirate* to take charge of the Foreign Office with Sir Samuel Hoare as foreign secretary and the youthful Anthony Eden as minister of League of Nations Affairs. Owing to an unsuccessful attempt, with Pierre Laval of France, to go behind the back of the League of Nations with a scheme to appease Mussolini at the expense of Ethiopia, Hoare lasted as foreign secretary for only six months, but his direction of foreign policy had a noticeable influence on the early stages of the Leith-Ross initiative. On the surface the direction of British China policy under Hoare remained unchanged. In his first formal review of foreign policy in Parliament on 10 July 1935, the new foreign secretary spoke, mainly in platitudes, of the importance of Anglo-Chinese relations. He stated that the broad bases of English policy in China remained to maintain "steady progress towards

[2]Vansittart, Minute, ibid.

order and stability" and to promote "good relations between China and Japan." Hoare coupled the "full recognition of China's right to control her own destinies" with that historically evolved principle for foreign penetration of China, "the maintenance of the principle of the Open Door." Without referring directly to Japanese claims to leadership in the Far East, Hoare asserted that if China was to regain her historic place in the world, she would "need help from the West as well as from the East." He mentioned that the government was sending one of its most distinguished civil servants and economists to China "on an economic mission of investigation."[3]

Within the cabinet itself, however, Hoare's appointment resulted in a strengthening of Treasury influence on far eastern policy at the expense of the more cautious Foreign Office. Treasury influence increased not because Hoare was weaker or more indecisive than Simon. On the contrary, at the first cabinet meeting the new prime minister scribbled a note to Ramsay MacDonald saying that he found it "very refreshing to hear 'I strongly advise . . .' from the F.O.!"[4] But unlike Simon, who was leader of the Liberal party faction in the national government, Hoare was a senior member of the Conservative inner circle, and he soon fell under the spell of Neville Chamberlain. Hoare shared Chamberlain's strong desire to rehabilitate the Anglo-Japanese relationship, and early in his tenure as foreign secretary he went out of his way to make a friendly speech at an Anglo-Japanese dinner in London. And in return for the attitude of the Conservative party, he told Japanese Ambassador Matsudaira that he expected some *quid pro quo* from Japan. He suggested Matsudaira warn his masters that it was the height of folly for Japanese soldiers to continue aggressive actions in North China at a time when a Conservative government was in power in London and there was "a real chance of better feeling," since he must have noticed "the hostility of our parties of the Left to Japan."[5]

Hoare also attempted to swing the Foreign Office around to support of Chamberlain's views. In one of his first requests to the Far Eastern Department, Hoare asked for a reappraisal of the non-recognition of Manchukuo and suggested the revival of spheres of influence in China with Japan in the North and Britain in the South "whilst we still have some bargaining

[3]304 *H.C. Deb.*, 10 July 1935.
[4]Baldwin to MacDonald, 26 June 1935, Templewood Papers, 7:1, Cambridge University Library, Cambridge.
[5]Hoare to Matsudaira, 2 July 1935, FO 19357/F4261.

counters."[6] Aware from earlier cabinet discussions that the Foreign Office was critical of Treasury ideas on China, Hoare told his advisers that there were objections to every possible course of action, but in his view there were even stronger objections "to any proposals for inaction." Hoare was anxious that Chamberlain's bid to seize the initiative in the Far East with the Leith-Ross mission should be successful, and he ordered that any suggestions Leith-Ross might make should be treated "with sympathy and impartiality." Underlining his strong feelings on the matter, he added that he would be glad to see the drafts of all important telegrams before they were despatched.[7] To officials in the Foreign Office who had grown accustomed to Simon's monumental capacity for looking at all aspects of a question, it came as a rude shock to find that Hoare had come to "complete agreement" with Neville Chamberlain on proposals for Leith-Ross's mission even before consulting with his own department.[8] With scarcely concealed anger and growing frustration at the reversal of normal procedures, permanent officials of the Foreign Office looked on while Sir Warren Fisher and the Treasury gradually usurped the vital function of preparing drafts for telegrams to the Far East.[9]

In the meantime Leith-Ross had his own arrangements to make before leaving for Japan and China. The first task was to ascertain the opinions and requirements of the British financial and merchant interests, and the second was to achieve some kind of understanding with the United States. A number of consultations took place with such groups as the Manchester Chamber of Commerce, the China Association, and the China market lobby (otherwise known as the "McGowan Committee").[10] In response to questions, Leith-Ross assured these groups that his enquiries would not in any way be limited to financial affairs. He regarded his mission to China

[6]Hoare, Minutes, 17 and 25 June 1935, FO 19331/F3856, F4099; see also Hoare to Vansittart, 25 July 1935, FO 19287/F4811. (The idea of "spheres of influence" in China had been formally renounced at the Washington Conference of 1921-22 in favour of the "open door" policy.)

[7]Hoare, Minutes, 10 and 20 August, 1935, FO 19243/F5081, F5195.

[8]Chamberlain, Minute, 31 July 1935, FO 19243/F5081. A former chairman of the Conservative party, J. C. C. Davidson, characterized Hoare as "an intriguer, really" and said he was "too subtle," "very suspicious by nature," and "although a very clever man . . . always splitting hairs" (Robert R. James, *Memoirs of a Conservative: J. C. C. Davidson's Memoirs and Papers* [London: Weidenfeld and Nicolson, 1969], p. 407).

[9]Wellesley, Minute, 3 September 1935, to which Vansittart added the comment: ". . . the right order has got reversed: it is for us to prepare our own drafts as a general rule, though we are open to suggestions in any joint affair—which this is." 4 September 1935, FO 19244/F5687. Also Wellesley, Minute, 27 November 1935, FO 19337/F7433; Vansittart, Minute, 3 May 1936, FO 20216/F1702, and Cadogan, Minute, 1 October 1936, FO 20219/F5993.

[10]See FO 19288/F4816; BT 11/388; and FO 19243/F4813.

as "a wide one, and he was going out to see how best she could be helped to put her affairs in order."[11] Questions raised on the order paper in Parliament showed that some M.P.'s wanted assurances that no new loans to China would be considered until past defaults in interest were made good and the existing issues brought up to date. Chamberlain and Hoare had replied evasively on 30 July that these points would be carefully born in mind.

Leith-Ross's most concrete discussions were held with Montague Norman, governor of the Bank of England, to whom he submitted a list of "Questions on China," seeking advice about the reform of Chinese currency and the possibility of raising a foreign loan. In his reply,[12] Norman favoured China going on to paper currency with a link to sterling at a devalued exchange rate of 1s.2d. (current rate, 1935, 1s.7d.) to give Chinese exports a fillip and provide foreign exchange stability. The argument for a sterling link was that China's relations were already greatest with the sterling bloc countries (up to 35 per cent) and London, being the most important world money market, was the best place to hold reserves. But the governor also recognized that political difficulties with the powers would be great since Japan, the United States, and France would all be opposed to a sterling scheme.

With respect to Leith-Ross's query about a loan, Norman believed that although China would not need one to carry out currency reforms, it would be desirable from a British point of view. However, he felt that a loan for £10 million could only be floated on the London market if 50 per cent of the service was guaranteed by an act of Parliament and 50 per cent by Japan and the other powers who might join in. Why was this qualification made? It may have revealed the fears and hesitations which British capital had about any further investments in that debt-ridden country. In this case it might be argued that British financiers were putting forward an impossible condition to avoid having to find money for some political scheme of the government. It must be remembered, however, that it was the Hong Kong and Shanghai Bank which originally took the initiative by requesting permission to renew lending to China. Another possibility, therefore, is that British bankers, through Montague Norman, were aware that the gov-

---

[11]Minutes, G. C. Papers—1935, 23 July 1935, p. 313.

[12]Norman replied after consultation with interested financiers and told Leith-Ross that "we have given a lot of argument and thought to your questionnaire," and that it would be a "great advantage to feel when you are in China that with you we all have a common platform," Norman to Leith-Ross (confidential), 17 July 1935, T 188/34. A letter of S. D. Waley to the Foreign Office on 14 October 1935 enclosed the questionnaire and the reply, "Provisional Answers by Mr. Governor to Questionnaire on China," private and confidential, FO 19245/F6479.

ernment, or at least the chancellor of the Exchequer, was potentially prepared to have the nation pay a price for some help in arranging a political détente in the Far East. In this case the minimum conditions necessary for the City of London to raise the money, which Montague Norman proceeded to outline in detail, provide a candid insight into the political-economic objectives which British financial capitalists had in China:

(a) specific security such as silver bullion, which could be sold if necessary, as well as the revenue of the Chinese Maritime Customs;

(b) a British subject to continue as administrator of the Maritime Customs;

(c) control over the spending of the loan for approved purposes;

(d) a British adviser to the Central Bank to exercise control, although the word "control . . . should almost certainly be avoided";

(e) reform of the Chinese budget "to restore confidence";

(f) a satisfactory stabilization standard—preferably sterling;

(g) due consideration of outstanding defaults of "respectable loans."

In almost every respect these conditions were similar to the tutelary British loan agreements made in China during the dying days of the Manchu Dynasty and now found so objectionable by the growing numbers in China and Britain who considered that the Chinese should be masters in their own house. A comparison with the Reorganization Loan of 1913 for £25 million is instructive. That loan was secured on the large Salt Tax revenues which were to be collected under the supervision of foreign inspectors, and the proceeds of the loan could only be spent for foreign-approved administrative purposes through a Bureau of National Loans under a foreign director.[13] The proposed loan in 1935 was to be secured on the largest source of central government revenue, the Maritime Customs,[14] in which a British subject was to continue as chief inspector; the loan would be spent for approved purposes under the control of a British adviser to the Central Bank. In addition, China was to be brought within the British sterling bloc. These conditions show that British financiers continued to hold the objectives of an earlier era to exercise control over China. These views in turn help account for the estrangement between business and the Far Eastern Department of the Foreign Office, where Sir John Pratt had long ago come to the conclusion that such objectives were no long operable in China.

Sir Frederick Leith-Ross, however, did not operate from the Far Eastern

---

[13]Addis to Foreign Office, 13 January 1913, FO 405/211, no. 44; also Jordan (Peking) to Grey, 17 May 1913, ibid., no. 540.

[14]In the years 1933-35, the Maritime Customs provided from 37 to 42 per cent of the central government's income, Feuerwerker, *The Chinese Economy*, p. 79.

Department of the Foreign Office, and armed with his information from the governor of the Bank of England he went to Neville Chamberlain with a highly ingenious scheme. He proposed that an international loan for £10 million be technically made to the Manchukuo government (which would get around the Four Power Banking Consortium of 1920 requiring that Britain, France, the United States, and Japan all share equally in public loans to China) but that the proceeds be paid to China as an indemnity for the loss of Manchuria under conditions which would assure that China did not waste the money.[15] If the other powers, particularly Japan and China, agreed, would it be possible, Leith-Ross wished to know, for the government to ask Parliament to guarantee a loan of this kind?

The response at the Treasury was enthusiastic. Sir Warren Fisher's comment was that if this resulted in China's recognition of Manchukuo, the political advantage to Britain was "self-evident." Presumably Britain and the rest of the world would be able to follow China's example. In a general recognition of Manchukuo a détente would develop in the Far East; Japan could return to the League of Nations; and Britain could expect a strong measure of Japanese gratitude and thereby be freer to concentrate on Germany. The disadvantage, of course, was that if the scheme failed, word would get around, and the government would be accused in Parliament and abroad of trying to sell out China and of undermining the decisions of the League of Nations. These negative possibilities either did not occur to or were not considered sufficiently dangerous to deter Fisher, Chamberlain, and the new foreign secretary, Sir Samuel Hoare. After talking it over informally with the foreign secretary (who did not consult his departmental advisers, nor, apparently, the new minister for League of Nations Affairs), Chamberlain told Leith-Ross that they wanted to proceed with the loan plan. If the necessary consents were obtained and it became a practical scheme, he had every confidence in putting the proposed guarantee before Parliament.[16] Chamberlain's willingness to give guarantees for a private loan illustrates the new and close relationship of enterprise and government. A generation earlier, when political factors in China were also at a fever pitch, Lord Salisbury had made it plain that Parliament would never consent to such a "very grave departure from policy" as a British government guarantee to investment enterprise.[17] D. C. M. Platt comments that there was no doubt many of Salisbury's audience of businessmen were in complete agreement.

[15]Leith-Ross to Hopkins and Chamberlain, 30 July 1935, encl. in Leith-Ross to Vansittart (personal), 7 August 1935, FO 19243/F5081g.
[16]Fisher and Chamberlain, Minutes, 30 July 1935, ibid.
[17]Platt, *Finance, Trade and Politics*, p. 289.

The other preliminary task facing Leith-Ross, arriving at some under-standing with the United States government on measures necessary for the rehabilitation of the Chinese economy, proved not only impossible but virtually unnecessary. Mutually strained relations on monetary policies, tariff questions, and the handling of Allied war debts inclined the British and American Treasuries to avoid discussion at a high level. For the sake of appearances, however, some gesture was needed, and it was arranged that Leith-Ross would travel to the Orient via Canada with a stop-over in Toronto in case the Americans wished to send a representative up for consultations. The British side soon learned that the American State De-partment was unable to convince the secretary of the Treasury that there was anything useful to be gained by meeting Leith-Ross.[18] Apart from the existing tensions, the American Treasury had the added embarrassment of its inexpedient domestic silver policy, the Silver Purchases Act of 1934, which was responsible for draining China of her traditional currency, as an additional reason for avoiding any face-to-face discussion with the high-ranking British economic expert. Leith-Ross concluded that there was no initiative for talks coming from the Americans and that Britain was "clearly absolved" from any accusation that she had declined the hand offered by America.[19]

It remained for the Foreign Office to learn of the plans for the Leith-Ross mission. Sir Robert Vansittart heard of the various proposals be-latedly, and C. W. Orde, head of the Far Eastern Department, managed to see Leith-Ross only on the eve of his embarkation from Southampton. For the sake of the record, however, Orde conveyed the scepticism of his department. In a remarkably accurate forecast, the Foreign Office pre-dicted that China would not consider the bribe of a loan, "at any rate of such moderate dimensions," sufficient for the signing away of part of Chinese territory, an act which seemed "particularly abhorrent to Chinese feelings"; China would not submit to foreign control under the guise of a loan, and any attempt to impose it would lead to serious trouble and was contrary to British policy as laid down in the *December Memorandum* of 1926; League of Nations circles and the United States would regard pressure on China to recognize Manchukuo as reprehensible; Japan would only finance China

---

[18]Morgenthau to Stamp, 9 July 1935, T 160/619. Also Lindsay to Wellesley, 12 August 1935, FO 19244/F5546. See Borg, *Far Eastern Crisis*, pp. 130-32, for a discussion of American attitudes to Leith-Ross.

[19]Leith-Ross to Fisher and Chamberlain, Minute, 18 July 1975, T 160/619. Fisher's reaction, shared by Montague Norman, was that this was "quite admirable." The Americans would of course continue to make accusations, "but that needn't disturb us." Minute, ibid. Blum, *The Morgenthau Diaries*, p. 212, shows Morgenthau was suspicious that Leith-Ross would try to put China on the sterling standard.

under conditions controlled by herself; and in Manchukuo, Japan was better off as things were now since isolation of Manchukuo gave Japan freedom to consolidate a monopoly of development along lines antagonistic to other foreign interest. In any partnership, the Japanese would try to make Britain "her catspaw" as she did during the latter years of the Anglo-Japanese alliance. The best solution, according to senior officials of the Foreign Office, was to have China appeal for help through the League of Nations.[20]

Although it did not approve of Leith-Ross's proposals, the Foreign Office, in response to Sir Samuel Hoare's desire for "sympathy and impartiality" toward the mission, sent a non-committal telegram to Ambassador Cadogan in Nanking giving the gist of Treasury plans for currency reform but omitting, on Chamberlain's request for secrecy, any reference to the Manchukuo deal. The Foreign Office understood that the object of his mission was to endeavour to secure the co-operation of Japan, and if possible the United States, in rendering assistance to China in line with the cabinet sub-committee's decision of 22 February 1935 stating that:

> In our view it is vital that any plan for assisting China, besides being technically sound, should be carried out with the friendly agreement of the other Powers, including of course, China herself.[21]

In the absence of any consultation or agreement between the permanent officials of the Foreign Office and the Treasury, Leith-Ross set off on his mission without any written instructions. Even though there had been informal conversations between the two ministers most directly involved, there was no direct cabinet minute on the subject of Leith-Ross's instructions. For an undertaking of this kind these procedures were most unusual, slightly irregular, and bound to create confusion. The oversight involved was not accidental. Nor, obviously, was it because Leith-Ross was merely going on some kind of fact-finding advisory trip as the Foreign Office press release had suggested. It reflected an already existing state of disagreement between the two departments of state and a feeling by the Treasury that it would probably have been impossible to reach agreement with the Far Eastern Department on any far-reaching definition of Leith-Ross's functions. Hoare had, in fact, asked Chamberlain to have Leith-Ross discuss his plans with the Far Eastern Department, but Chamberlain had left this up to Leith-Ross. The latter decided not to contact the Far Eastern De-

---

[20]Orde, Wellesley, and Vansittart, Minutes, 7 and 9 August 1935, FO 19243/F5081g.

[21]See Pratt, Memorandum, 25 November 1935, FO 19247/F7505.

partment because he was pressed for time and because "the idea . . . can't be much further explored at this end."[22] The desire for extreme secrecy to avoid any premature disclosure of the Manchukuo deal may also have been a factor in minimizing advance discussion.

The effort to keep the broad political-economic aims of the Leith-Ross mission hidden did not, of course, prevent the press from speculating. From their respective clipping services, Leith-Ross and the Foreign Office were soon aware of the intense international interest in the mission. *The Times* kept its comments close to the official line, but the *Economist* suggested that the mission was to test whether Japan really intended to challenge the right of the rest of the world "to hold intercourse with China directly and freely." The Tokyo *Asahi* said that the price of Japanese co-operation in China was greater freedom for Japanese goods in the British Empire. *Pravda* thought that English interests in China must have suffered a heavy blow for London to mobilize its best economic counsellor in what was "not a purely economic mission but also a political one"; the question of special interest, according to the Russians, was "who is to pay for the 'conversations' between Tokyo and London?" The *China Times*, a large Chinese-language paper in Shanghai, wrote that the mission was connected with the struggle over foreign markets and the attempt to control the world supply of raw materials; another prominent Chinese paper believed the British were "noted realists" who in return for concessions elsewhere, might sacrifice some of Britain's interests and the "White Man's prestige" in order to make an accommodation with Japan's aim of dominating the Far East. And finally, the *New York Times*, whose correspondent discovered that Leith-Ross had the support of the Bank of England and Treasury chiefs but the misgivings of the Foreign Office, described the mission as an attempt "to flatter and cajole the Japanese."[23] These particular newspaper comments, some of which seemed to be based on inside information, had little visible effect except that they heralded the mission and tended to heighten the expectations which other people, and perhaps Leith-Ross himself, placed on the outcome of his work.

While the press speculated, Leith-Ross sailed across the Pacific Ocean aboard the *Empress of Asia* and wrote out the plan he had outlined to Chamberlain. In his proposed "Treaty of Peace and Good Understanding

[22]Leith-Ross to Vansittart, 7 August 1935.

[23]*Economist*, 17 August 1935, pp. 320-21; *Asahi*, 2 September 1935, quoted by *The Times*' Tokyo correspondent, 3 September 1935, and in Clive to Hoare, 3 September 1935, FO 19244/F5687; *Pravda*, 25 August 1935, translation in T 160/619; The *China Times*, 11 September 1935 (Reuters Translation Service), ibid.; *Shun Pao*, 10 September 1935 (Reuters Translation Service), ibid.; *New York Times*, 17 and 27 November 1935, FO 19267/F7654, F7744.

Between China and Japan," which has been described by an eminent British historian as "both realistic and imaginative,"[24] Leith-Ross spelled out some of the details of his scheme: the loan would be used to re-habilitate the Chinese economy through a currency reform; China would abandon silver and go on to a managed paper currency linked to a suitable foreign exchange standard and issued by a reformed Central Bank of China. A few important points such as the proposed British adviser to the Central Bank and the sterling link for Chinese currency were omitted, but otherwise Leith-Ross spoke frankly to his Japanese hosts on his arrival in Tokyo and indicated that he pinned the hopes of his mission on winning agreement for a British or a joint Anglo-Japanese loan. The funds thus provided, he said, would pacify the Chinese over the loss of Manchuria and pay for the rehabilitation of China; the resulting political détente would achieve a general recognition of the state of Manchukuo. This would relieve Japan of the political isolation resulting from her withdrawal from the League of Nations, and it would still ensure Japan's requirements for raw materials and a population outlet in Manchuria. British interests would be served by increased peace and stability, which would lead to improved trade and security for "important investment and other interests in China."[25] Japan would have to agree to some face-saving formula for the wording of Manchukuo independence which would follow the Egyptian or Tibetan precedents, making it easier for China to accept the loss of her four northeastern provinces. In return for British recognition of Man-chukuo, Japan would have to pledge to abstain from intervening in the politi-cal and administrative affairs of China south of the Great Wall. But having re-cemented Anglo-Japanese relations by this pledge, Japan would be en-titled to demand the abandonment of the anti-Japanese boycotts in China proper.

As there was something of benefit for Britain, China, and Japan in his proposals, Leith-Ross told Japanese officials that Britain was prepared to go ahead provided Japan and China accepted, even if the other powers would not agree. The optimism which infused Leith-Ross's initial presenta-tion was based on the premises that there was room for both Britain and Japan in China and that both Japan and China could be persuaded to co-operate, on British terms, in bringing order to the affairs of China. Leith-Ross entertained hopes for a favourable Japanese response, because Japanese sources had earlier hinted that an invitation to Japan alone to

---

[24]Medlicott, *British Foreign Policy*, p. 158.
[25]Leith-Ross to Waley, 19 October 1935, T 160/620 and in "Notes," August 1935, Leith-Ross Papers, T 188/34.

join Britain in assisting China might not be unwelcome,[26] but his hopes were more imaginative than realistic.

The Japanese reaction to Leith-Ross's proposals was not favourable. He found that the officials with whom he talked, from the Emperor down, were personally friendly but non-committal or sceptical about his proposals, and the tone of the Japanese press was none too cordial. Japanese leaders, as the Foreign Office had predicted, were not eager to induce China to recognize Manchukuo, and they thought that China would be the last to take this step. Unfortunately for Leith-Ross's plan, the Japanese already had Manchuria without paying for it. A great variety of reasons, some contradictory, were given by Japanese politicians, soldiers, bankers, and journalists for disapproving British proposals for the rehabilitation of Chinese currency. One conviction was that before any new lending took place there should be a settlement of existing indebtedness. On the other hand, it was suggested that if Britain raised a loan and allowed Japan to direct its expenditure there could be co-operation. It was also argued that a new foreign loan would prove mischievous, be of no benefit to China, and merely enrich personally and strengthen politically the anti-Japanese "Sung Dynasty" (Soong family) which stood as the present government of China. The Japanese language *Shanghai Nichi Nichi* advised Leith-Ross against trying to strengthen the position of the financiers of Chekiang Province because

> China is different from other capitalistic states. She has her own peculiar economic structure. The rise and fall of the financial group centering at Shanghai may not fundamentally affect the economic structure of whole China. This is the view held by the Japanese.[27]

High ranking Japanese military officers conducted press interviews in which they let it be known that they were absolutely opposed to the Leith-Ross mission if it meant "joint investigation or joint assistance" to China because the British had to recognize that Japan was the "sole stabilizing influence" in East Asia. These officers expressed the opinion that it would be cheaper to allow China to lapse into complete financial chaos than to have to take military measures to turn out the unfriendly government at Nanking.[28]

---

[26]See Clive to Simon, 30 January 1935, FO 19238/F652; Cadogan to Simon, 29 April 1935, FO 19241/F2751; Clive to Simon, 4 May 1935, FO 19241/F2885; Cadogan to Simon, 8 and 11 May 1935, FO 19241/F2921, F2996.

[27]*Shanghai Nichi Nichi*, 25 September 1935, from Tokyo Correspondent. Translation sent to Leith-Ross by H. H. Kung, 7 October 1935, T 160/620; for similar sentiments see *Japan Advertiser* (Tokyo), 25 September 1935, and "China Annual Report," Peking embassy, 2 June 1936, FO 20275/F3111.

[28]Clive to Hoare, 16 September 1935, FO 19244/F5940.

At the face-to-face meetings with Japanese officials during his three week visit to Tokyo in September 1935, Leith-Ross encountered no overt opposition, but, sensing the lack of any genuine response, he reported to Sir Warren Fisher that he "could get nothing out of them" and that there was "little chance of the wider settlement" which had been contemplated in London.[29] It was too soon to draw final conclusions, but it seemed possible, in spite of A. H. F. Edwardes's assurances, that the Japanese attitude invalidated the premise that there was expansion room for both Britain and Japan in China.

In view of the British cabinet's injunction about securing the friendly agreement of the powers, the logical step now might have been for Leith-Ross to return home without creating further complications. This was the view within the Far Eastern Department of the Foreign Office. But there were pledges to British business interests about the rehabilitation of China's economy, hopes had been raised in Nanking, and Leith-Ross's own prestige and that of the government he represented were already too deeply involved to permit any drawing back. This was the view of the British Treasury.

Leith-Ross went to China in the last week of September 1935 and arrived in Shanghai like a "gale of wind."[30] He proceeded to tell Chinese leaders of his proposal for China to recognize Manchukuo. Premier Wang Ching-wei, who had the reputation of being the most pro-Japanese politician in Nanking, replied that the British suggestions would be extremely difficult. The premier feared that China would lose her "moral as well as material position" in the eyes of the world and that furthermore such an act might create fresh revolution and disruption in China.[31] Ambassador Cadogan was also appalled when he learned of Leith-Ross's proposed Manchukuo deal and pulled him aside to warn him to go slow. But Leith-Ross pressed on regardless in interviews with H. H. Kung, T. V. Soong, and Wang Ching-wei both at Nanking and Shanghai. Cadogan found this behaviour fantastic:

> He does not know the first thing about the political situation here. God save us from our amateur diplomats. . . . Our name will be mud in China very soon. Found L. Ross discussed Manchukuo with Soong after I left. I don't like his methods. . . .

[29]Leith-Ross to Fisher, 4 October 1935, T 160/620; Leith-Ross to Fisher (secret and personal), 11 October 1935, FO 19244/F6415g; Clive to Hoare, 17 and 30 September 1935, ibid., F6006, F6163.

[30]Clive to Vansittart, 6 January 1936 (5 December 1935), FO 20241/F156.

[31]Cadogan to Hoare, from Leith-Ross for Treasury, 30 September 1935, FO 19244/F6159.

Why do they send me abroad at great expense and then always send someone to cut the ground from under my feet."[32]

The British government was soon forced to abandon further attempts to reach a Sino-Japanese détente through "the sphere of finances" in Manchuria. Cadogan cabled home that if Leith-Ross's proposals became known in Europe it would be hard to predict what effect they might have at a moment when Britain was "contemplating possibly extreme steps" for upholding the principles of the League of Nations over the Italian invasion of Ethiopia. The Treasury, however, would not agree to a "categorical instruction" to abandon a line approved before Leith-Ross's departure, but he was tactfully asked to bear in mind the situation in Europe when discussing with the Chinese "any proposal which may involve suggestion of recognition."[33] Diplomatic enquiries from various embassies and questions in Parliament forced a showdown, and the foreign secretary was obliged to rise during question period in the House of Commons on 24 October 1935, and, with slight regard for veracity, state:

> The Hon. Member's question is doubtless prompted by somewhat misleading press reports. . . . But the recognition of the existing régime in Manchuria has not been urged upon the Chinese Government either by His Majesty's Government or by Sir F. Leith-Ross personally.[34]

Since he was unable to proceed with his Manchukuo scheme, Leith-Ross turned to proposals for rehabilitating the sagging Chinese economy through currency reform. After two weeks of conferences with T. V. Soong and Finance Minister H. H. Kung, Leith-Ross was able to report that the Chinese government had worked out a programme based on a sterling standard of foreign exchange which was not very different from that which he had sketched out with the Treasury and Bank of England before leaving London. As had been suspected by the governor of the Bank of England, China had such large reserves of silver—which she was able to sell to the United States government—that no foreign loan to support the currency reform would be necessary, except "for window-dressing purposes."[35] The

---

[32]24 and 25 September, 1935, Cadogan Papers—Diary.

[33]Cadogan to Hoare, 30 September 1935, FO 19244/F6160; Hoare to Cadogan, 2 and 8 October 1935, ibid., F6160, F6368, Outfile, and Minutes by Vansittart, Hoare, and Waley.

[34]305 *H.C. Deb.* This reply followed the lines of a letter which Hoare's private secretary drafted in reply to enquiries from Lord Apsley and Captain Erskine-Bolst, M.P., FO 19245/F6717.

[35]Leith-Ross to Fisher, 11 October 1935, FO 19245/F6415g and 4 October 1935, T 160/620.

Chinese ministers, however, wanted the window-dressing. Leith-Ross considered that their preliminary response to British conditions for a loan were satisfactory, and, illustrating an aspect of the interlocking relationship of government and finance in England,[36] he strongly recommended that the Treasury authorize the Hongkong and Shanghai Bank to issue a loan for £10 million.

While Leith-Ross and Cadogan were still trying to persuade London to approve the loan to China, without Japanese participation if necessary, the Chinese government lost patience and told Leith-Ross that they were going to proceed, without the window-dressing loan, to issue a unified, unconvertible paper currency based on the nationalization of all silver reserves in the country. Leith-Ross regretted this development since it foiled his efforts to recover British prestige by taking the lead in the reconstruction of China and to obtain some satisfaction and "promise of supervisory conditions for British investors and traders."[37] However, he did not take it too "tragically." Disclaimers to the contrary, he undertook several actions to ensure the success of the currency reform. On the basis of advance knowledge,[38] he and Ambassador Cadogan prepared a King's Regulation to appear simultaneously with the Chinese Currency Decree on 4 November 1935. This regulation ordered all British subjects, banks, and firms in China to comply with the Chinese order prohibiting the payment in silver of any debt in China on pain of imprisonment with or without hard labour for a period not exceeding three months or a fine not exceeding £30 or both.[39] In this fashion the British government helped the Chinese government to overcome the extraterritorial rights enjoyed by

[36]The London Stock Exchange imposed an embargo on British capital exports at the request of the chancellor of the Exchequer following the financial crisis in 1931. Although there was no statutory legislation for enforcing the embargo, its observance was closely monitored by the Stock Exchange through the Kennet Committee on Foreign Investment. By the summer of 1934, when the financial outlook had improved, the chancellor was ready to consider exceptions, provided the proceeds of any investment were tied to purchasing industrial equipment in Britain or would stabilize exchanges within the sterling bloc. See Chamberlain's speech, 292 *H.C. Deb.*, 19 July 1934; also Addis to Leith-Ross, 3 June 1936, T 188/49.

[37]Leith-Ross to Treasury, 29 October 1935, FO 19245/F6767, F6768, F6769; Cadogan to Hoare, 7 November 1935, FO 19246/F6962.

[38]Leith-Ross maintained, with respect to the Currency Decree, that Nanking was solely responsible for "this bold step" (*The Times*, 23 June 1936). But in the face of Japanese displeasure, the Chinese government also tried to avoid responsibility for the decree, and Kung ostentatiously wrote to Leith-Ross expressing "grateful appreciation" for his assistance to the Chinese government (5 November 1935, FO 19246/F6940). T. V. Soong conveyed the Chinese decision to Leith-Ross a full week in advance—five days before the Japanese and others were informed.

[39]Cadogan to Hoare, 1, 3 and 4 November 1935, FO 19245/F6865, F6867, F6889.

foreign banks (allowing them to ignore Chinese law) which, otherwise, would have vitiated the monetary reform. Most foreign governments, with the notable exception of the Japanese, followed suit. Leith-Ross also arranged, through the press department of the Foreign Office, for *The Times* to give prompt, sympathetic notice to the Chinese decree, as an "important scheme for modernizing the finances of China," thus ensuring moral support in the leading money market of the world.[40] Finally, the British government agreed that British banks would hand over their silver reserves to the Chinese government in exchange for the new "fapi" or paper currency, if such a call was made upon them.[41]

After Leith-Ross went to Shanghai, Japanese pressure on China escalated rapidly, and it continued to intensify during the following twelve months. To what extent was his mission the cause of Japan's increasingly forceful penetration of China? Professor J. B. Crowley unfortunately does not refer to the Leith-Ross mission in his detailed study of Japan's quest for autonomy in the 1930's. The answer to this question must depend partly upon the extent to which the Chinese were encouraged by Britain's interest to offer resistance to Japanese pretensions, an aspect which has already been referred to and will recur. But the recent revelations about Japanese policy toward China in the 1930's show that in fact the decision of the Japanese government to prevent Nanking's influence in the provinces of North China was taken as early as 1933. This decision was reaffirmed by the Okada Cabinet on 7 December 1934.[42] In *Japan's Imperial Conspiracy*, David Bergamini suggests that by the end of 1934 Emperor Hirohito and his inner cabinet had already planned the power play in North China which took place in mid-1935.[43] While interpretations may vary on details, it seems abundantly clear that aggressive Japanese action would have proceeded irrespective of Britain's initiative. This confirms the perceptive analysis which G. B. Sansom, commercial secretary in Tokyo, had provided for the British cabinet in January 1935.

The British initiative in sending the high-ranking Leith-Ross to China may nevertheless have stoked the fires of Japanese resentment. British

[40]*The Times*, 4 November 1935; FO 19246/F6887.
[41]Hoare to Cadogan, 4 November 1935, Outfile, FO 19245/F6893.
[42]Crowley, *Japan's Quest*, pp. 194-95, 211.
[43]D. Bergamini, *Japan's Imperial Conspiracy* (New York: Morrow, 1971), p. 588. Because of the nature of Bergamini's sources, some of which are verbal and privileged, many scholars find it hard to accept his thesis that it was Emperor Hirohito himself, "a formidable war leader: tireless, dedicated, meticulous, clever and patient" (p. xxviii) who masterminded Japanese imperialist expansion in the 1930's. On the other hand, lack of knowledge about the emperor's personal role may account for "a fog of uncertainty" which Professor J. B. Crowley says still envelopes the details of inter-ministerial discussion of the China problem (*Japan's Quest*, p. 220).

intelligence sources reported that the Japanese were alert to "certain powerful influences being exerted" on the British government to act in China, in consequence of which Japan was more than ever anxious to further her aims in China "with the least possible delay."[44] British observers also heard Japanese officials make pointed remarks that Britain was out to thwart Japan in every possible direction.[45] Whatever the combination of motive forces, the drama of Japan's increased drive for control of China began to unfold before the eyes of half-incredulous, half-resigned British officials.

On 4 October 1935, the Japanese government formally notified the Chinese ambassador of its "new China policy" which was to serve as a basis for negotiating a Sino-Japanese Friendship Treaty. This policy became known as Hirota's Three Principles.[46] The preamble to Hirota's principles stated that the fundamental basis of Japanese foreign policy was to secure stabilization in East Asia, to uphold the great cause of justice, and to work for the common prosperity of Japan, Manchukuo, and China through mutual assistance and co-operation. The three key principles to achieve these desired ends were:

(1) China should stop all anti-Japanese speeches and activities and put an end to her dependence on European and American countries.

(2) China should give tacit consent to the independence of Manchuria, and in North China at least enter into co-operative economic and cultural relations with Manchukuo and Japan.

(3) China should co-operate with the Japanese army in the suppression of the menace of communism, especially in northwest China.

In view of previous Japanese activities in China, the Far Eastern Department of the Foriegn Office observed that there was "nothing new in

---

[44]Director of Naval Intelligence (Admiralty) to Foreign Office, 3 April 1935, FO 19313/F2211.

[45]Gull, Report of interview with Eiji Amau, Japanese Foreign Office spokesman, 12 August 1935, G. C. Papers, April-December 1935, pp. 242-43.

[46]*Asahi* (Tokyo), 29 September 1935, quoted by Clive to Hoare, 28 September 1935, FO 19314/F6159; also Admiral Dreyer, "China General Letter," no. 32, October 1-31, 1935, ADM 116/3081; Crowley, *Japan's Quest*, p. 230. The full text was translated from the confidential files of the Japanese Foreign Office for use at the war crimes trials in Tokyo, where Hirota was sent to the gallows after World War II (Hirota to embassies in China, Manchukuo et al., 28 September 1935, IMTFE Exhibit 3254, T 29625-8). The Three Principles were first drafted by the Asiatic Bureau of the Japanese Foreign Office in July 1935; they were amended and approved by the army and navy ministers by September and adopted by the cabinet on 4 October, 1935. Hirota restated them in his foreign affairs speech in the Diet on 21 January 1936.

all this."[47] The employment of terms such as "common prosperity," "co-operation and mutual assistance," and "the great cause of justice," by Japanese propagandists made the Hirota Three Principles subject to many glosses and misunderstandings in some quarters in the years to follow. Confusion also arose from the fact that the Japanese cabinet kept secret a fourth principle, reaffirmed on 4 October 1935, which was to intensify the army's efforts to create puppet governments in North China and eliminate the Kuomintang from the area. But there was little doubt in the minds of Western observers that the Hirota principles, in spite of fair words, were only a restatement of previous claims to Japanese hegemony in East Asia. Many foreign diplomats held the belief, which has since coloured many accounts of Japanese foreign policy, that the army was following an independent policy in North China at odds with official national policy.[48] Japanese scholars in the postwar period have found that there were deliberate plans by army officers to upset Hirota's efforts to engage Chiang Kai-shek in a Sino-Japanese Friendship Treaty, but, according to Professor Akira Iriye, the concept of a civilian-military split evaporates in the light of the new evidence being released by the War History Office of Japan. Foreign ministers such as Hirota and Arita "were as much interested as the military in a new order in Asia," and the bureaucrats of the foreign ministry "were in close touch with their army and navy counterparts."[49] British Ambassador Clive was apparently somewhat of an exception among contemporary observers because his despatches tended to stress the unity of purpose among the civilian and military elements in their policy towards China. In one typical despatch in 1935 Clive wrote that while the army showed their teeth in China, the Japanese Foreign Office, like a nervous child, "very gently pat them on the back, whispering good dog, but you mustn't bite the foreigner."[50]

From secret intelligence and other sources, the British government was led to believe that Japan had followed up the adoption of the Hirota Three Principles by increased diplomatic pressure on China to take some positive action which would improve the climate for a Sino-Japanese friendship treaty. According to these reports, the Chinese Ambassador,

---

[47]Harcourt-Smith, Minute, 28 September 1935. FO 19341/F6156.

[48]Crowley, *Japan's Quest*, pp. 229-331, 231. In his diary, the American ambassador to Tokyo spoke of the existence of liberal, saner heads in the government, who tried to hold the army in check (Grew, *Ten Years in Japan*, pp. 147, 167).

[49]E. M. Robertson, ed., *Origins*, p. 257. See also James Morley, ed., *Dilemmas of Growth in Prewar Japan* (Princeton: Princeton University Press, 1971), pp. 14-15, for a discussion of the Japanese documentary collection, *Taiheiyo senso e no michi*.

[50]Clive to Wellesley, 29 September 1935, FO 19243/F4890.

Chiang Tso-pin, was given a list of demands which allegedly included:[51] the expulsion of Leith-Ross from China immediately; the organization of an independent government in North China; the placement of all railways under the control of Japan; the withdrawal of China from the League of Nations; the avoidance of European and American friendship; and co-operation with Japanese troops in exterminating communist bandits. Whether or not the demands were exactly as reported, there was no doubt that the "duck" policy of Minister Ariyoshi in 1934 gave way to the loud and knocking "woodpecker"[52] diplomacy which was the specialty of Japanese Consul-General Yakichiro Suma in Nanking. The "woodpecker" policy continued throughout the remainder of 1935 and 1936 as Japan provoked or took advantage of anti-Japanese incidents in China in order to renew her demands on the Nanking government.

In the military sphere Japanese activities were even more visible. On the pretext of the murder of two pro-Japanese newspaper editors in Tientsin in May 1935, Japanese forces had been augmented in North China and various aerial demonstrations and troop manoeuvres staged to cow the local populace. Provocative demands were placed before bewildered or conniving local Chinese rulers, who were charged with being "insincere" in their attitude to Japan. In June 1935, Japanese military officers demanded the removal of the provincial governor and his army from Hopei and insisted that in future no Chinese officials should be appointed to North China whose employment might, in the judgment of the Japanese, be detrimental to Sino-Japanese relations. This was a clear violation of the Nine Power Treaty by which Japan and the other powers had pledged to respect the administrative integrity of China, but the Chinese authorities agreed to these Japanese demands in a secret exchange of letters which became known as the "North China Agreement" or the "Ho-Umetsu Agreement."[53]

The Ho-Umetsu Agreement set in motion a Japanese offensive in yet another arena: the economic penetration of China south of the Great Wall. A Japanese press agency announced the formation of the "North China Exploitation Company," with initial capital of Yen 10 million and its head office in the International Settlement in Shanghai, designed to

---

[51]Colonial Office to Foreign Office, 17 January 1936 (21 November 1935), A. Gascoigne, Minute, 18 January 1936, FO 20241/F306.

[52]This phrase was coined by Suma, as reported in Colonial Office to Foreign Office, 12 April 1935, FO 19294/F2424.

[53]Texts of the letter of General Umetsu, North China Garrison, Japanese army, and the reply of General Ho Ying-chin, head of the Peiping Military Council and minister of war in Nanking, are given in Knatchbull-Hugessen to Eden, 9 February 1937, FO 405/276, no. 9.

accelerate the economic development of North China through the co-operation of Japan, China, and Manchukuo. It was founded following a conference attended by high ranking Japanese military and economic officials. As part of this economic offensive, the Japanese navy disarmed the Chinese Maritime Customs Preventive Service in the waters off East Hopei, and the way was opened for smuggled goods to pour into Tientsin and the rest of China from Dairen and Mukden.[54] From his flagship at Chingwangtao, the pro-Japanese British commander-in-chief took photographs and watched, scandalized by the manner in which strings of armed men and donkeys loaded with rayon of Japanese manufacture and sugar wended their way through breaches in the Great Wall "in broad daylight" to be loaded on trains for Tientsin. The smugglers, who did not "condescend to pay even their railway fares," undersold Chinese manufactures in Tientsin and Peking and smuggled out silver.[55] To the growing alarm of British and American bondholders and traders, armed smuggling reached its height in April 1936, when an estimated CN\$2 million per week was lost to the Maritime Customs revenue, and did not abate until the summer of 1936.[56] By that time North China had become saturated with smuggled goods. Preventive measures along the Tientsin-Pukow railway, out of reach of Japanese guns, finally halted the flow of goods heading southwards. In a post-mortem of the smuggling episodes, the Foreign Office concluded that the damage done to British trade and China's credit by the contraband in North China was very much less than was at one time anticipated.[57]

From time to time, mainly as a result of pressure in Parliament, where the "bellicose pacifists" of the Opposition clashed with the "impotent militarists"[58] in the seats of power, the Foreign Office had to take the public notice of those Japanese actions in China which seemed to breach the Nine Power Treaty or directly threatened British interests. The government had little faith that Japanese actions would be deterred by public opinion in other countries or even by remonstrances on the part of other

[54]Clive to Hoare, 17 December 1935, FO 19314/F7874.

[55]Admiral Dreyer, China General Letter, no. 32.

[56]Gull, Report, 30 October 1936, G. C. Papers 1935-38. In a *Times* leader, "Chinese Bondholders and Japan," 19 May 1936, it was pointed out that between August 1935 and May 1936 an estimated loss of £1.8 million out of £23 million customs revenue had occurred as a result of Japanese activities in North China.

[57]Knatchbull-Hugessen to Eden, 19 July 1937, "Memorandum Respecting Smuggling in North China 1935-37, its Origin and Effect on British Interests and on the Chinese Maritime Customs," gives a comprehensive summary of the issue, FO 436/1, no. 112; see also FO 20267-8, File 991, and Irving Friedman, *British Relations with China: 1931-1939* (New York: Institute of Pacific Relations, 1940), pp. 71-78.

[58]Morgan P. Price, 307 *H.C. Deb.*, 5 December 1935.

governments. But it accepted the suggestion of Ambassador Cadogan that "a brake can be put to some extent on their policy of aggression" by intimation of disapproval or even only of doubt as to the correctness of their policy.[59]

Following this advice, requests for assurances about the "open door" in China were made to Japan in 1935, and more strongly worded representations over armed smuggling and Japanese political demands on China were made in 1936.[60] In all cases direct reference to the Nine Power Treaty was minimized because mention of the treaty "irritated" Japanese leaders "like a red rag to a bull."[61] Care was also taken to avoid any impression of concerted Anglo-American action at British initiative because such representations "would have inflamed the Japanese."[62] British representations to Japan, "lame and ineffective" as they were, were met with "truculence and injured innocence."[63] However, the clerks in the Foreign Office were able to use the replies from Tokyo to piece together comforting assurances or suitable evasions for the game of parliamentary questions and answers.

At the time of the Chinese currency reform in November 1935, British relations with Japan suddenly became strained. The H. H. Kung-Leith-Ross currency reform received a sensational press in Japan, where the papers featured a charge by the minister of war that Britain was launching a severe counter-attack against Japan in retaliation for the Manchurian incident and intended to confront Japan with a financial protectorate in China.[64] In North China, General Doihara of the Kwantung army began action to create a second Manchukuo out of the five Chinese provinces immediately south of the Great Wall. By means of an army of *agents provocateurs*, incidents were staged in Tientsin and along the boundary of the demilitarized zone created by the Tangku Truce of 1933 in order to give the impression of a popular demand for autonomy. Through a "reign of terror . . . and imprisonment of any Chinese officials who opposed

[59]Cadogan to Hoare, 1 July 1935, FO 19311/F4218.

[60]Hoare to Clive, 14 June 1935, FO 19311/F3818; Hoare to Wiggins (Tokyo), 26 November 1935, FO 19337/F7319; Eden to Clive, 30 April 1936, FO 20267/F2326, and 8 October 1936, Outfile, FO 20277/F6132.

[61]Clive to Hoare, 17 and 18 June 1935, FO 19311/F3856, F3895.

[62]Cadogan to Clive, 5 November 1936, FO 20277/F6812. See also Wellesley to Lindsay, 2 March 1935, where Wellesley said it was "essential" to avoid seeking joint Anglo-American action, even though he admitted that the appearance of common Anglo-American interests was "the one thing short of force which had a chance of restraining the Japanese military." Outfile, FO 19311/F4218.

[63]Leith-Ross to Fisher, 13 December 1935, T 188/28; Wiggins to Hoare, 28 November 1935, FO 19337/F7509.

[64]Clive, Political Diary, no. 7, FO 19338/F7776; *The Times*, 12 November 1935.

them,"[65] the Japanese demanded the creation of an autonomous bloc which would be financially and administratively independent of Nanking.

The permanent officials at the Foreign Office became thoroughly alarmed at the possibility of a confrontation with Japan. The most inflammatory issue was Leith-Ross's determination to proceed with a £10 million loan to support the Nanking government's currency reform and establish British control over China's financial resources, even if Japan was reluctant to co-operate on British terms. Leith-Ross held the opinion, shared by the Hong Kong and Shanghai Bank, that the Japanese bankers would be so anxious to participate in any loan approved by His Majesty's government, that the Japanese government would come around and that this might help restore better state relations.[66] To the surprise of the Foreign Office, Leith-Ross's determination was strongly supported by Ambassador Cadogan, who held that Britain should maintain her self-respect and independence and not be frightened off a desirable action merely by fear of incurring Japan's displeasure. Cadogan emphasized that attention had been focussed on the whole situation by Leith-Ross's mission, and the demands of the China market lobby were also apparently firmly imprinted on the mind of the ambassador. If it became known, he said, that Britain had refrained from a line intrinsically sound because of ill-founded Japanese objection, leading British business firms who had "been clamouring" for a "stronger policy" would consider that the signal had been hoisted and that the watchword was "scuttle." For a while, officials in Whitehall were unable to decide "on which horn of the dilemma"[67] they preferred to impale themselves: to accept the veto of the Japanese meant British prestige was gone and her trade ruined, while to go forward would incite the Japanese to promote separatist movements to split China into fragments and destroy the very government which Leith-Ross was trying to bolster up.

Ambassador Clive in Tokyo brought the issue to a head. While not opposing the loan categorically, he warned that the Japanese would certainly be hostile to a loan floated through the Hong Kong and Shanghai Bank in which they were merely invited to participate. Japan had little economic interest in solving Shanghai's financial crisis, Clive said, and if the British firms pulled out as a result of further deterioration, Japanese firms would be able to step in to take their place. Since this was the case, why, asked Clive, should Japan participate in a loan the "main object of which is to serve British interests?" Although Japanese military activity in

[65]Leith-Ross to Fisher, 2 January 1936, T 188/26.
[66]Ibid., 4 and 11 October 1935, FO 19245/F6415g; T 160/620.
[67]Cadogan to Hoare, 25 October 1935, FO 19245/F6711; Waley to Orde, ibid., F6704; Orde, Memorandum, 28 October 1935, ibid., F6729g.

North China was "nominally directed against communist activities," it was really aimed at the British-favoured Chiang Kai-shek, T. V. Soong, and H. H. Kung whom the Japanese detested.[68] At the Treasury Sir Warren Fisher dismissed Clive's message, saying disdainfully that he had "very little opinion of Clive's judgment at any time" and that it was "not improved by his childish jealousy of Leith-Ross."[69] But as Sir Robert Vansittart read the files of telegrams and minutes which began piling up on his desk at the Foreign Office, he wrote:

> I do not understand the working of Sir Warren Fisher's mind. . . . He is continually urging us to adopt a more friendly attitude to Japan, although we are already doing all we can in that direction; and he continually dwells, with the Admiralty, on the paramount necessity of not antagonizing Japan, at any rate until we are in a stronger position. Yet here we seem to be embarking on a course obviously bound to excite great Japanese hostility—a challenge to Japan, in fact—while we have our hands full in the Mediterranean. What *exactly* is the amount of the offset to such a risk? Why *precisely* is it worth while?[70]

As it turned out, an unexpectedly firm front to Japanese encroachment by the Chinese took the pressure off the British government. Fortified by a meeting of the National Conference of the Kuomintang in Nanking, the central government withstood the pressure in North China to a certain extent, and the Japanese were frustrated in the major coup for which they had hoped. Instead they had to be satisfied with the establishment of a semi-autonomous Hopei-Chahar Political Council and the creation of a "puppet government"[71] in the smaller, demilitarized zone of the Tangku Truce. The latter régime was called the "East Hopei Anti-Communist Autonomous Council" and had Yin Ju-keng, a pro-Japanese Chinese administrator, as its head. To show they were serious, Japanese military forces took swift measures to prevent any Chinese armed interference with their protegé in East Hopei, and Yin Ju-keng promptly seized the Customs and Salt revenues and the receipts of the Peking-Mukden Railway.

Foreign Secretary Hoare, who had been afraid of creating "bad blood with the Treasury,"[72] finally raised the question of the Leith-Ross mission

---

[68]Clive to Hoare, 29 October 1935, ibid., F6750.
[69]Fisher, Minute, n.d., Hopkins Papers, T 175/91. Public Record Office, London.
[70]Vansittart, Minute, 29 October 1935, FO 19245/F6729.
[71]Howe to Eden, "China/Annual Report," 2 June 1936.
[72]Paul Mason to Hoare, 24 October 1935, FO 19245/F6704.

at a cabinet meeting late in November 1935. But since the urgency had gone out of the situation in North China, his report was only for information purposes, and he did not press for the recall of Leith-Ross.[73] This was to be Hoare's last involvement in the affairs of China; he soon left the cabinet as a result of the furore created by the Hoare-Laval plan over Abyssinia.

Hoare's greatest difficulties as foreign secretary seemed to have arisen out of British commitments to the League of Nations. On the one hand, while he and Chamberlain were planning, without success, to undermine and if possible reverse a League decision not to recognize the state of Manchukuo, Hoare went to Geneva and, on 11 September 1935, with Ethiopia in mind, delivered a resounding speech in favour of collective maintenance of the Covenant in its entirety and particularly for steady resistance to all acts of unprovoked aggression. Threats, however, did not stop Mussolini and neither did partial sanctions. After the British general election was safely won in November 1935, Hoare, apparently on Baldwin's urging and with Vansittart's support, found it prudent to try to climb down from the high plane of collective sanctions against Italy. But fortune and political colleagues temporarily deserted him, and he was forced to resign.

Perhaps the best that might be said for Hoare was that he had been an energetic foreign secretary. In his hurry, however, Hoare's ideas on policy and his conduct of affairs were uncertain and even erratic. This did not seem to bother him. If British foreign policy lacked "continuity dictated by clear-cut logic," he maintained, in one of the six major speeches he made between June and December 1935, the reason was that it was based "upon qualities of the heart, rather than of the mind." He claimed a "sound instinct upon the big issues" for British policy and tried to justify himself by saying it was not possible to give sweeping definitions about policy because "like an English gentleman, you cannot define him but you know one when you see one."[74]

By the time he handed over the seals of his office to Anthony Eden, Hoare, not surprisingly, had still been unable to make any progress towards convincing his Japanese friends that if China was to regain her historic place in the world, she would need help from the West as well as from the East. The impact of the Leith-Ross mission, to date, had been to raise, rather than lessen, tensions in the Far East.

In the Far East, Eden's immediate problem was what to do with the Leith-Ross mission. The permanent officials of the Foreign Office

[73]Cab 49(35)4, 27 November 1935, CAB 23/82.
[74]At Chatham House, 26 November 1935, Templewood Papers, 8:2.

continued to feel that it was urgent for Leith-Ross to come home because "as long as this bull remains in the China Shop, there is no knowing how much political crockery may be broken."[75] Eden's dislike of political struggles[76] as distinct from diplomatic negotiation limited his effectiveness in rallying support for the proposals of the Foreign Office when they differed from the methods and viewpoints of others, especially from Chamberlain's. Although he was no match for Chamberlain, Eden was less reticent about raising his doubts than Hoare had been. He sent several letters to Chamberlain stating in firm language that the Foreign Office was determined to recall Leith-Ross quickly, because there was nothing further to discuss with Japan and his activities and the suspicions of him in Japan "might stir up once more the nationalist passions that led to the aggression in North China and culminated in the recent murders in Tokyo.

By this time, as a result of Japanese sabre-rattling, unorthodox economic practices in China, and the assassinations of several leading statesmen by certain army forces in Tokyo during the February 26th Incident of 1936,[77] Leith-Ross himself felt that it was hopeless to try to strike a bargain with Japanese leaders. He wrote Sir Warren Fisher that their fundamental policy was "(a) to get control over North China through Chinese puppets whose actions they will dictate, and (b) to weaken the Nanking government so that it can be disregarded as a military factor." This would mean the "eventual disruption of Chinese credit and trade and ultimately possibly some fresh wave of communism." Almost from the time he had arrived in China, he had found Japanese officials there even more difficult to deal with than their superiors in Tokyo:

> They have got their tails up and say openly that they intend to control China and to get rid of British and American influence. They are frankly hostile to my mission here and the Japanese papers this morning tell me that the sooner I go home the better.

Leith-Ross felt that the Japanese leaders, especially the military, were "mad" and the "only arguments that would avail with them are big guns."[78] The question was whether he should be recalled from the Far East on some pretext and await developments, as he preferred, or whether the

---

[75]Wellesley and Vansittart, Minutes, 22 January 1936, F0 20215/F320.

[76]See for example, *Facing the Dictators*, pp. 218-19.

[77]Eden to Chamberlain, 7 April 1936, Outfile, FO 20216/F1702. See Crowley, *Japan's Quest*, chapter five, for background to this traumatic event.

[78]Leith-Ross to Fisher, 3 March 1936, T 188/27; 17 October 1935, T 188/28; 3 March 1936, T 160/619, T 188/27.

British government could find some other approach and act in some vigorous fashion now in order to avoid worse troubles in the future.

Chamberlain, however, wanted neither a confrontation with Japan nor a termination of the mission. He clung to the hope that a loan under British control and supervision would be possible "without either a Japanese crisis or Japan's co-operation."[79] Although admitting, in his enigmatic phrase, that events "had been telescoped,"[80] he successfully ignored the arguments of Eden and Leith-Ross without really challenging or even meeting them. Both Chamberlain and Fisher were much influenced by the knowledge that the British community in the Far East was greatly heartened by Leith-Ross's presence, and they were afraid that any sudden end to the mission would be seen as a defeat at the hands of Japan and would involve "a damaging loss of prestige everywhere in Asia."[81] They decided that Leith-Ross should stay on in the Far East to make a political fence-mending trip to Japan.[82] In another of those breaches of normal procedure and protocol which led career diplomats to complain in their memoirs of the twilight of diplomacy,[83] Fisher by-passed Eden and arranged for an invitation from Koki Hirota (now prime minister) for Leith-Ross to revisit Japan.

Anticipating Foreign Office objection to this *fait accompli*, Chamberlain wrote to Eden pointing out that if the invitation were now refused, "the Japanese would inevitably regard it as a rebuff, in which case we should have prejudiced any chance there may be of improving our relations with Japan in the future." As a result, Leith-Ross was instructed to proceed to Tokyo and try the standard diplomatic sparring technique of proposing "as his own idea" some plan for demarcation of world markets.[84] Leith-Ross found this instruction unacceptable and cabled home for further explanations. Since the main complaint of Japan was colonial and Indian quotas, he wanted to know if the Board of Trade would be prepared to

---

[79]Hoare, Minute, 18 November 1935, FO 19247/F7430.

[80]Cab 49(35)4, 27 November 1935.

[81]O. Harvey, Minute, and Eden to Cadogan, drafted by Treasury, 21 February 1936, FO 20216/F1210-13.

[82]The chief of the Imperial General Staff was also urging a political agreement with Japan to compensate for Britain's weak strategic position in the Far East. See Duff Cooper, "The Importance of Anglo-Japanese Friendship," C.P. 12 (36), CAB 24/259.

[83]Sir Walford Selby, *Diplomatic Twilight, 1930-1940* (London: J. Murray, 1953); Frank Ashton-Gwatkin, *The British Foreign Service* (Syracuse, N.Y.: Syracuse University Press, 1949).

[84]Chamberlain to Eden, 30 March 1936, FO 20216/F1702; Eden to Cadogan (drafted by Treasury), 29 February 1936, ibid., F1213.

modify these, and if so, in return for what assurances about other markets?[85]

Leith-Ross's question prompted a round of discussion between the various departments of state. The Colonial Office took the Treasury suggestion to mean the abandonment of colonial quotas and stated that it would be "only too happy" to do this, since the quotas had originally been imposed at a sacrifice of colonial interests "in favour of a wider Imperial interest."[86] However, in a manner which revealed the powerful political influence of the Lancashire manufacturers, both the Treasury and the Board of Trade said they had no such definite concessions within the Empire in mind. Treasury thinking about commercial negotiations with Japan had been summed up rather bluntly in the following sentence: "We believe some planned limitation of Japanese exports is in the interests of both countries."[87] And the Board of Trade rejected proposals to lift colonial quotas because the colonies provided "the one bright spot in the cotton industry's export markets" and because such action would meet with the strong opposition of Lancashire manufacturers, "for whose benefit they were imposed."[88]

When Leith-Ross finally returned to Japan in June 1936, without any fresh proposals, he was told by the Japanese Foreign Ministry that Japanese industrialists "were in no mood" for trade discussions; the old British proposals of 1934 for reductions in Japanese exports, they said, were quite unacceptable, and no agreement could ever be made on that basis. After a talk with General Rensuke Isogai about Japanese policy in China, in which he could find no common ground, Leith-Ross left Japan.[89]

On the way back to England, he made a brief stop-over in Shanghai, to have a farewell meeting with Chiang Kai-shek and to issue a press release. Then Leith-Ross returned to London after almost a year in the Far East, without any Anglo-Japanese understanding, but with a briefcase full of ideas about the British position in China on which he would make a report to the cabinet.

[85]Leith-Ross to Board of Trade, 9 March 1936, BT 11/516, doc. 19A.

[86]S. Caine to Orde, 11 May 1936, and C. G. Eastwood to Orde, 26 May 1936, ibid., doc. 49.

[87]Draft telegram from Treasury for Leith-Ross, 3 September 1935, FO 19244/F5687.

[88]A. E. Overton to Orde, 3 May 1936, BT 11/516.

[89]Clive to Eden, 12 June 1936, ibid., and 18 June 1936, FO 410/97. The latter gives General Isogai's answers to a number of questions put to him by Leith-Ross: "Memorandum Respecting Japanese policy in China." Isogai was military attaché in Peking.

Plate 1. (*right*) The Bund, Shanghai, in the 1930's. The Shanghai Club and the clock tower of the Customs House flank the domed Hongkong and Shanghai Bank building.

Plate 2. (*below*) "The Leith-Ross Dollar." The new one yuan standard dollar, issued by the Nanking government, was linked to sterling and printed in London on the advice of Leith-Ross as part of the Chinese currency reform of November 1935.

Plate 3. Sir Frederick Leith-Ross, the chief economic adviser to the British cabinet, leaving Waterloo Station, London, in August 1935, on the first lap of his mission to China.

Plate 4. Archibald Rose (*centre*) at Peking Airport, July 1934. A former member of the British consular service, Rose paid frequent visits to China as director of the British-American Tobacco (China) Co., to deal with problems and smooth relations with Chinese politicians. He was also a prominent member of the China Association in England.

Plate 5. Sir Harry McGowan

Plate 6. Sir William Keswick

Plate 7. Vice-Admiral Sir Charles Little

Sir Harry McGowan, chairman of Imperial Chemical Industries Ltd., Sir William Keswick of Jardine, Matheson Co., and sometime chairman, Shanghai Municipal Council, and Warren Swire of John Swire and Sons were among the most prominent businessmen urging a strong British forward policy in China. Sir John Pratt was far eastern adviser of the Foreign Office, 1925-1937. Vice-Admiral Sir Charles Little, deputy chief of naval staff, was commander-in-chief of the China Station, 1936-1937.

Plate 8. Sir John Pratt

Plate 9. Warren Swire

Plate 10. H. H. Kung, Minister of Finance

Plate 11. T. V. Soong, Chairman, National Economic Commission

Plate 12. Dr. L. Rajchman, Member, League of Nations Secretariat, was appointed to advise the Chinese government, 1933-1934.

Plate 13. Sir Arthur Salter, member of the British cabinet's Economic Advisory Committee, was adviser to the Chinese government, 1933-1934.

Plate 14. (*right*) Sir Samuel Hoare (*right*), Foreign Secretary (June-December, 1935) and Anthony Eden, Minister for League of Nations Affairs. Eden succeeded Hoare as Foreign Secretary in December, 1935.

Plate 15. (*below left*) Neville Chamberlain, Chancellor of the Exchequer, 1931-1937, and then Prime Minister until 1940.

Plate 16. (*below right*) Sir John Simon, a leading Liberal, was Foreign Secretary in the National Government, 1931-1935.

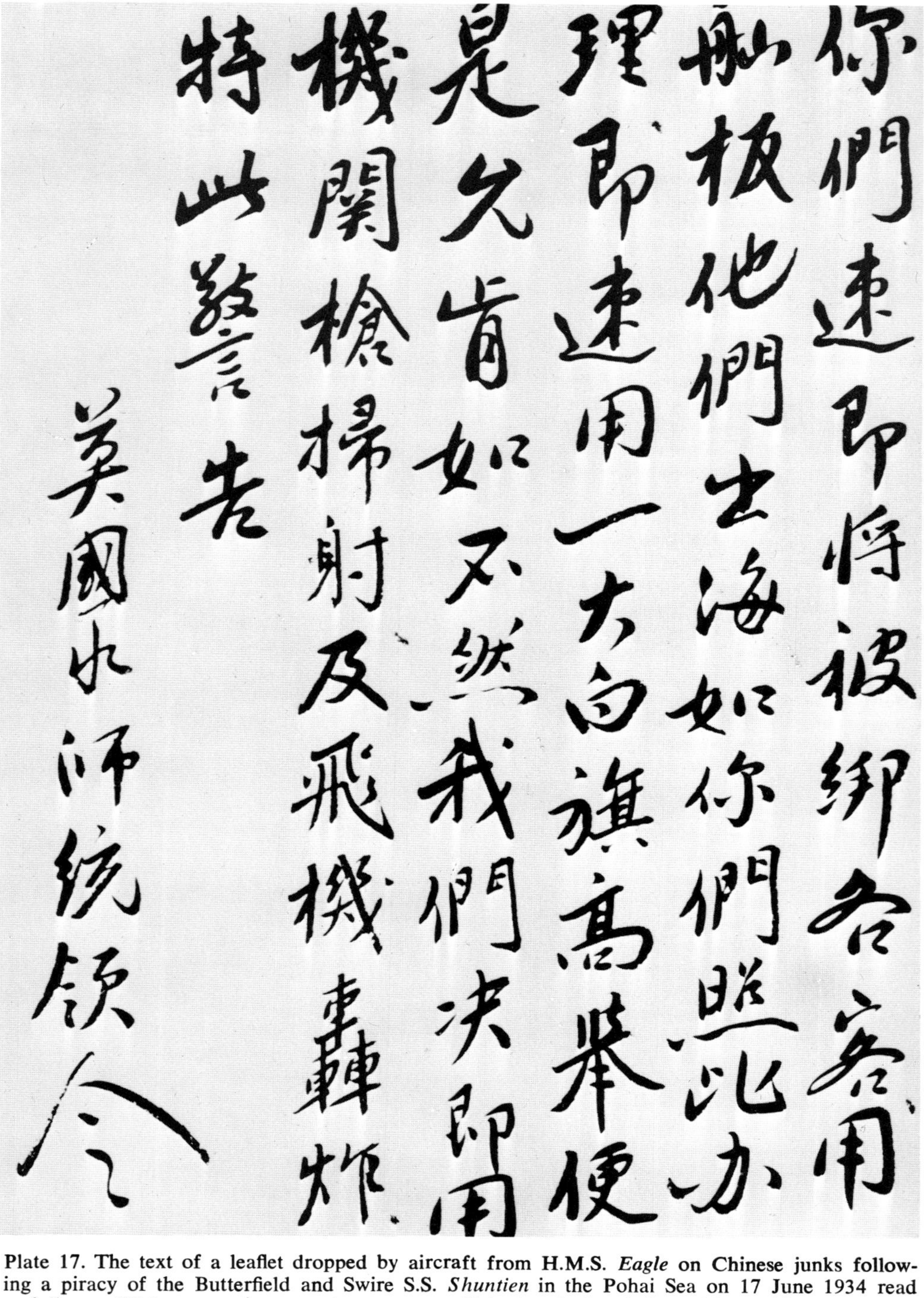

你們速即將被綁各客甬
舢板他們出海如你們照此功
理即速用一大白旗高舉便
是如不然我們決即用
機關槍掃射及飛機轟炸
特此警告

美國北師統領令

Plate 17. The text of a leaflet dropped by aircraft from H.M.S. *Eagle* on Chinese junks following a piracy of the Butterfield and Swire S.S. *Shuntien* in the Pohai Sea on 17 June 1934 read
as follows: "Unless you give up prisoners you will be bombed and shot with machine guns. Next
time these bombs will hit. Put all prisoners in sampan and send them to sea. Display a large white
flag to show you understand. If you do not, you will be fired on. By order of the British Naval
Commander-in-Chief."

Plate 18. Ambassador Cadogan and family with Admiral and Lady Dreyer and staff aboard H.M.S. *Suffolk*, flagship of the China Fleet, holding consultations following the violation of Chinese airspace and strafing Chinese junks near the mouth of the Yellow River by British naval aircraft during the S.S. *Shuntien* incident.

Plate 19. H.M.S. *Sandpiper*, last of the famous shallow draught gunboats, built for the Yangtse River Flotilla of the British Navy in 1933.

Plate 20. The two principals involved in the kidnapping of Chiang Kai-shek (4) at Sian in December, 1936, were General Chang Hsueh-liang (2) and General Yang Hu-cheng (5). Madame Chiang Kai-shek (3) and her brother, T. V. Soong (1) flew in from Nanking to help arrange Chiang's release.

Plate 21. On his return from discussions following the Sian Incident, Chou En-lai (in white helmet) was greeted by his comrades at Yenan airport. Mao Tse-tung is fifth from the left.

6

The Leith-Ross Mission Phase Two: from London

Sir Frederick Leith-Ross's report to the cabinet in the summer of 1936 was arranged with almost the same informality as his departure to the Far East had been a year earlier. His findings were the subject of an inter-departmental conference at the level of senior departmental officials, and a summary of his recommendations was distributed to the office of every minister, but the cabinet itself did not make any overt conclusion about the mission.

There were probably several reasons for this. One was that other matters, including a new crisis in the Mediterranean over the outbreak of civil war in Spain, claimed the attention of the ministers. Another was that Leith-Ross had returned to London immediately prior to the long summer vacation in August and September, when the ministers tried to avoid having meetings of any kind. A further factor was the highly specialized nature of some of the topics covered in Leith-Ross's report. His broad political recommendations proposed that the government make firm diplomatic representations to Japan to adopt a "more reasonable policy towards China"[1] and suggested the continuance of appropriate British financial assistance to China. But these principles were elaborated through recommendations about such technical topics as the personnel of the Chinese Maritime Customs, Chinese tariffs, export credits, use of indemnity funds, British banks, consular services, defaulted bond issues, and new loans which were far too detailed for consideration by the full cabinet.

But in addition to these reasons, Neville Chamberlain and Sir Warren

---

[1]C.P. 251 (36), 29 September 1936, CAB 24/264.

Fisher probably preferred an informal way of dealing with the matters raised by Leith-Ross. They undoubtedly did not wish to face tiresome arguments from Anthony Eden and the Foreign Office, who stubbornly continued to view the mission as a failure.[2] Eden, in fact, wanted to sound a note of caution about telling British merchants and industrialists that there was an adequate basis for a forward policy in China, and he also wished to warn against attempts to impose foreign tutelage on the Chinese government in any new loans or other financial arrangements.[3] But when the cabinet reassembled in the fall, it decided, on 14 October 1936, to pass Leith-Ross's report and recommendations on to the Cabinet Committee on Political and Economic Relations with Japan. Eden was thereby out-manoeuvred, because this committee did not meet again. The result was that Leith-Ross's report was never formally dealt with at the cabinet level, and Eden's comments were buried in the files of the defunct committee. In the meantime, Leith-Ross's ideas were percolating through the Board of Trade, Department of Overseas Trade, and the Export Credit Guarantee Department, and various actions were being initiated.

When Leith-Ross had set out on his mission to the Far East, the main preoccupations of his sponsors had been to secure an understanding with Japan, to encourage a Sino-Japanese détente, and, on that basis, to help revive British economic interests in China. Back in London a year later, his concerns were the same, but, almost imperceptibly and in unacknowledged fashion, the last named desiderata came to take precedence.

During his prolonged sojourn in the Far East, Leith-Ross had been a critical observer of the Chinese scene and the involvement of British subjects therein. He saw that Britain was not dealing with a primitive people in China, as was sometimes the case within the Empire, but with a people who had their own ideas for the development of their vast country. The Nanking government would have to conciliate vested interests of all kinds, and the most that could be expected would be that they would gradually improve things in their own rather haphazard way, with many special concessions and a good deal of waste. But this method seemed to suit China, where the government rarely did anything with complete efficiency and yet succeeded in avoiding any real breakdown. Leith-Ross foresaw that ultimately China would become a world power and that it was not the Japanese but the Chinese who would eventually "oust us from our privileges there."[4]

---

[2]Orde and Eden, Minutes, 10 and 12 June 1936, FO 20217/F3176.
[3]P.E.J. (35)5, 3 November 1936, CAB 27/596.
[4]Leith-Ross to Fisher, 22 February 1937, T 188/53.

Consequently, rather than waiting until these privileges were taken a-way, he considered that Great Britain should gradually renounce her extraterritorial rights against adequate safeguards. Such a step might be a hard pill for the British community in Shanghai to swallow, but that community, in Leith-Ross's view, was itself partly to blame for the depression into which British business in China had recently fallen. British merchants, who had won a reputation for integrity and straightforward dealing, continued to rely on their Chinese compradors. In the past they had "made money easily without special efforts"[5] by using this kind of intermediary, but Chinese opinion was becoming increasingly hostile to compradors. Unlike his German competitor, who went out among the Chinese without extraterritorial protection and made friends, the aloof British businessman was reluctant to emerge and was "tinged with a suspicion of conscious rectitude" which estranged his Chinese counterpart.[6] One entrepreneur had told Leith-Ross that he had never received a Chinese in his house "and never would" because it was unsound policy to cultivate Chinese connections.[7]

If the British government was going to invest time and treasure in re-habilitating the China market for British trade, Leith-Ross believed that there would have to be some major alterations in the attitudes and practices of the old British China firms. As a first step toward tearing down the out-moded extraterritorial system, for example, he tried, in vain, to secure the co-operation of British enterprises in voluntarily applying the new Chinese Income Tax law to their employees and clients.[8] He also made "suave but ruthless" attacks on the Hongkong and Shanghai Bank. In his opinion, this bank had become enormously wealthy by operating its business as a "godsend" to the speculators but a detriment to the legitimate interests of Sino-British trade,[9] and he suggested that the governor of the Bank of England be asked to look into the matter. In the interests of efficiency, he supported Louis Beale, commercial counsellor in Shanghai, in advocating the fusion of competing British houses in China. Only in this way could Britain counter the ordered strength of the Mitsubishi and the

---

[5]C.P. 251 (36), 29 September 1936; also 23 July 1936, FO 20218/F4498.

[6]Memorandum on "British Policy in the Far East," 19 March 1937, T 188/53.

[7]C.P. 251 (36), 29 September 1936.

[8]See Leith-Ross and A. H. Ferguson correspondence, 2 December 1936 to 29 January 1937, and Leith-Ross to Fisher, Minute, "Chinese Income Tax Law," 20 October 1936, T 188/70.

[9]Phillips, Minute, 21 July 1936, T 188/27. R. S. Henchman, Shanghai manager of the bank, described the currency manipulations of 1935 as the most exciting of his career (Maurice Collis, *Wayfoong: The Hongkong and Shanghai Banking Corporation* [London: Faber and Faber, 1965], pp. 207-9).

South Manchurian Railway Co., of Japan, or Siemens of Germany, who possessed their own banks, fleets, and insurance organizations. He backed proposals of some of the younger British businessmen in China, such as W. J. Keswick of Jardine, Matheson & Co., who were willing to establish joint Sino-British combines for the development of railways, industry, and shipping.

Leith-Ross was convinced by the arguments of Jean Monnet and Sir Arthur Salter that in the long run it was only this association of British and Chinese capital which would create vested interests among decisive Chinese groups, so that any future efforts of a perfervid nationalism to expel British capital from China could be defeated. This seemed to be the answer to the problem which had perplexed the deputy under-secretary of state for foreign affairs a decade earlier when he said what Britain ought to do was "to try and capture the nationalist movement by sympathizing with it and endeavouring to get it on the right line," but how precisely this could be done, he had "not the faintest idea."[10]

Now, in return for evidence that some British China firms were at last prepared to change with the times, Leith-Ross advocated a more generous attitude in offering medium term credit facilities to China by the government's Export Credit Guarantee Department. Since conditions under which the department gave guarantees in other parts of the world did not apply in China (where, for example, there was no bankruptcy law and where payments were usually guaranteed by a Chinese government agency), Leith-Ross suggested longer terms and a reasonable premium of 5 rather than 12 per cent.[11] Although no credits were guaranteed by the cautious department before the Sino-Japanese war started in July 1937, the presence of its representative, William Kirkpatrick, who was sent to China in October 1936, had a considerable psychological impact on Japanese and German as well as on British and Chinese traders as evidence of the earnestness of the British government.[12]

[10]Wellesley, Minute, 18 January 1926, FO 11620/F119.

[11]Leith-Ross to Fisher, Minute, 13 October 1936, T 188/27; also C.P. 251 (36), 29 September 1936.

[12]The German government and industrialists reacted by proposing a gentleman's agreement on credit terms and demarcation of markets, but British firms, who thought the German position was weakening in China, were only interested in an understanding to fix prices. See W. J. Keswick to D. G. M. Bernard (Matheson and Co.), 1 March 1937, FO 20972/F2027; also Department of Overseas Trade to Foreign Office, 15 January 1937, ibid., F298. For Japan's negative reaction to Kirkpatrick's mission see A. H. F. Edwardes to Sir Horace Wilson, 14 October 1936, T 188/27. German ambassador Trautman saw his country's interests running parallel to the British in China and was pleased to "let the British do our work for us without running any risks." *DGFP*, 1936, 5:604.

Leith-Ross's proposals for the gradual abolition of extraterritorial privileges and for the reform of the attitudes and the reorganization of British China Houses were long-term projects; a matter of more immediate concern was how to bolster trade and re-start the flow of British capital into China. British industrialists and engineering and shipping firms were pressing for the flotation of new loans for railway construction. A British railway expert, General Hammond, had been engaged by Chiang Kai-shek to rationalize the structure of China's railways, and Leith-Ross was impressed at the progress the Chinese were making with their limited capital resources. Over 1,500 km. of new construction had been completed the previous year and another 2,500 km. was under way. On the basis of the trend illustrated by the figures in Table 8, Leith-Ross worried that if British interests did not act with enterprise and imagination, the market would soon be pre-empted by others—especially the Germans, "who have neither capital nor credit" but were providing both in China.[13] According to the figures in Table 8, British interests were getting less than 5 per cent of the very substantial contracts which were being negotiated. These figures do not actually represent the complete picture. For example, the British and Chinese Corporation negotiated a Shanghai market loan for £2.6 million in partnership with T.V. Soong in 1936, and through the British Boxer Indemnity Fund purchases had been made to complete the Canton-Hankow Railway with British equipment.[14] Nevertheless, in a field where British interests had long been predominant, the trend was not encouraging.

Before any new lending could be considered, the backlog of millions of pounds of defaults on thirty-three existing railway loans had to be settled. Leith-Ross considered that the Chinese authorities, who were anxious to redeem their credit standing for fresh borrowing, made fair offers during negotiations on defaulted loans and recommended that they be accepted. Details varied according to the security of particular loans, but overall their proposals amounted to a cancellation of £4.6 million, or four-fifths of the arrears of interest, in return for immediate resumption of interest and amortization payments on all loans. Leith-Ross's greatest difficulty was in getting the British Chinese Bondholder's Committee[15] to be

[13]Leith-Ross to Addis, 8 April 1936, T 188/49. A précis of Hammond's confidential report to Chiang Kai-shek was contained in Waley to Orde, 28 November 1935, FO 19252/F7504.

[14]D. G. M. Bernard, "Annual Report to the British and Chinese Corporation," *The Times*, 11 June 1936; also Maze Papers, 12:177-80.

[15]The composition and work of the committee which was formed on the initiative of the governor of the Bank of England, is summarized in "Chinese Bondholder's Committee to Mr. Eden," 8 June 1937, FO 405/276, no. 60.

reasonable. With railway debts so high as to outstrip the Chinese capacity to pay, the bondholders had no sense of reality in pointing to their bonds and claiming the fulfillment of obligations laid down therein. Leith-Ross remonstrated with bondholder representatives arguing that China had been through a series of civil wars which had wrecked many of the railways and much of the rolling stock and that it was absurd to imagine that bondholders could recover arrears of interest accumulated in that period. If the bondholders were treated like the shareholders in British shipping companies, he said, they would be asked to write off all arrears, to accept some sort of income bonds for their capital, and to agree to new capital being raised in priority to their claims. The Chinese were still offering priority to the old claims, including 20 per cent of the interest in arrears, so that Leith-Ross was "astounded that the bondholders do not jump at the proposal."[16]

Since the Chinese government was rapidly making settlements with the bondholders of other countries, the British bondholders were eventually forced to abandon their demand for full payment of interest arrears. However, they prevailed upon the Chinese government to improve their original offer by agreeing to appoint British personnel to act as watchdogs on particular railways. The Foreign Office representative objected vainly that this apparent denial of the right to run their own affairs would be an unnecessary irritant to Chinese public opinion. Furthermore, since the salaries and positions offered did not permit the employment of first class men, they would be side-tracked and humiliated, "an act of which the Chinese were unrivalled masters," and they would be able to do little or nothing to prevent corruption, promote efficiency, or secure orders for British industry.[17] In spite of the rigid attitudes of the bondholders, settlements were reached and by mid-1937 the Bondholder's Committee was able to report that no Chinese bonds issued on the London market remained in serious default. The striking rise in capital values which resulted from the settlements is shown in table 7.

Although the loan defaults were not finally settled until 1937, by the summer of 1936 Leith-Ross already considered that the promising attitude of the Chinese government warranted immediate preparations for a fresh inflow of British capital into Chinese railways. With this in mind, he proposed to the cabinet that Britain should "contribute to the financial and economic rehabilitation of China, on which our trade depends,"[18] by

[16]Leith-Ross to Addis, 8 April 1936.
[17]Foreign Office Memorandum, "Leith-Ross's report on his financial mission to China," P.E.J. (35)5, 3 November 1936.
[18]C.P. 251 (36), 29 September 1936.

initiating an international railway loan of up to £15 million raised through the China Consortium banks.

To avoid cause for friction with Consortium partners, Leith-Ross proposed that the proceeds of the suggested loan would be distributed among participants for expenditure in their respective countries in proportion to the amount of their subscriptions to the loan. The orders for materials would not be tied to open tender, as prescribed by existing Consortium rules, and the Consortium would be broadened to include Belgian, German, and Chinese banks. In a supplementary recommendation, Leith-Ross proposed that if a loan could not be arranged in this fashion, then Britain should withdraw from the Consortium and the government give guarantees for a purely British loan.

For reasons which have already been outlined, the cabinet itself did not pass judgment one way or another on these important proposals. But Chamberlain, in his capacity as chancellor of the Exchequer, approved. On 9 October 1936, Sir Charles Addis was authorized to contact Japanese authorities and prepare the way for Leith-Ross's programme.[19] According to this plan, first priority would be given to floating a loan on a broad international basis and through "friendly agreement of the other Powers."

Unfortunately for the international orientation of British plans, unexpected political developments in South China made the rehabilitation of the country through co-operation with other powers more difficult. In the summer of 1936, the long-simmering antagonism between the ruling South-West Political Council of the Kuomintang in Kwangtung and Kwangsi provinces and the central government erupted. The immediate cause of the conflict was the doubling by the Japanese of their North China garrison under cover of the Boxer Protocol of 1901. The South-West leaders found in this act both a fresh rallying point for anti-Japanese sentiment and an excellent stick with which to beat Nanking for its failure to resist Japan. In the first week of June 1936, the South-West Political Council issued a circular telegram to the other provinces urging the central government to give a lead to the nation in a practical policy of armed resistance to Japan. Its own troops were re-named the "Chinese Revolutionary Anti-Japanese National Salvation Army," and some detachments began marching northwards through Nanking-held territory.

In trying to decide whether these political and military moves should be taken at face value, British embassy officials found it difficult to disentangle the truth from a welter of conflicting evidence. There were indications that the Japanese not only did not take the threat to themselves

---

[19]Leith-Ross, Minute, 13 October 1936; Leith-Ross to Addis, 9 October 1936, T 188/47.

seriously but were actually in touch with the southwest leaders and supplying them with funds and munitions.[20] To those familiar with the Orient there was nothing improbable in the paradox: the Kwantung-Kwangsi leaders might well intend to fight the Japanese in North China—if they ever got so far—and borrow arms and money from Japan for that purpose; Japan might be willing to supply arms and money, knowing full well that it would be against Nanking that they would have to be used. However, Chiang Kai-shek's astute political manoeuvring resulted in a massive defection of civilian and fighting forces in Kwangtung. Questions of war and peace, Chiang declared, in reply to the circular telegram of the South-West Political Council, could only be decided by a plenary session of the Central Executive Committee of the Kuomintang which he undertook to call into session within a month; meantime he pledged not to be the first to fire a shot in a civil war which might well invite foreign aggression. By June 15th the Kwangtung troops were retreating and the semi-independent southwestern administration rapidly collapsed. In response to a request for asylum in July, the military governor of Kwangtung, Marshall Chen Chi-Tang, was spirited away to exile in Hong Kong aboard the British gunboat H. M. S. *Moth*.[21]

Chiang Kai-shek returned to the South, for the first time in almost ten years, in a triumph which the British Foreign Office thought could "only be described as masterly."[22] He moved swiftly to incorporate Kwangtung province into the National Government system and read local officials a stern warning against corruption, emphasized by the execution of Dr. Feng Jui, head of the Bureau of Agriculture and Forestry, on charges of embezzlement.[23] The British embassy speculated that if the central government was allowed time to consolidate its control, Chiang would be in a position to speak to Japan in a very different tone from the past.

Within a few weeks of the collapse of the southwest rebellion, the Japanese government, which had been conducting a major policy review in the summer of 1936 with a view to strengthening its self-sufficiency in national defence,[24] put Chiang Kai-shek's new position to the test. On the pretext of the murder of several Japanese civilians in August 1936, the Japanese ambassador presented a list of major demands to the Chinese

---

[20]Cowan (Peking) to Eden, 16 June 1936, FO 20249/F3419, and Howe (Peking) to Eden, 16 September 1936, FO 20251/F5612.

[21]Admiralty to Foreign Office, 21 July 1936, FO 20250/F4383.

[22]G. W. Aldington, Minute, 23 July 1936, ibid., F4446.

[23]Knatchbull-Hugessen to Eden, 14 January 1937 (27 November 1936), FO 405/276, no. 2.

[24]See Crowley, *Japan's Quest*, pp. 289-300, for details of the "Fundamental Principles of National Policy" adopted by the inner cabinet on 16 August 1936.

Foreign Minister, Chang Chun, in September in the hope that the National-ist Government would agree to negotiate a series of treaties or agreements. Ambassador Kawagoe wanted: 1) Sino-Japanese co-operation against the Communists to extend all over China and not only to North China; 2) the establishment of a special area in North China; 3) economic co-operation throughout China; 4) the employment of Japanese advisers in all govern-ment organs; 5) the reduction of tariffs on articles of special interest to Japan; 6) the eradication of anti-Japanese feeling and suppression of anti-Japanese propaganda, including the revision of school text books; 7) the establishment of an air service between Fukuoka and Shanghai.[25] There was such a close similarity between these demands and those allegedly given to Ambassador Chiang Tso-pin in November 1935, at the time of the Leith-Ross–H. H. Kung currency reform, that it seemed a continuation of the Japanese policy of keeping up relentless pressure on China.

But for the first time since the Manchurian crisis of 1931-33, the Chinese government reacted in a firm and formal manner to the demands from Japan. The British embassy learned that on 23 September 1936, the Chinese foreign minister had replied that while China was doing all in her power to combat communist activities she was not prepared to take any action which might seem to be aimed at a friendly power. China was willing to explore possibilities for genuine economic co-operation but would not agree to the establishment of any special area in North China; tariffs could be modified, but not irrespective of their effect on Chinese revenue or the commerce of other powers; Sino-Japanese air services could be con-sidered when illegal Japanese flights in North China were brought to an end; Japanese subjects might be employed as technical advisers, but not in the army or navy. Outright rejections of Japanese demands were avoid-ed, but in each case consideration was hedged by various conditions. In addition, Foreign Minister Chang made certain counter-demands on Japan: the abolition of the East Hopei Autonomous Government, the cancellation of the Tangku Truce, and the suppression of smuggling in North China.

The Japanese ambassador took "immediate and violent exception"[26] to the Chinese reply and broke off the interview. Within a few hours of this interview another Japanese was murdered, and the Chinese could not be-lieve that now the Japanese government would hold their hand. Nanking envoys were hastily sent to Canton to report to Chiang Kai-shek and take his instructions, while the reactions of the Japanese government were anx-iously awaited. As it turned out, the Japanese were not prepared to push

[25]Knatchbull-Hugessen to Eden, 14 January 1937.
[26]Ibid.

matters to a showdown. It was arranged that the Kawagoe-Chang talks should be resumed, while the Japanese military contented themselves with larger and longer than usual autumn manoeuvres of the North China garrison, near Peking, from 26 October to 4 November 1936.[27] The incident, however, was a clear indication of things to come. Sino-Japanese détente the British hoped for was not likely to result from increased Chinese resistance to ever-expanding Japanese pressure.

The stiffening of the Chinese attitude to Japan had immediate implications for the financial and economic programmes which the Leith-Ross mission was attempting to set in motion. From the British point of view, the new aspect of the situation was that "owing to hatred of Japan," Canton was " 'pro-British' for the first time in a hundred years."[28] As a result of its victories in the southwest, the Nanking government put the whole question of the Consortium at issue by inviting special British assistance in a vast plan of new railway construction south of the Yangtse River. The projected railways would run in a great arc from Chungking in Szechuan, southwards through Kweichow and Kwangsi Provinces to Canton, and then northwards towards Shanghai. Construction would begin with a two-hundred-mile stretch from Canton to Meihsien, a town near the border of Fukien Province. The Chinese authorities indicated that they had strong objections to any dealings whatever with the Japanese south of the Yangtse River and that if Britain insisted on sharing with her consortium partners, then China would have to turn to German or French financial groups. Chiang Kai-shek indicated that he wished Britain to contract to build the new railways so that he could answer Japanese protests with a *fait accompli*: "We have entered into definite agreements with the British and we cannot now alter them."[29]

On other questions as well, the Nanking authorities were inviting Great Britain to establish a sphere of influence south of the Yangtse River. Until the present, Chiang Kai-shek had been relying mainly on a large military mission from Germany, under General von Seeckt, for assistance. Now he requested the advice of British officers on how Canton's defences could best be co-ordinated with those of Hong Kong.[30] He also urged

[27]Howe to Eden, 10 November 1936, FO 20229/F6841.

[28]Ashton-Gwatkin, Minute, 11 January 1927, FO 20231/F7999.

[29]Knatchbull-Hugessen to Eden, 2 October 1936, T 188/47; Knatchbull-Hugessen to Eden, 30 November 1936 (20 September 1936), FO 20232/F7346; and Eden to Knatchbull-Hugessen, 23 February 1937, FO 20994/F881.

[30]War Office to Foreign Office, 30 September 1936, FO 20244/F5897. Vansittart feared Japan would raise a "considerable storm" if British officers were engaged by China just now, but felt such a move could be camouflaged by agreeing that the Chinese could hire certain retired officers "on regular contract" rather than by lending active officers.

Britain to establish a protectorate over the island of Hainan to forestall a Japanese seizure of the territory.[31]

These were the pressing questions that faced Britain's new ambassador, Sir Hughe Knatchbull-Hugessen, on his arrival in China in the autumn of 1936. Knatchbull-Hugessen, who started his career in 1908, was regarded by the Foreign Office as "a safe man"[32] and a highly skilled practitioner of his trade by the time he was posted to China. In his first major review of the British position, Knatchbull-Hugessen showed a surprising lack of caution. He assumed that sooner or later China "must try conclusions with Japan," but this did not deter him from advocating, in line with Leith-Ross's report which he had received before leaving London, that Britain should grasp "whole-heartedly" any advantageous economic proposals which came her way in South China.[33] His attitude was partly based on an idea that China could be divided into spheres of influence. In addition Knatchbull-Hugessen appeared to be relying on the development of increased Chinese resistance: the Chinese were already showing Japan that she could not have her own way in China.

Obstacles to British economic penetration of South China, Knatchbull-Hugessen pointed out, had been (a) the separatist southwest régime with its peculiar ideas of state monopoly and control, and (b) the Japanese Amau declaration. He was of the opinion that central government control over the southwest was likely to be effectively maintained over a fairly long period and that Britain should shape her policy on that assumption. As to possible Japanese reactions to British economic expansion in the South, Knatchbull-Hugessen fell back on the wishful thinking, first expressed by Sir John Simon in April 1934, that the Amau declaration was not directed in any serious way at Britain. If the Chinese were prepared to face the possible consequences of ignoring the Amau declaration, Knatchbull-Hugessen thought there was "every reason" why Britain should also do so in South China. He naïvely cited "categorical assurances" by Japan of her intentions to respect British rights and interests in China as reason to believe that attempts to prevent, by forcible or even diplomatic measures, the conclusion or exploitation of contracts entered into by British subjects in China were very remote.

Knatchbull-Hugessen freely acknowledged that the Chinese invitations were not actuated solely by motives of friendship. They wished to develop the South for economic and military reasons and were compelled to look abroad for help because they lacked internal resources. The choice of

[31]Knatchbull-Hugessen to Eden, 14 November 1936, FO 20270/F6968.
[32]*The Times*, obituary, 23 March 1971.
[33]Knatchbull-Hugessen to Eden (secret), 30 October 1936, FO 20231/F6096.

Britain rather than Germany or the United States was dictated by military reasons. The Americans seemed to be pulling up stakes (leaving the Philippines), and the Germans were not at present in a position to apply force in the Far East. Britain, on the other hand, was already entrenched at Hong Kong and Singapore and clearly intended to protect her interests in those regions. It was not unnatural for the Chinese to hope, Knatchbull-Hugessen went on, that if British investments became sufficiently important, Britain would in an extremity take all necessary measures—diplomatic certainly and military possibly—for their protection, and in doing so would protect the interests of China. But he also believed that it would be possible to avoid encouraging the central government to hope that Britain would enter into any commitments or schemes for mutual defence against Japanese attacks. On the premise that political obstacles to British economic expansion in South China were no longer a deterrent, he proposed that every encouragement should be given to British subjects to go ahead and seek business openings in the usual way.

The apparent indifference of the ambassador to the possibility of complications with Japan may have been encouraged by his chief military adviser, Vice-Admiral Sir Charles Little. Little, who had been deputy chief of naval staff until posted to the China Station as commander-in-chief early in 1936, did not share the pro-Japanese sympathies of his predecessor, Admiral Sir Frederick Dreyer. Little was convinced of the correctness of the chiefs of staff recommendation of "showing a tooth" to Japan, and he thought Britain over-rated the Japanese. When Japanese police ill-treated three sailors of a British submarine flotilla visiting Keelung, Formosa, in October 1936, Little was "immensely pleased"[34] at the opportunity to show the Japanese that he was not at all impressed with them by cancelling the British China Fleet visit to Japan, scheduled for 30 October to 10 November, and demanding an apology.[35]

Vice-Admiral Little's negative attitude towards Japan was matched by a strong belief in the latent capacity of the Chinese to resist Japanese aggression. Little, who was born in Shanghai, agreed with those who felt that it would be impossible to deal China a vital blow owing to her vast size and lack of industrial centres. Japan could conquer the Chinese forces but could never conquer China. If Japan tried to take over China, she would experience the bandit troubles of a vaster Manchuria and temporarily ruin the market which she was anxious to build up.. This being the case, a Chinese policy of active resistance to Japan might call the Japanese bluff

[34]Little to Chatfield, 18 February 1937, Chatfield Papers.
[35]Admiralty Memorandum no. 1041, 3 November 1936, ADM 116/3682. An acceptable apology was not forthcoming for several months.

that under present conditions was peacefully dividing China piecemeal.[36] The only difficulty in Little's position was that if Japan was prepared to take stern measures on a large scale, the trade of the China coast, where British interests mainly lay, might be ruined for some years.

The long and important despatch from Knatchbull-Hugessen received an unexpectedly passive treatment in the Foreign Office. Foreign Secretary Eden was absent in Geneva for several weeks at the time, and the message was handled within the Far Eastern Department. Sir John Pratt had already dismissed Vice-Admiral Little's ideas about Chinese resistance as "receptive and gullible,"[37] since a rabble could not fight a modern equipped army. But he was strangely quiet about Knatchbull-Hugessen's proposal for British economic expansion to proceed in spite of the unmistakable possibility that the Chinese government would use this added strength to fight Japan. Such a line was contrary to the Foreign Office's thesis about quietly cultivating Chinese good will while doing nothing to antagonize Japan. Pratt was apparently deferring to Leith-Ross, who, he told a friend, was "the acknowledged authority now on China" and the "agent of the new policy."[38] Pratt and C. W. Orde, head of the Far Eastern Department, both noted that the ambassador was in substantial agreement with Leith-Ross's proposals for a more ambitious policy in China, and concurred with Knatchbull-Hugessen's line because the Cabinet was "in the mood to run considerable risks rather than see everything go by default."[39] After the Treasury had made the necessary consultations within the City of London, a decision was apparently arrived at informally, and the Foreign Office despatched the Treasury-drafted instruction to Knatchbull-Hugessen to go ahead in the following terms:

> We are inclined to agree with your view that political obstacles are not such as should deter us from entertaining proposals . . . provided that they are kept on a strictly economic basis. We realize, of course, that the Chinese in making any railway projects are moved by political as well as by economic considerations. Nevertheless, provided the lines proposed can be shown . . . to be sound business propositions . . . we see no reason why [the] Minister of Railways should not be encouraged. . . . We await with interest . . . further reports.

The Treasury's eagerness to handle the Chinese railway financing was further underlined by its message that if the Hongkong and Shanghai

[36]Little to Secretary of the Admiralty, Report of Proceedings, Commander-in-Chief, China Station, 8 March 1936, 4 April 1936, ADM 1/8862, MO 3106/36.

[37]Pratt, Minute, 15 April 1936, FO 20271/F1847.

[38]J. H. Cubbon to Maze, 22 February 1937, quoting Pratt, Maze Papers, 13.

[39]Pratt and Orde, Minutes, 7 October 1936, FO 20231/F6195.

Bank and the British and Chinese Corporation, a joint creation of the Bank and Matheson and Co., were going to "resume activities and meet German competition," they should become adequately organized for negotiating with the Chinese government on a large scale and ought to strengthen their representation in China.[40]

The fateful decision to give active diplomatic backing to the Matheson-Hongkong and Shanghai Bank group for the renewal of British capital investment in Chinese railways brought with it certain immediate complications. One difficulty was the claim of France and Japan to special spheres of influence, stemming from pre-World War I agreements covering Kwangsi and Fukien Provinces, the areas of the proposed new railways. The Far Eastern Department admitted privately that the position had drifted back to the pre-war régime of spheres of foreign influence in China. Britain, despite any soft words, would not welcome Japanese participation in any loan for railway construction in Central or South China.[41] But officially, the position remained that of the Nine Power Treaty of 1922 by which, in place of spheres of influence, the signatories had pledged to respect the territorial and administrative integrity of China and the "open door" for all nations. Therefore when C. R. Morriss, secretary of the British and Chinese Corporation, asked for advice about French and Japanese complaints over projected railways in Kwangsi and Fukien Provinces, the Foreign Office chose to rely on legalities and concurred in the suggestion of Morriss that, unless there were specific prior agreements, these protests and pressures could be ignored on the grounds that "alleged 'spheres of influence' are no longer applicable."[42]

The China Consortium of banks was another complication which, however, was not so easily ignored because the United States government was involved and that quarter was "pregnant with adverse reactions."[43] On Treasury advice, Sir Charles Addis of the Hongkong and Shanghai Bank wrote his American, French, and Japanese partners in the Consortium and asked them, in view of the Chinese objections to the Consortium, to relinquish their claim to participate in a loan for the Canton-Meihsien railway. In the Far Eastern Department, it was recognized that Addis's approach to the other groups was only a manoeuvre: whatever answer Addis received, the money would "be lent somehow," provided security

---

[40]Eden to Knatchbull-Hugessen, 26 October 1936, T 188/47; also FO 20231-2/F6664.

[41]Chaplin and Pratt, Minutes, 9 and 26 February 1937, FO 20972/F785, F1047.

[42]E. R. Morriss (British and Chinese Corporation) to Foreign Office, 15 June 1937, and Foreign Office reply, FO 20973/F3476.

[43]Chaplin, Minute, 22 January 1937, FO 20972/F408.

was adequate. The French and American groups declined to waive their claims, while the Japanese declined and then changed their stand ten days later.[44] Clearly a battle for concessions was looming, and since the results of the Addis initiative were inconclusive, the only alternative was British withdrawal from the Consortium.

The Consortium, for reasons of high policy and because it had been formed "at the behest of the Governments behind the Groups,"[45] could not be dissolved otherwise than at the initiative of the governments. And since the Americans had originally sponsored its creation, it was considered essential that Britain preface her withdrawal by frankest consultations with the U. S. government. Consequently, on 10 February 1937, Sir Alexander Cadogan, who had been recalled from China by Anthony Eden for promotion to deputy under-secretary of state (and later to permanent under-secretary), saw the U. S. Chargé d'Affaires, Ray Atherton, and handed him a "Memorandum Respecting the China Consortium," in which British arguments for dissolution were fully and skilfully expounded:[46] the Chinese government objected to group treatment which, "like the unequal treaties," seemed to them to touch the independence of China as a sovereign state. Therefore, it was turning to German, French, and Belgian groups outside the Consortium to finance construction of new railways. Another reason for dissolving the Consortium was that the "open tender" principle of the group was in conflict with policy adopted by Consortium governments in regard to foreign lending in their markets, and, therefore, instead of promoting the economic progress of China, as its authors intended, the Consortium was an obstacle standing in the way of any such action. Cadogan said that he understood that the American group as at present constituted could not in fact take any active share in a consortium operation. But, he wanted to know, was there any method by which, while restoring to its individual members the required liberty of action in industrial enterprises, the major objects of the consortium could be attained by retaining co-operation between the governments concerned, including the Chinese government? Cadogan asked for a prompt reply.

In due course the American government indicated that, subject to the views of the banks, it was favourably disposed to the dissolution of the

[44]Addis to Orde, 20 January 1937, ibid., Chaplin, Minute, 22 January 1937, Addis to Orde, 4 February 1937, FO 20972/F741; Hall-Patch to Treasury, 9 February 1937, ibid., F785; H. Kano (Yokohama Specie Bank) to Addis, 19 February 1937, ibid., File 79. In reporting the Japanese change of heart, Addis suspected they intended to make a similar request in North China.

[45]Chaplin, Minute, 22 January 1937.

[46]Eden to Knatchbull-Hugessen, 23 February 1937, T 188/48; also in FO 20994/ F881, *FRUS*, 1937, 4:568.

Consortium as presently constituted; but it was apparent to interested parties in Britain that the process of dissolution was going to be long and drawn out.

In the meantime the Chinese government was becoming impatient with the lack of definite responses to its proposals. In order to meet this Chinese pressure, several steps were taken. In Hong Kong, British officials encouraged the formation of an unofficial committee of leading British businessmen to work out means for co-operating with the new régime of Chiang Kai-shek in Canton, and contracts were accepted for the development of power, water, and transportation utilities in several municipalities in South China.[47] Considerable thought was also given to Chiang Kai-shek's suggestion for advancing a British interest on Hainan Island, the strategic outpost which lay astride the communications between Hong Kong and Singapore. British officials felt that strategic objectives would be assisted if there were some British commercial firms "prepared to go in and to become objects of our solicitous protection."[48] Article three of the Nine Power Treaty of 1922 technically precluded Britain from seeking any monopoly or preference in Hainan, but this clause could be "circumvented" if British mining interests formed an *ad hoc* combine "to eliminate competition" and "assume a Chinese complexion by co-operation with Chinese interests" to obtain prospecting concessions.[49] The formation of a combine proved to be impossible, for no British company could be induced to take the initiative, and British officials deplored the present lack of the adventurous spirit which had characterized British merchant venturers "in the old days."[50] The only action which the government could devise on this matter was an instruction to the ambassador in Tokyo to "intimate tactfully" to the Japanese government, in the event a suitable

[47]Knatchbull-Hugessen to Eden, 28 December 1936 (14 November 1936), FO 20232/F7999.

[48]N. B. Ronald (Far Eastern Department), Minute, 22 December 1936, FO 20270/F6968.

[49]J. T. Henderson (Far Eastern Department), Minute, 4 January 1937, FO 20232/F7999.

[50]G. C. Pelham, Commercial Secretary (Hong Kong), to Leith-Ross, 19 November 1936, T 188/51. Leith-Ross eventually got Sir Henry Strakosch of Union Corporation and Selection Trust to send an engineer out to investigate possibilities. The British engineer found Hainan to be a plague-ridden, burnt-over island with numerous rock exposures. He reported that observant Aborigines were in the habit of sending specimens of unusually heavy rocks to places visited by Chinese traders for evaluation. Mineralization, however, appeared to be weak. Leith-Ross later wrote to Strakosch regretting the trouble, adding wryly that he was "glad the observant Aborigines did not send any specimens of unusual or heavy rocks directly on to your representative." ibid.

opening arose, that Britain would take "a grave view" of any change in the territorial *status quo* in South China.[51] But the most insistent Chinese pressure was on British financiers for a decision on the Canton-Meihsien and other railway loans. After some delay, but without waiting for agreement among the powers, Leith-Ross gave an undertaking to the Matheson-Hongkong and Shanghai Bank group that "it is the policy of His Majesty's Government so to arrange with the Consortium countries that a Sterling Issue in London for the Canton-Meihsien Railway will be possible within a period of two years."[52] The Foreign Office did not question the authority of the Treasury's high official to give such assurances but considered it too dangerous to give written evidence of these funeral arrangements for the Consortium. Sir Alexander Cadogan, however, gave confidential, verbal confirmation of Leith-Ross's understanding of the government's intention that the Hongkong and Shanghai Bank could safely make cash advances in order to keep the Chinese railway business in British hands.[53]

Although British economic prospects were improving in China, another object of the Leith-Ross mission—creating a friendly understanding with Japan—was not meeting with any similar success. The return of Leith-Ross to London in July 1936 had coincided with the appointment of Shigeru Yoshida as ambassador to the United Kingdom, and the scene of Anglo-Japanese conversations shifted to London. Over the next year, Yoshida conducted an erratic personal diplomacy in the British capital which, in the opinion of the British Foreign Office, often amounted to little more than pious aspirations. In fairness to Yoshida, his performance may have reflected not so much his ineptness as the difficulty of putting an acceptable face on the intentions and actions of his government.

Yoshida had been vice-minister of foreign affairs in Tokyo, but he was said to be unpopular with the army and had been sent to London to save his face when the army refused to accept him as foreign minister. He was the son-in-law of Count Makino and therefore connected with the immediate advisers of the Emperor, but he had supposedly made blunders which annoyed the court. Rumour had it that Yoshida, who was to become prime minister of Japan after World War II, was not taken very seriously in Japan and that he was not of the same calibre as his predecessor in Britain, Tsuneo Matsudaira, the Emperor's father-in-law. Unfortunately

[51]Eden to Clive, 16 January 1937, FO 20270/F8055.
[52]O. J. Barnes (Hongkong and Shanghai Bank) to Cadogan, 12 February 1937, FO 20972/F914.
[53]Cadogan, Minute, 26 February 1937, ibid.

for the Japanese, Yoshida's credibility was weakened by all the rumours which accompanied his arrival in Britain.[54]

The main themes which Yoshida put forward as the basis for Anglo-Japanese friendship were in a familiar refrain: a gentlemen's agreement about the Soviet Union (as first suggested in the Shigemitsu-Edwardes talks in 1934), joint tutelage of China under Japan's leadership, and re-opening of markets for Japanese textiles within the British Empire.

In his first contact after arriving in London, Yoshida suggested that if Britain would come to "some arrangement" with Japan about the Russian menace, he had no doubt that the two countries could "find a satisfactory solution to our differences about China." The British side thought he was being "more earnest than coherent" about the Russian menace and did not respond to this suggestion.[55] Yoshida then proposed a co-ordination of policy toward China in which, according to Anthony Eden's report, Japan would be charged with the maintenance of law and order while Britain would be charged with the irrigation of China. The "obscure proposal"[56] perplexed Eden, and he wondered whether the Chinese would not prefer to be responsible for exercising law and order themselves and whether the United States would not have to be included in any under-standing. Moving closer to British views, Yoshida proposed a conference in London of China, Japan, and Britain for the purpose of co-operation in railway construction in China. But this idea was side-tracked by senior Japanese officials in China, who said such approaches were premature and indicated that British railway proposals "tended to encroach on a Japanese preserve."[57]

There is a strong possibility that Yoshida's next initiative was prepared in close co-operation with the British Treasury. A long memorandum which, by Yoshida's own admission, was prepared by someone else was given to Neville Chamberlain (instead of to the Foreign Office as required by protocol) in which proposals were made that closely paralleled Fisher's and A. H. F. Edwardes's thinking about China. According to this plan Britain would agree to joint Anglo-Japanese representations to the Nanking

[54]F. O. Lindley, Memorandum, 21 July 1936, FO 20277/F4808; Cadogan, Minute, 7 August 1936, ibid.; Cadogan, Minute of conversation with Ray Atherton (U.S. embassy), 17 December 1936; FO 20286/F2926; E. Drummond (Rome) to Cadogan, December 1936, FO 20287/F7427; Clive to Eden, 27 January 1937, FO 371/F570/28/23; S. Yoshida, *The Yoshida Memoirs* (Boston: Houghton Mifflin, 1962), p. 14. (These memoirs contain little on the Anglo-Japanese talks of 1936-37.)

[55]Cadogan, Memorandum, 10 August 1936, FO 20277/F4808.

[56]Eden, Memorandum, 31 July 1936, ibid., F4625.

[57]See Knatchbull-Hugessen to Eden, 25 September 1936, T 188/49, and 11 November 1936, FO 20232/F6891.

government on matters of mutual interest in return for Japanese pledges to respect the territorial rights and sovereignty of China south of the Great Wall and the "open door" everywhere in China. Britain would encourage the Chinese central government to employ "an adequate number" of Japanese military officers in order to secure order and combat communism in China and would approve of any Sino-Japanese agreement that China should buy all her arms from Japan; Britain would agree to a "defensive agreement" embodying the principle of "benevolent neutrality" on the part of Great Britain in the event of war between Japan and the Soviet Union, in return for Japan's undertaking to protect British possessions and trade routes in the East in the event of Britain being engaged in war elsewhere. Japan would accept a reasonable quota for textile exports to the British Empire.[58]

In a conversation with Yoshida, Eden raised doubts about many of these points in terms of Britain's existing commitments to the League of Nations and the need for "patience and restraint" in face of the disappointments which were bound to occur in the social and political reorganization of such a vast country as China.[59] But when it came to formulating a written reply, there developed, according to Cadogan, a "wrangle with the Treasury who *will* try to put rubbish into our draft reply to Yoshida"; it was only after Sir Warren Fisher had "tinkered quite unnecessarily" that the British aide-memoire was given to the Japanese ambassador.[60] In the meantime the latter had apparently gone ahead of his government, which had recently concluded a pact with Germany, and he was afraid to send the British note to Tokyo. Instead, he came back to the Foreign Office and proposed a short statement calling for "frank discussions," which would, in Cadogan's opinion, simply be a bit of paper to say that "we should like to kiss and be friends. Quite easy but useless." Cadogan continued to record his frustration at the artificial and contrived nature of what was heralded in some quarters as evidence of warmer Anglo-Japanese relations in the spring of 1937:

> That ridiculous Yoshida sent me round his aide-memoire (which he had written at my dictation). This process of negotiations, whereby I have to draft his communications as well as ours, is both laborious and embarrassing, and likely to prove unfruitful.[61]

[58]Eden to Clive, 6 November 1936, FO 410/97, no. 39.
[59]Eden to Clive, 18 January 1937, FO 410/98, no. 14.
[60]See 15 January 1937, Cadogan Papers, Diary, and Eden to Yoshida, Aide Memoire, 18 January 1937, FO 410/98, no. 14.
[61]21 and 28 January 1937, Cadogan Papers, Diary.

The quarrel between the Treasury and the Foreign Office over how to approach Japan led to confusion and resentment within the policy making group in Whitehall, but, in spite of an opinion of Sir Warren Fisher to the contrary,[62] it does not in itself appear to be the cause of the failure to reach an Anglo-Japanese agreement. This failure lay in the absence of sufficient common interests between Britain and Japan in China or elsewhere. A British policy dictated by financial and economic considerations in China without a concurrent improvement of political-diplomatic relations with Japan was unworkable. But political relations with Japan were unlikely to improve without British recognition of Manchukuo, an action not possible unless China could be persuaded to take that unlikely step first. And the Treasury's plans for rehabilitating China involved imposing foreign tutelage on Nanking—a political device in which Japan might have been willing to co-operate, but which the Foreign Office rejected as an outmoded, unworkable, and fruitless attempt to turn back the clock.

By the end of 1936, when Japanese difficulties in China were increasing because of stiffening Chinese resistance, the urgency for an Anglo-Japanese understanding diminished, even in the minds of its most ardent supporters in the British cabinet. Time, it seemed, was on Britain's side. This tendency was strengthened by the signing of the German-Japanese Anti-Comintern Pact in November 1936. Although the coming together of Germany and Japan had been a main fear of the cabinet during the defence debates of 1933-34, the foreign secretary was "not prepared to take this agreement tragically" because it was merely a registration of a situation that already existed and did not bring any fundamental change in the international situation.[63] The Hirota Cabinet hoped the pact would promote favourable developments in Sino-Japanese negotiations. The agreement with Hitler, even though vaguely worded, was seen by Japan as a tool to persuade the Chinese Nationalists and the Western powers of the dangers of relying upon the Soviet Union as a deterrent to Japanese policies in North China. It was also seen as a means of promoting a *modus vivendi* with Britain.[64] In the eyes of the British, however, the pact as it applied to the Far East only strengthened the feeling that Britain could rely on the Soviet Union to hold Japan in check. The German-Japanese agreement was even wel-

---

[62]In a minute written 21 July 1936, Fisher complained of the lack of "any reciprocal attitude on the part of the Far Eastern Department of the F.O." for cordial relations with Japan, T 188/27.

[63]Eden, Minute, 13 December 1936, FO 20286/F7504g, and Eden to I. Maisky (Ambassador of the U.S.S.R.), 21 December 1936, FO 20286/F7927.

[64]See Crowley, *Japan's Quest*, pp. 305-6; for German aims and location of all relevant documents, see *DGFP*, Series C, 5:899, 1138.

comed by the permanent under-secretary of the Foreign Office as extinguishing a "potentially disquieting" rapprochement between Russia and Japan which had been developing in the autumn of 1936.[65] To the extent that the pact antagonized Russia, it would produce a stalemate in Russo-Japanese relations and tend to discourage Japan from adventures further south.

In these circumstances, Sir Frederick Leith-Ross and even some members of the Foreign Office began to think that Japan could be got around and that her power was exaggerated. In the spring of 1937, this feeling led high officials to re-evaluate British policy in the Far East. It is ironic that just as these officials were reaching a more optimistic assessment of the British position, powerful forces were germinating in China which would challenge Japan and soon lead to war in Asia and the withering of British hopes.

[65]Vansittart, Minute, 5 November 1936, FO 20286/F6478.

7

British Policy and the End of Peace in 1937

After the failure of the Chamberlain-Hoare plan for recognition of Manchukuo in 1935, the British government could no longer be accused of following an overt policy of appeasement towards Japan in China. Neville Chamberlain still kept this plan in his contingency file and spoke of it with favour to the dominion prime ministers at the Imperial Conference in London in 1937, but there was no counterpart to the "Munich agreement" of 1938 in the Far East. There was, instead, an element of recklessness in the drive to establish a British sphere of influence south of the Yangtze. By 1937, policy makers turned a blind eye to the growing signs of danger to Britain's desire for "peace, security and sound trading" in China.

In their effort to "rehabilitate" China under British tutelage, a proposal which Chamberlain and Fisher had originally put before the cabinet committee in February 1935 and which found expression in the Leith-Ross mission, responsible British officials and statesmen made several profound miscalculations. They failed to assess correctly the dynamic of Chinese nationalism. They knew that increased British trade and investment would be a psychological and material aid to China in her struggle to check Japan, but they did not foresee that the growing anger among China's population against Japan's activities would lead to national unity and an effective demand for armed resistance. Only belatedly did they come to realize that this unity had arisen and that it included a renewal of a united front between erstwhile deadly foes, the Communists and the Kuomintang, to oppose Japanese aggression. British policy makers never envisaged China's anti-Japanese resistance going to such lengths.

British officials also underestimated the strength, determination, and exclusiveness of Japanese imperialism. Therefore, when Japanese officials raised questions and complaints about the implications of what looked to them like a British protectorate over China, British officials turned a deaf ear and countered with the Disraeli maxim that "in Asia, there is room for us all." British self-confidence was such, moreover, that various suggestions for an international political effort to block the aggressor, which arose early in 1937, were rejected in favour of an unavowed, but nevertheless definite, effort by Britain to check Japanese expansionism south of the Yellow River by helping to build up China's strength.

The extent to which British statesmen misjudged the situation in the summer of 1937 is illustrated by Neville Chamberlain's remark to the dominion prime ministers on 8 June 1937, that Japan "appeared to be in a more reasonable mood than for some time past."[1] In the same vein, Anthony Eden told the House of Commons on 25 June that there were "encouraging signs of improvement in the international situation in the Far East." It was true that the new Hayashi Cabinet, which lasted from February to May, 1937, adopted a less belligerent attitude towards China and that Japanese army economic experts had begun to revise their earlier insistence on the importance of having the resources of North China under Japanese control.[2] Nevertheless, on 7 July, just two weeks after Eden's reassuring remarks to the House of Commons, the Marco Polo Bridge incident marked the outbreak of a long and bloody war between China and Japan. This war, lasting eight years, resulted in the immediate expulsion of the Japanese and eventually of Chiang Kai-shek as well as the British from China.

The roots of this complacent and faulty assessment of the political balance in the Far East are to be found in official interpretations of events in the winter and early spring of 1937, and they are reflected in a subsequent joint effort, mainly by the Treasury and some younger members of the Foreign Office, to clarify British far eastern policy.

In what was supposed to be a long-term forecast in November 1936, the British War Office considered that anything in the nature of a full-scale war between China and Japan was "extremely improbable."[3] Minor

---

[1]E(P.D.)37, 15th meeting, Imperial Conference, London, 8 June 1937, CAB 32/128.

[2]Crowley, *Japan's Quest*, pp. 316-21; a general staff memorandum on 6 January 1937 stated; "We must purge ourselves of the idea that North China is a special region and revise the strategy of encouraging the independence of the five [northern] provinces." *Gendaishi shiryo* [Documents on Contemporary History], (Tokyo, 1964-66), 8: 380, cited in Robertson, *Origins*, p. 265.

[3]M.I. 2, "Appreciation of the Probable Course of a Sino-Japanese War," 26 November 1936, WO 106/115.

skirmishes might occur, but M. I. 2, the authors of the report, felt that for Japan it would be unnecessary, if not positively disadvantageous, to wage war on China in view of the "inevitable" war with Russia. Strategically Japan's aim in China was to secure the western flank of Manchukuo against communist infiltration, and economically she hoped to gain control of Chinese sources of raw material and to develop China as a secure market for Japanese manufactured goods. The economic aims were thought by M. I. 2 to be more important than the strategic, and they would be vitiated if Japan were forced to resort to arms. Rather than waging war, which would compromise the fundamental object of Japanese policy— readiness for war with Russia[4]—Japan would take advantage of existing internal dissatisfaction in China in order to divide the country into three or more independent areas, each more or less under Japanese influence, which could be played off against each other as occasion arose.

The War Office found it more difficult to formulate precise Chinese objectives. If the Chinese as a whole had an object, it was to maintain their national sovereignty. But British military intelligence analysts felt that there was no real feeling of patriotism in China and therefore that there "was nothing to be gained by discussing the possible action of a United China." It boiled down to considering the possible action of Chiang Kai-shek, the most serious obstacle to Japanese ambitions and consequently their most likely target. The courses open to Chiang were so many as to defy listing. The most probable was that he would temporize and devise some face-saving expedient whereby he could (without serious personal embarrassment) arrive at a bargain with the Japanese on economic questions in North China. Alternatively, he might offer armed resistance to some well established act of Japanese aggression as a basis for an appeal to the League of Nations and then withdraw, either as head of a government, or as an individual, to a prepared position in Western China. This theory was borne out by the fact that he was known to have withdrawn his personal troops to the west and northwest in recent months and to have accumulated in this area most of the available stocks of ammunition, petrol, and money. This, however, was likely to be his final recourse. A

---

[4]This may have been an erroneous assumption by 1936 because the Imperial Way faction of the Japanese army, which favoured a strike north against Russia, had already been eclipsed at the time of the Tokyo mutiny on 26 February 1936 by the Control faction, which favoured expansion into China and the South Seas. Kanji Ishihara, who was chief of the operations section from 1935, nevertheless continued to be actively interested in strategic planning towards Russia, and a memorandum drafted by his department in July 1936 declared that preparation against the Soviet Union should be completed by 1941 (*Gendaishi shiryo*, 8:682, cited in Robertson, *Origins*, p. 266).

declaration of war against Japan or the continuation of passive resistance were the most unlikely courses, since they would lead to financial ruin and his personal downfall.

The War Office showed a thorough grasp of many important facts in the situation, but it underestimated the extent of Japanese ambitions in China, and it miscalculated the strength of Chinese patriotic feeling. While the exact nature of future Japanese plans may have been difficult to determine, there is no obvious or objective explanation for the underestimation of the spirit of Chinese patriotism because, as the following summary shows, the political correspondence of the Foreign Office is filled with evidence about this phenomenon—especially after the Chinese realized that the Japanese were attempting to set up an autonomous puppet régime in the five provinces of North China in 1935. One of the earliest British observers to detect a new attitude in Nanking was E. M. Gull, secretary of the China Association, who was making an extended tour of the Far East in 1935. After a meeting with high officials of the Nanking government, Gull reported that any further Japanese demands involving the sacrifice of territory or of important sovereign rights would be resisted by force. "Everywhere," he wrote on 6 November 1935, "one encounters a steadily growing sentiment in favour of resistance, whereas four or five months ago the general attitude appeared to be one of hopelessness."[5]

The spectacular growth of anti-Japanese public opinion was described in historical perspective by the China Secretariat of the Colonial Office in Singapore, in a report titled "Modern Literary Developments in China."[6] The Colonial Office had gained certain insights through reading confiscated mail from China intended for overseas Chinese in Malaya. As a rule, it found, anti-Japanese movements in the previous twenty years were short-lived, fizzling out almost as soon as the incidents which provoked them were settled. But the present movement, originating in the Manchurian incident, had been maintained for five years and instead of waning was increasing, spurred on by repeated acts of aggression by the Japanese in North China. It included distribution of anti-Japanese circulars and leaflets, but also novels, short stories, poems, films, and plays with Japanese aggression in China as their setting. By 1935, the popularity of this kind of literature became widespread, and hundreds of periodicals either wholly or partly devoted to the publication of these articles sprang into existence "like bamboo shoots after spring rain." They also appeared in influential newspapers, particularly those critical of Nanking, and were "clamouring

[5]J. Swire and Sons, encl. from Gull to Orde, 29 November 1935 (6 November 1935), FO 19314/F7516.
[6]Colonial Office to Foreign Office, 19 December 1936, FO 20248/F7821.

for armed resistance against Japan." In June 1936, all writers of "National Defence Literature," as it came to be called in 1935, joined to form the "Chinese Literary Writers' Association," calling for a "united front against Japanese aggression in China."

Public opinion in China was further stirred by large and militant student demonstrations which took place in Peking, Shanghai, and elsewhere on and after 9 December 1935. Trains were seized by students and professors in an endeavour to force the railways to convey them to Nanking to put pressure on Chiang Kai-shek to resist Japan.[7] By 2 January 1936, Leith-Ross reported that, although the Nanking government was trying to keep things quiet, "even sober and reasonable men take the view that war with Japan is becoming inevitable."[8]

Reports of stiffening Chinese reactions to Japan came from a broad cross-section of sources. Rear-Admiral Lewis E. Crabbe of the Yangtse Flotilla, China Station, reported in the spring of 1936 that "there was evident anticipation of armed resistance to Japan,"[9] as did the representatives of many British China firms. Lord Riverdale, representing Sheffield steel interests, for example, called on Sir Maurice Hankey, secretary of the cabinet, more than once in 1936 to tell of the feverish Chinese activity and their requests for credits for heavy armaments and for the building of underground arsenals. Riverdale's agents told him that the Chinese intention was to abandon coast lines and ports and resist on interior lines, with the possible support of the U.S.S.R.[10] In notes, which Hankey distributed to undisclosed persons in mimeographed form, Riverdale suggested that England might be willing to supply, indirectly through another country, the necessary plant and munitions to enable China to fight England's battle with Japan. "It might be far cheaper," he said, "for England to spend 300,000,000 Chinese dollars to hold Japan, whilst any repayments received could be regarded as profit."[11] The Conference of Missionary Societies of Great Britain and Ireland also prepared confiden-

---

[7]Cadogan to Eden, 30 December 1935, FO 19338/F8055.

[8]Leith-Ross to Fisher, 2 January 1936, T 188/26.

[9]Admiralty to Foreign Office, 18 May 1936, FO 20246/F2776.

[10]Hankey to Orde, 23 April 1936, FO 20242/F2268. For a discussion of the way in which the mainstream of Chinese nationalism was transformed from Social Darwinism, which blamed China's frailty on her own faults, to anti-imperialism following the May Fourth Movement of 1919, see Jerome Ch'en, "Historical Background," in Jack Gray, ed., *Modern China's Search for a Political Form* (London: Oxford University Press, 1969), pp. 8-12. For a detailed account of the December 9th student movement see John Isreal, *Student Nationalism in China 1927-1937* (Stanford: Stanford University Press, 1966).

[11]M.O. (36) 5A, 15 June 1936, Hankey Papers (CAB 63/51), Public Record Office, London.

tial reports which showed a close contact with the Nanking government and reflected much searching of heart among the thousands of foreign Christian missionaries at the way China was being "robbed and bullied" by Japan. It might come as something of a shock, one report to the Foreign Office said, to hear that there are many of our Chinese Christian leaders who think that the time has come for China to resist.[12] The general secretary of the International Missionary Council, William Paton, who visited China in 1935, warned that in despair the Nanking government might "stop fighting the Reds," and, even at the risk of the communist threat "to property and institutions," get them to join against Japan.[13]

The British ambassador, Sir Hughe Knatchbull-Hugessen, was no exception to those who noticed the growth of Chinese desires to resist Japan in 1936. It was a chemical truth, he observed, that "the more you compress a substance, even cotton wool, the more resistant it becomes." Public opinion, he declared, "seemed to have woken up in China" and he stressed in March 1937 that "anti-Japanism is indeed the most potent driving force in China today."[14]

Against the objective evidence of growing anti-Japanese opinion in China flowing into Whitehall offices, officials there continued to harbour doubts about it turning into any effective or united resistance. Most of the evidence came from the "educated circles"; what about the "vast masses of Chinese people," particularly the commercial elements, "who would regard war as a national disaster?" The Chinese method of survival was not through military resistance but through the age-long process of "impregnating its conquerors with its own system of values." All the courageous talk about resistance to Japanese aggression was a cover by Chinese leaders for the congenial task that they had set themselves of making "our flesh creep" with the ultimate object of "dipping their hands into our pockets."[15] These were typical of the sceptical attitudes in the Far Eastern Department.

Another reason most British officials were reluctant to entertain the idea of serious Chinese resistance to Japan was the disastrous effect such action would likely have on British property and interests. Nevertheless, this fear led Anthony Eden to seize every possible occasion to urge moderation

[12]Cadogan to Eden, 7 April 1936, encl. from R. D. Rees, FO 20242/F1934.

[13]Paton to Lothian, copy to Chatham House, "Memorandum on Chinese Policy to Japan," 9 December 1935, Lothian Papers, GD 40/17/313.

[14]Knatchbull-Hugessen to Cadogan, 22 December 1936 (4 November 1936), FO 20246/F7891; Knatchbull-Hugessen to Eden, 14 April 1937 (2 March 1937), FO 20970/F2170.

[15]Harcourt-Smith, Minute, 14 April 1936, FO 20242/F1934; H. Maxse, Minute, 14 January 1936; Pratt, Minute, 15 April 1936, FO 20271/F1847.

upon the Nanking government. The hope that this advice would be followed may well have obscured, in British minds, the true state of Chinese opinion. When the Chinese Foreign Minister, Chang Chun, refused Ambassador Kawagoe's demands in October 1936, for example, Eden cabled Nanking that His Majesty's government hoped that all questions at issue would be speedily disposed of in "a friendly and reasonable spirit." Similarly, suggestions that China avoid "anything savouring of over assertiveness" were made when Japanese mercenaries advanced into Suiyuan Province in November 1936, and again when a Japanese economic mission, under Kenji Kodoma, visited China in the spring of 1937 seeking tariff revisions.[16] In keeping with this attitude, British authorities also took measures to curb any anti-Japanese activities which took place in British concessions or the International Settlement in Shanghai. The breaking up of student demonstrations and the arrest of leaders of the Chinese National Salvation Movement by the British-led Shanghai Municipal Police force earlier in 1936 had led to the inevitable questions and evasions in Parliament[17] but did not cause the government to change its general point of view.

A further reason for the reluctance of British officials to believe that Chinese resistance to Japan would become serious was their suspicion that much of the agitation was communist or communist-inspired propaganda designed to embarrass the Nanking government rather than to unite the country to oppose Japan. Chiang Kai-shek's attitude lent support to the view that the Chinese would not unite against Japan because his government continued, until 1937, to promulgate emergency measures for the maintenance of public order which prohibited anti-Japanese student demonstrations, writings, or speeches that endangered "the safety of the state" in the face of possible Japanese retaliation, and which authorized police to arrest ringleaders and suspects.[18]

The idea that resistance to Japan was some kind of communist plot led to the most serious and damaging failure of British analysis after the famous Sian Incident of December 1936. At that time, Chiang Kai-shek was kidnapped and held prisoner in Sian, capital of Shensi Province, for two weeks by subordinates, including the young marshal Chang Hsueh-

---

[16]Eden to Knatchbull-Hugessen, 2 November 1936, Outfile, FO 20245/F6551; Knatchbull-Hugessen to Eden, 30 November 1936, FO 20259/F7232; Eden to Knatchbull-Hugessen, 27 April 1937, FO 20965/F2302.

[17]99 *H.L. Deb.*, 5 February 1936; 308 *H.C. Deb.*, 14 February 1936; 309 *H.C. Deb.*, 26 February 1936; also Cadogan to Eden, 29 April 1936 (20 March 1936), encl., "Police Report on Student Demonstration in International Settlement," 3 September 1936, FO 20249/F2389, F2187.

[18]Cadogan to Eden, 29 April 1936.

liang, commander of the Tungpei (northeastern) army, who was supposed to be fighting the Communists in the northwest. Chang's main point in seizing Chiang Kai-shek was to convince him that it was high time to stop pouring out vast sums of money in fighting the Communists while Japan, the greater enemy, was allowed to absorb China piecemeal. He had taken this action, according to W. H. Donald, the British subject who was a personal adviser to both men, because he had been unable to get the ear of the generalissimo in Nanking owing to Chiang's pro-Japanese entourage. The young marshal and his associates placed eight demands calling for the end of civil war, the release of the patriotic leaders arrested in Shanghai, and reorganization of the Nanking government to admit all parties to share the joint responsibility for saving the nation before Chiang Kai-shek and broadcast them to the nation.[19] Chiang Kai-shek apparently refused to talk to his captors. Meanwhile, in Nanking a conservative faction of the government in favour of sending a punitive expedition to Sian, regardless of the consequences for the generalissimo, was defeated by the group headed by Madame Chiang Kai-shek and her brother, T. V. Soong, who then flew to Sian. Suddenly and unexpectedly, the generalissimo was released on Christmas Day and returned immediately to Nanking. He was followed by young marshal Chang, who placed himself in the hands of the government for investigation of his conduct and punishment if the government should find he had been at fault.

Many explanations were suggested for this surprising dénouement. The payment of a huge ransom, coupled with the acceptance of some of the young marshal's demands and a promise of immunity, were the most popular, according to Ambassador Knatchbull-Hugessen. W. H. Donald told the ambassador that there was no question of a ransom and that the generalissimo himself had promised nothing. T. V. Soong, however, gave certain undertakings as a condition of Chiang's release, the chief of which, according to Donald, were the cessation of civil war, the reorganization of the central government, and a strong national policy against Japan.[20] Unfortunately for the ambassador, W. H. Donald omitted telling him that the chief reason for Chiang's release was the intervention on his behalf of Chou En-lai, representing the Chinese Communist party and the Red Army. The Tungpei army officers had been unwilling to release Chiang and demanded his death until the Communists dissuaded them. Although the Communists took no part in the kidnapping plot and details of the

---

[19]Knatchbull-Hugessen to Eden, 22 February 1937 (28 December 1936), and "Quarterly Political Report," 14 April 1937 (2 March 1937), FO 20969/F1048, FO 20970/F2170.

[20]Knatchbull-Hugessen, "Quarterly Political Report," 14 April 1937.

discussions were never officially released, Chou En-lai apparently convinced the Tungpei army high command that Chiang Kai-shek was the only commander-in-chief who could unite the entire nation in the struggle against Japan.[21] It is not clear why Donald who later claimed to be the one who proposed bringing the Communists into the negotiations for Chiang's release,[22] failed to advise the British embassy of the critical role which the Communists played in the resolution of the Sian Incident. Possibly he feared it would taint Chiang in the eyes of Knatchbull-Hugessen and cause Britain to lose confidence in the Chinese leader. In the published version of Chiang's Sian diary, no mention is made of his talks with Chou En-lai, an omission which a contemporary American observer thought was natural "as such a revelation would have intensified the suspicions of the conservatives at Nanking and of Japan."[23]

Whatever motivated Donald's behaviour, his failure to inform Knatch-bull-Hugessen of this aspect of the situation led the ambassador to give an incorrect assessment of the probable course of events to the British government. Knatchbull-Hugessen first reported that there had indeed been a cessation of the anti-communist campaign in the northwest and that he did "not know what to make of this." It was undoubtedly the result of some understanding reached in Sian, but "a situation in which communist forces remain in undisturbed occupation of parts of Chinese territory clearly cannot last indefinitely."[24] Knatchbull-Hugessen was basing himself partly on a homily that Chiang issued to his captors before leaving Sian, in which he said that "you have today decided in the interest of the State to send me back to the capital without forcing me to sign any document, issue any order or accept any extraordinary demand." The whole statement, which in the circumstances Knatchbull-Hugessen thought was a master-piece that bid fair to become a classic of Chinese political literature, was important, he said, because of the allegations made by the Communists that Chiang had undertaken to declare war on Japan.[25] The leader of the Chinese Communists, Mao Tse-tung, also thought that Chiang's statement "with its ambiguity and intricacy" was "indeed an interesting piece of

[21]Lyman P. Van Slyke, ed., *The Chinese Communist Movement: A Report of the United States War Department* (Stanford, 1968), pp. 41-42; Shen Po-chun, "The Sian Incident," *China Reconstructs* 11 (December 1962): 30-33.

[22]Earl A. Selle, *Donald of China* (New York: Harper, 1968), p. 333.

[23]Bisson, *Japan in China*, p. 173.

[24]Knatchbull-Hugessen to Eden, 31 December 1936, telegram 957, FO 676/332.

[25]Knatchbull-Hugessen, "Quarterly Political Report," 14 April 1937, FO 20970/ F2170, no. 29. The noted American sinologist, Paul Linebarger, has written that the Chinese "have long delighted in ingenious formulae with which to meet *de jure* impasses, while proceeding *de facto* in quite another direction" (*The China of Chiang Kai-shek: A Political Study* (Boston: World Peace Foundation, 1941), p. 175.

writing among China's political documents"; but the significant point which Mao picked out, in contrast to Knatchbull-Hugessen, was the assertion that "all promises will be kept and action resolutely taken." These promises, according to Mao, in an article published on 28 December 1936, included the reorganization of the national government, the release of the patriotic leaders in Shanghai, an end to the policy of "annihilating the Communists," and an alliance with the Red Army to resist Japan.[26]

The British ambassador may not have had immediate access to Mao Tse-tung's article, but he was not without independent information about the new attitude of the Chinese Communists to Chiang Kai-shek. Captain R. Scott, of the Royal Scots regiment, an intelligence officer attached to the embassy, had an interview with Chou En-lai at the latter's request in Sian on 19 January 1937. Scott reported that Chou, who had been alleged to be in hiding and whom Scott called the "principal Red agent in Sian," came to the guest house accompanied by a local banker. Scott received and noted down a full report of the Communist's change of policy, which had been brought about, he said, by increasing Japanese aggression. Chou En-lai told him that the Red Armies would fight under Chiang Kai-shek's orders against the Japanese. In response to questioning, he stated that they were not assisted by Russia in any way, and as to losing the coast in an anti-Japanese struggle, "Mr. Chou said that as things stood they would lose it anyway." Scott's report was marked "Secret," and when it reached England the level of interest in the Foreign Office was indicated by the single comment, from a third secretary, that it was "Much too long."[27]

Foreign Office officials ignored Captain Scott, but they also doubted the reliability of W. H. Donald's account of the events at Sian and the political situation out of which they arose. Something was missing. Donald's honesty had never before been questioned, but Sir John Pratt believed, correctly, but for the wrong reason, that Donald's explanation was "most unconvincing."[28] Pratt and the other officials in London thought the incident reflected old-style warlord politics rather than high-minded patriotism or co-operation with the Communists. They rejected the notion that high-minded patriotism could have motivated the plotters in Sian.

The men in Whitehall were further reassured by Ambassador Knatchbull-Hugessen's unperceptive report of the plenary session of the Kuomintang's

[26]Mao Tse-tung, "A Statement on Chiang Kai-shek's Statement," *Selected Works*, 1: 254-57.

[27]Knatchbull-Hugessen to Eden, 24 March 1937 (4 February 1937); Minute by Chaplin, Far Eastern Department, 30 March 1937, FO 20971/F1750.

[28]Pratt, Minute, 1 March 1937, FO 20969/F1048.

Central Executive Committee in Nanking from 15 to 23 February 1937.[29] Knatchbull-Hugessen said that it was clear that there was to be "no compromise with Communist armies, Communist doctrines, or common front" and that the government proposed to pursue exactly the same policy as in the past. Chiang was now going to use the central government's forces to break up the Communist armies. So far as Knatchbull-Hugessen could learn, the Kuomintang meeting had been harmonious, no serious difference of opinion had appeared, and the feeling in the country seemed overwhelmingly to support government policy. The line taken on the Communist question should "allay Japanese fears," and coupled with the conciliatory tone of recent Japanese statements to China by the new Foreign Minister Sato, Knatchbull-Hugessen was led to hope that a "new atmosphere is about to enter Sino-Japanese relationships." C. W. Orde found it encouraging that the Kuomintang had rejected any compromise with the Communists for the purpose of resisting Japan. And Sir Alexander Cadogan, from his Olympian perch as deputy under-secretary at the Foreign Office, commented that it would be "quite fatal if the Chinese were to get above themselves and adopt a forward policy as regards Japan." He was sure that their only line was "passive (and courteous but firm) resistance to any outrageous Japanese demands. Fortunately they seem to have come back to this idea."[30]

It was only in June 1937 that Ambassador Knatchbull-Hugessen began to see through the smokescreen which the Chinese had thrown up in February. Although the Plenary Session of the Kuomintang Executive Committee in February had verbally confirmed a policy of non-cooperation with the Communists, the Nanking government had actually taken steps "to reorganize the Chinese Communist forces and to incorporate them into the National Army"[31] at that time. Knatchbull-Hugessen now realized that the seemingly forbidding preconditions for any reconciliation laid down by the Kuomintang—the complete abolition of the Red Army and the soviet government and the absolute cessation of Red propaganda and class struggle in any form—were actually complementary to the subtly worded offers made by the Communist party to place its army and local governments under the nominal control of the central government. On 7 June

[29]Knatchbull-Hugessen to Eden, 25 February 1937, ibid., F1136.

[30]Orde, Minute, 27 February 1937, FO 20969/F1136; Cadogan, Minute, 16 March 1937, ibid., F1048.

[31]Chiang Kai-shek, *Soviet Russia in China: A Summing-up at Seventy* (New York: Farrar, Strauss and Giroux, 1965), p. 65. Knatchbull-Hugessen to Eden, 14 April 1937, reported the exchanges which took place between the Kuomintang and the Communist party in February, but Knatchbull-Hugessen thought they represented an impasse.

1937, without expressing any opinion or feeling on the question, Knatchbull-Hugessen mailed a despatch to Anthony Eden, in which he affirmed that the truce between the central government forces and the Communists continued in the northwest and that there was "no doubt that negotiations have indeed been proceeding" between Chiang Kai-shek and the Communist leaders for the purpose of organized resistance to Japan.[32] But by the time this despatch reached Eden, on 26 July, the Sino-Japanese war was about three weeks old.

Would the British government have acted any differently if they had been able to penetrate the reality of Chinese political development? Given her weak military presence in the area, the options open to Britain were not very wide. If Britain had seen that war was coming and had abandoned a forward policy, her interests and possessions in China would immediately have become an object of Chinese contempt and perhaps even hostility. This hostility was what the "old China hands" feared, and they had convinced the government to forestall it by the forward policy. British support to China was real, but it was working on a longer time-scale than the moods or plans of either of the protagonists in the Far East would allow.

Theoretically, Britain could have taken the long view that ultimately China could never be conquered by Japan and that, therefore, Britain could profitably risk a few million pounds now to help China create for Japan "the bandit troubles of a vaster Manchuria," as suggested by Vice-Admiral Little. But the concept of a "people's war" and guerilla warfare tactics were not yet well-known, and British statesmen, anyway, were not prone to engage in such long range or speculative exercises. Even though the Chinese would have been displeased at a halt to the forward policy, it is inconceivable that new investments and extended credits for capital construction would have been undertaken by private enterprise and approved by the government had war been expected.

The dilemma created by the prospect of Chinese armed resistance to Japan would have forced the British government to reconsider its lines of high policy. Britain would have had to either contemplate a strategic and economic retreat from the Far East and face the repercussions which came five years later in any event, or make an effort to associate the U.S.S.R. and, if possible, the U.S.A. with herself and China in a common front to Japan. As long as British statesmen continued to believe that this particular war was "extremely improbable," they avoided the trouble of facing these awkward alternatives. As it was, the self-chosen role of arbiter, gently

[32]Knatchbull-Hugessen to Eden, 26 July 1937, FO 20970/F4531.

protesting any "unreasonable" demands by Japan on China and quietly encouraging China's "legitimate," i.e., *non-military*, reconstruction suited the temper of neither China nor Japan. By encouraging China and thereby provoking Japan, the British government was in fact contributing to the very forces which were making war inevitable.

Lack of understanding of the stirrings of Chinese patriotism was only one of the factors which contributed to the failure of the British government's hopes for "peace, security and sound trading" in the Far East. Another was its underestimation of the power and wide plans of Japanese imperialism. Once again, there were many warnings. Japanese officials spoke with increasing emphasis to British officials about their fears of the probable results of British policy in China. In February 1936, Yakichiro Suma, Japanese consul-general in Nanking, had told Leith-Ross that China would have to choose between Britain and Japan. If she flirted with Britain, "there was a risk of a collision between British and Japanese interests in China."[33] A year later, Suma and the Japanese ambassador to China both told Knatchbull-Hugessen that the recent increased interest in British commercial expansion in China had created suspicions in Japan. It was believed that the Nanking government was "being encouraged" in its "definitely anti-Japanese" attitude by the British government. The first secretary of the Japanese embassy in Peking had asked Knatchbull-Hugessen outright whether it was "the object of Great Britain to drive out Japanese trade from China."[34]

These Japanese intimations were treated lightly on the British side. Ambassador Knatchbull-Hugessen had replied to his questioners that anyone who entertained such notions "had better be placed in a lunatic asylum" since China "was big enough for all" and Britain had "no intentions of impinging upon legitimate Japanese interests."[35] In the Far Eastern Department of the Foreign Office, First Secretary J. T. Henderson thought it was "interesting to see how angry they get when they think we are doing what they announced their intention of doing themselves, i.e., turning China into an economic protectorate." He believed that the Japanese were probably contributing towards an increase in British prestige rather than frightening the Chinese "by their cries of alarm" about British activity in China.[36]

---

[33]Leith-Ross to Eden, 3 February 1936, FO 20215/F638.
[34]Knatchbull-Hugessen, Minute, 17 February 1937, FO 676/332; Knatchbull-Hugessen to Eden, 15 March 1937, FO 20948/F1551.
[35]Ibid.
[36]J. T. Henderson, Minute, 28 April 1937, FO 20994/F2380.

Leith-Ross summed up the new British feeling that Japanese power was exaggerated in a memorandum to Sir Warren Fisher and Neville Chamberlain in February 1937. His reasoning, which received the endorsation of Chamberlain shortly before he became prime minister, ran as follows:[37] Japan's position was "essentially weak locally" with a powerful Soviet army and air force on their north and a rapidly organizing China on their south. The test of Japanese power to secure control down to the Yellow River had come in 1936, and the failure of successive Japanese governments "to coerce either Russia or China" had left them in an unstable condition: they were short of money, faced with popular discontent, and could not contemplate "a serious continental war." In these conditions Japan was "anxious to get on better terms with us." While the precise proposals put forward by Yoshida "may be purely his personal ideas," the objective he had in mind would be welcome to both military and civil authorities in Japan. The Japanese "would be prepared to pay more than they would ask" for an understanding with Britain. Britain would contribute capital, which Japan lacked, in order to make China prosperous and therefore useful "for projects in which Japan is interested." The British Treasury expert, in short, was strangely optimistic that the Japanese government, now under General Hayashi, realized that their China policy had failed, that aggression in China was futile, even dangerous, and that they would turn to co-operation with the Nanking government to secure the economic outlets which Japan needed in China; a friendly understanding between Japan and China would be cemented by the British loans and credits which were in the process of being negotiated by British financial diplomacy in China.

Almost as an afterthought, Leith-Ross added that Britain should make herself stronger so as not to "tempt aggression." Since Britain would never be able to wage war with Japan single-handedly, Leith-Ross suggested that in addition to seeking an understanding with Japan British defences should be supplemented by linking up her interests with those of other powers, such as the United States, the U.S.S.R., and China, who were in a better position than Britain to exert force in the Far East.

In the spring of 1937 several suggestions arose independently for such a "Pacific Pact" to check Japan, but they were all in effect rejected by the British government as being unhelpful, unreliable, or irrelevant. The first such proposal came indirectly from China and Russia. Chiang Kai-

---

[37]Leith-Ross, Memorandum, 22 February 1937, with marginal notations by Chamberlain saying "a very interesting paper; I am disposed to pursue the subject on these lines," 23 February 1937, T 188/53.

shek had intimated that he was considering an alliance with Russia and had asked for Britain's opinion about the possibility of co-operation with other powers for a joint understanding to keep the peace in the Far East.[38] Knatchbull-Hugessen had taken up a variation of this theme with the Foreign Office. It seemed clear, he said, that no Sino-Japanese understanding was possible without Russian participation. China could not side with either neighbour against the other and Japan would agree to nothing without some solution of her strategical problems *vis-à-vis* Russia. He thought the other powers might help arrange a tri-partite understanding.[39] Officials in the Foreign Office, however, were unwilling to entertain such a suggestion, and they continued to feel that, for British interests, there were "certain advantages in mutual distrust between Russia and Japan."[40] Such antagonism would prevent Japan from turning southwards. One Assistant Under-Secretary of State, Orme Sargent, went so far as to argue that a "nicely constructed system of checks and balances" was "more likely to serve the cause of peace" than "agreements between nations." Anthony Eden did not hold such an extreme view, but he felt that the "triangle for us to work in is ourselves, Japan and China, with the U.S.A. constantly in touch." Russia could be left where she was, "not an unhealthy cause of anxiety in Tokyo."[41] As long as Britain, which had little direct military power in the East, refused to move beyond that triangle, there was no hope that the Japanese militarists could be stopped.

Early in April 1937, another idea for a Pacific pact came from President Roosevelt. He sent a message through his adviser, Norman Davis, to the British government suggesting a pact for the neutralization of the Pacific. This would be a step towards removing war from an important part of the world and would further the standstill Washington Four Power Treaty of 1921. Roosevelt's idea was defortification of the Aleutians, the Philippines, and Guam by the United States, the East Indies by the Dutch, Hong Kong by the British, Formosa and the Mandated Islands by Japan. However when the British side asked Davis if there would be an American guarantee of neutralization or of the status quo, he drew back. The Foreign Office soon came to understand that the president had in mind "a 'moral' obligation only." In view of the worthlessness of a Japanese

---

[38]Howe to Eden, 25 June 1936, FO 20250/F3715. A similar Chinese initiative was repeated in May 1937, Leith-Ross to Cadogan, 18 May 1937, T 188/56.
[39]Knatchbull-Hugessen to Cadogan, 4 March 1937, FO 21024/F1325.
[40]Memorandum, 31 March 1937, ibid.
[41]Sargeant and Eden, Minutes, 25 March 1937, ibid.

signature, Davis reportedly agreed that the proposal for neutralization of the Pacific was, for the moment, impracticable.[42]

The other suggestion for a Pacific pact came from Prime Minister Lyons of Australia when he came to London for the Imperial Conference in May 1937. Lyons's proposal received a good deal of publicity, but it was without much real substance. Apparently it was put forward in the hopes of making "political capital" back home in view of the forthcoming general election in Australia.[43] In any case, Anthony Eden had little difficulty in sweeping the Australian proposal under the carpet along with other suggestions for a Pacific pact.[44] The British government preferred to rely on the ever-elusive Anglo-Japanese conversations with Ambassador Yoshida for a détente in the Pacific, and still more, it wished to concentrate its energies in the Far East on strengthening relations with the Nanking government for the purpose of developing British economic prospects in China.

The problem of a British advance in China under the shadow of Japan's preponderate position in East Asia was never far from the minds of officials in Whitehall. A major review of policy on this question was initiated by younger members of the Far Eastern Department, who were apparently more subject to the influence of Leith-Ross and the Treasury than was Sir John Pratt. In consultation with seven other government departments over a period of four months, from February to May 1937, these men produced a report which concluded that it would be "over-timorous" to abandon the China trade to its fate while any gaps in Britain's defences were being made good. There were still large areas of the country where Japan had not arrogated to herself a "special position," and there were development schemes to be financed which not even Japan would be concerned to regard as inspired by strategic considerations. There was here "a position to be maintained and further business to be won." A difficulty was that Chinese nationalism was now strong enough "to insist on doing things wrong in the Chinese way rather than right in a Japanese or British way." Consequently, Britain would have to approach the matter from a standpoint which fully acknowledged "Chinese sovereignty in China." It was felt that there was a faint hope of "inducing Japan to

[42]Eden to Lindsay, 16 April 1937, Outfile, FO 21024/F2214; also Cadogan, Minutes, 25 April and 4 May 1937, ibid., F2348, F2586; Borg, *Far Eastern Crisis*, pp. 247-48; *FRUS*, 1937, 3:975.
[43]Dominions Office to Foreign Office, message from G. Whiskeard, U.K. High Commissioner in Australia, 19 May 1937, FO 21025/F2919.
[44]325 *H.C. Deb.*, 25 June 1937, when Eden replied to parliamentary questions; see also 4th, 11th, and 15th meetings of the principal delegates, Imperial Conference, 22 May, 2 and 8 June, 1937, for discussion of the Australian proposal, CAB 32/128.

agree to this condition," as the result of the "growth of more moderate views in Japan" in recent months. But before approaching Japan with any proposals for co-operation, Britain would have to show that "we are able and determined to defend and improve our own position" in the economic sphere, since no nation would consent to share if there seemed to be "every prospect" of getting it all for themselves. The adoption of a forward commercial policy and co-operation with Chinese in the development of China might, it was realized, arouse the displeasure of the Japanese. The latter might increase military pressure upon China with a view to persuading the central government to restrict British activities; but "it is difficult to conceive that the resentment would find more drastic expression." Insofar as Britain was able to co-operate with the Chinese and make them feel that "their interests and our interests are the same, they will protect us against this form of indirect Japanese pressure."[45]

It was on the background of such unwarranted government optimism that City hopes for economic advance increased in May-June 1937, during the visit of the Chinese Minister of Finance, H. H. Kung, to the British capital as leader of a delegation to the coronation ceremonies of King George VI.

At this time Sir Charles Addis was successful in calling together the council of the China Consortium for their first meeting since 1925. With Addis in the chair, the American representative, Thomas W. Lamont, moved, and the council agreed, to raise no objection to the British group entering into independent negotiations for the Canton-Meihsien Railway. The British group made a formal pledge "so far as it lay in their power," to offer sub-participation to the other groups, but this was on the understanding that none of the other banks would take up the offer. In this way the principle of the Consortium was kept intact, but even so it was a considerable victory for British financiers. In communicating the results of the council meeting to the Foreign Office, Addis expressed satisfaction with the results and said that he had been afraid of going further and making a general resolution for dissolution of the Consortium for "fear of scaring my colleagues off."[46]

Having got the door open, however, the Matheson-Hongkong and Shanghai Bank group, possibly under the pressure of H. H. Kung's presence in London, became emboldened and, to the astonishment of everyone,

[45]Memorandum, "British Policy in the Far East." For early version (22 February 1937) see Leith-Ross Papers, T 188/53, and for revised version (6 May 1937) see FO 21024/F2638. The seven departments consulted were: Overseas Trade, Colonial Office, Admiralty, War Office, Air Ministry, and Treasury.

[46]Confidential Print, 10 May 1937, FO 405/276, no. 46; *FRUS*, 1937, 4:590.

enlarged their scheme five-fold. On 26 May, less than three weeks after the meeting of the Consortium council, Addis wrote to his foreign colleagues that the Canton-Meihsien project for £2.7 million had now been "carried a step further," and if his colleagues had no objection, it would include an extension from Meihsien to Kweichi and from Samshui to Kuchow (aggregating £8 million) and from Pukow to Siangyang (£4 million) to be issued in instalments as a Consolidated Railway Loan of £15 million.[47] On learning of this amazing démarche, Leith-Ross told Addis that the Treasury was "surprised to find that the proposal had grown overnight" and noted that Addis's letter had "considerably fluttered the American and particularly the Japanese dovecotes."[48] J. P. Morgan and Co. had cabled from New York that they were "frankly rather puzzled" by the British move and added that they had not intended the recent Consortium council to be interpreted in a "permissive spirit" which would enable any one group "to stake out large claims so to speak far in advance." In an attempt to allay suspicions, Addis wrote a "soft answer" to his Consortium colleagues, saying he had no idea of pre-empting the field but was only trying to forestall further resort by the Chinese to the dangerous financial practice of short and middle term credits for railway building.[49]

As a result of the furore caused by the Hongkong and Shainghai Bank, officials at the Foreign Office found the atmosphere of rivalry and suspicion "very disquieting."[50] Something needed to be done to counteract the "spasmodic antics" of Leith-Ross and Addis. The Far Eastern Department would have preferred to drop further discussion of loans of any kind because Britain was getting into rather deep water. In the case of the Japanese, it looked as if Britain were "trying to browbeat them into running before they had really made up their minds to walk."[51] But it was not possible to evade all loan discussions because Kung was in London pressing for a revitalization of Leith-Ross's abortive 1935 currency loan. It was also clear that the Hongkong and Shanghai Bank, with the verbal assurances which it had received from Leith-Ross and Cadogan in February, was already too heavily committed to abandon the railway

---

[47]*FRUS*, 1937, 4:619. Chang Kia-ngau, *China's Struggle for Railway Development* (New York: J. Day, 1943), part 3, chapters 9 to 11.

[48]Leith-Ross to Addis, 31 May 1937, T 188/48.

[49]Addis to Leith-Ross, encl. from J. P. Morgan and Co. to Morgan, Grenfell and Co. (London), 31 May 1937, T 188/48.

[50]Cadogan, Minute, 30 May 1937, FO 20945/F3066.

[51]Chaplin, Minute, 28 May 1937, ibid.

projects.[52] To decide whether it was necessary to become involved in further cash advances a hurried interdepartmental meeting, at the level of senior permanent officials, was held at the Foreign Office. Leith-Ross's opinions in favour of negotiations for a currency loan were to prevail. The arguments in favour of the loan were still much the same.[53] It was considered that a second large reconstruction loan similar to the one given to Yuan Shih-kai in 1913 would be of great value to British trade and prestige in China and would help Dr. Kung consolidate the internal market. It would be the means of securing such British aims as the abolition of the Chinese coast trade duty, the reform of the Central Bank under a British adviser, the maintenance of the Chinese Maritime Customs under a British administrator, and assurances for additional recruitment and better treatment of British officials in the Customs and Salt Administrations.

The only nagging doubt Leith-Ross had entertained from the internal point of view, during his protracted negotiations on the subject in 1935, had been the lax standard of personal honesty of the Chinese administration. Though by their own lights patriots, the Chinese ministers were all said to take bribes. Leith-Ross had learned that Kung had amassed a very large fortune in the short period he had been in power. T. V. Soong had the best reputation, but his brother, T. L. Soong, was the leader of the speculators, ably assisted by his sister, the wife of the minister of finance. The system of "squeeze" permeated the whole administration. Leith-Ross had written to Fisher of his interview with Messrs. Kung and T. V. Soong when he tackled them on this point. Leith-Ross told his Chinese friends that he had "not been impressed" with some of the names to be appointed as members of the currency board under the reformed Central Bank, for they included notorious speculators like T. L. Soong and Mr. Tu (Yusheng). His report of this illuminating conversation continued:

> Dr. Kung replied that these could not be left out. T. L. Soong was the head of too many important banking institutions. Mr. Tu on the other hand had special claims. He was undoubtedly a speculator; he was also leader of the gangsters; but one hundred thousand men in Shanghai obeyed his orders; he could create a disturbance at

[52]By August 1937, the bank had signed contracts worth £6.7 million with the Chinese government. L. Oliphant to ambassadors of France, Japan, and the United States, 11 August 1937, T 188/48.

[53]See Leith-Ross to Norman, 24 May 1937, T 188/57; Addis to D. G. M. Bernard, encl. in Bernard to Warren Swire, 15 March 1937, Swire Papers—1076; W. H. Lock (Butterfield and Swire) to J. Swire and Sons, Swire Papers, China and Japan Box 51; Leith-Ross to Addis, copy to Treasury and governor, Bank of England, 20 May 1937, T188/49.

any moment. Further, apart from the question of power which made his support necessary to the Government, he was really becoming a reformed character. He had given up gambling and attended Dr. Kung's private Sunday services. No doubt there was a lot of gossip in Shanghai about speculation. Some people might say that he himself (Kung) speculated or that T. V. Soong speculated. I said that I had not heard this of Soong but I certainly had heard it about Dr. Kung. Kung replied rather hotly that it was absolutely untrue. He would take proceedings against anyone whom he could definitely pin down as having circulated such stories. He had lost a lot of money since he was Minister of Finance.[54]

Even though it was unfortunate that people popularly regarded as speculators should be in charge of the currency board, Leith-Ross thought that if T. V. Soong were in control, the risk of corruption would not be fatal to the loan scheme; it would just add to the overhead.

The veteran adviser of the Far Eastern Department, Sir John Pratt, continued to oppose the currency loan on the grounds that the currency reform had already succeeded without a loan. There was a danger, in Pratt's view, that Chiang Kai-shek's domestic enemies might well use the loan to represent him "as a puppet of the British," while in the eyes of the world it would appear that Britain had "decided to bolster up Chiang Kai-shek in order to promote our own interests."[55] In spite of the opposition from the Foreign Office, the view dictated by the Treasury prevailed. The main heads of a programme for a currency loan of £20 million, twice the original size proposed, were agreed to by the interested British parties and were handed to Dr. P. W. Kuo, head of the Chinese Bureau of Foreign Trade. The Chinese delegation agreed to the seven British conditions for a loan, virtually the same as those put forward in 1935. This time, however, the British government asked for written confirmation by Dr. Kung of his acceptance of the points in a memorandum, it being "of course understood that this document will not be published."[56] On 21 June 1937, Cadogan handed the ambassadors of the United States, France, and Japan an official memorandum on the proposed loan. The memorandum, which was confirmed in August 1937, stated that His Majesty's government favoured the loan if certain conditions were fulfilled, and they understood that the Chinese, who were likely to accept

[54]Leith-Ross to Fisher, 4 October 1935, T 160/620, T 188/28.

[55]Cadogan to Leith-Ross, 20 July 1937, T 188/57; Pratt, Minute, 8 July 1937, FO 20946/F3894g.

[56]Waley to T. K. Tseng (Chinese Corporation Delegation), 21 July 1937, T 188/57.

these conditions, were in communication with the Hongkong and Shanghai Bank to settle the terms.[57]

It is impossible to estimate the precise influence of Britain's decision to support China's currency reserves upon the renewal of Sino-Japanese hostilities in July 1937. British action certainly did not cause the war to break out: the war was the product of the fundamental clash between Japanese imperialist expansion and Chinese nationalism. But there is no doubt that after weeks of disturbing rumours of an Anglo-Japanese understanding about China,[58] the Nanking government was encouraged in its determination to resist Japan by Britain's decision. T. V. Soong had agreed with British Treasury representative, Hall-Patch, that technically the loan was not for covering budget deficits, which were increasing rapidly owing to heavy military expenditures. But Soong had added that while the loan "would not ostensibly be used for budgetary purposes," it would help the budget situation.[59] From this it was clear that the Chinese leadership interpreted the British loan as an initial payment to support the Chinese effort to drive Japan out.

The Japanese also saw that the British loan proceeds could be converted to uses other than those stipulated. The fact that Eden told Yoshida that Britain was not seeking any exclusive advantages but was anxious for the issue of a loan "entirely from the point of view of helping China" did nothing to reduce Japanese nervousness. They believed that by deciding to act alone Britain was "actuated by political motives." And the Japanese ambassador complained that China carried on propaganda showing off her intimacy with Great Britain.[60] The Japanese government had long ago decided, in Hirota's words, to stabilize East Asia. It would gain its wishes in China either by "co-operation" or by conquest. But the proposed British loan agreement with China may have spurred the Japanese military into action in the belief that any further delay would only make the operation more costly.

It will probably never be known who was responsible for the actual incident which unleashed large scale fighting between China and Japan in the summer of 1937. Apparently a company of Japanese soldiers stationed

---

[57]Eden to Knatchbull-Hugessen, 24 June 1937, Outfile, FO 20946/F3488; also Oliphant to ambassadors of France, Japan, and the United States, 11 August 1937; *FRUS*, 1937, 4: 603, 605.

[58]See telegrams 40-45, 47-49, 57 between Nanking and London, 4 to 22 May 1937 (confidential print), FO 405/276.

[59]Hall-Patch to Treasury, 19 July 1937, T 188/57.

[60]Eden to Knatchbull-Hugessen, 8 June 1937, T 188/57, FO 20945/F3292; Hall-Patch to Treasury, 19 July 1937, T 188/57; Yoshida to Leith-Ross, 16 July 1937, ibid.

at Peking under the Boxer Protocol of 1901 was holding provocative night manoeuvres near a camp of the Chinese 29th Army when some shots were exchanged. As was customary since the Tangku Truce of 1933, the problem was at first handled locally. Bowing to the demands of the Japanese army commander, the Chinese General Sung Che-yuan apologized for the entire incident, promised to punish the officers responsible, and agreed to withdraw his forces from the vicinity of the Marco Polo bridge. Sporadic firing continued, however, and within a few days, on 11 July, the Japanese General Staff received the cabinet's approval to send a punitive expedition of about 40,000 men to China. Chiang Kai-shek, meanwhile began sending reinforcements from the south. When Tokyo demanded on 17 July that Chiang stop sending troops northwards and that he recognize the puppet government set up in North China by General Doihara, Chiang gave a defiant answer. Reflecting the growing popular feeling in China, he stated that China's sovereign rights could not be sacrificed even at the expense of war. The war which was to last until 1945 was not officially declared, but with the arrival of the Japanese troop ships at Tsingtao and Shanghai heavy fighting with Chinese forces began within Britain's traditional sphere of influence in Central China.

In view of the continuous acts of Japanese armed expansion in China since 1931, the question of who fired the first shots on the night of 7 July 1937 may be of minimal historical importance. J. B. Crowley feels safe in concluding that the incident was not caused by a "conspiracy" of Japanese army officers as it had been in Mukden in 1931.[61] The British Foreign Office also thought that the Marco Polo Bridge incident of 7 July was not deliberately engineered, but Cadogan believed that it was "seized upon and exploited for the furtherance of a policy of blatant aggression."[62]

The problems facing the makers of British policy in China during the course of the Sino-Japanese war fall beyond the scope of this study, but it should be noted that in spite of the war crisis British economic activities in China continued to have considerable momentum. Even though the new railway contracts of the Hongkong and Shanghai Bank were not floated on the London market and the currency loan was never

[61]J. B. Crowley, "A Reconsideration of the Marco Polo Bridge Incident," *Journal of Asian Studies* 22 (May 1963): 309-26.
[62]Cadogan, Minute, 13 September 1937, FO 20955/F6115. According to Ikuhiko Hata in *Taiheiyo senso e no michi*, vol. 4, as cited in Robertson, *Origins*, p. 252, the extension of hostilities from the Japanese side is blamed on a "plot" by the pro-war faction in Japan which consisted primarily of the Operations and China sections of the general staff, the navy, and independent actions by the expeditionary forces.

consummated, British interests tried to ignore the war and were moderately successful in carrying on business as usual. British railroad investments suffered immediate war damage, and British shipping found itself subject to restrictions, but the trade of many British companies within the Japanese occupied zone even improved slightly. The giant Unilever Company, for example, was encouraged on the basis of increased soap sales of 25 per cent in 1939 over 1937 to think that China was one of the markets "to which we can look over the next few years for very considerable expansion."[63] The Kailan Mining Administration in Hopei and certain subsidiaries of J. Swire and Sons and Jardine, Matheson and Co. announced improved operations in annual reports of 1938 and 1939. J. W. Keswick reported that in 1938 the profits of his cotton mills in Shanghai were the highest in the company's history.[64] The returns of the Chinese Maritime Customs showed an over-all decline in British-China seaborne trade beginning in 1938, but it was not until 1939 that the Japanese were finally able to undermine the trading market based on the new paper currency which Leith-Ross had helped to sponsor in 1935.

To many British observers, the Sino-Japanese "incident," as it was called, was possibly just an inconvenient prelude to a creative restructuring of the China scene. The well-polished speeches of Foreign Minister Hirota contributed to this comforting thought. Hirota assured the world in 1938 that Japan had "no territorial ambitions in China," and for the purpose of promoting the welfare of the Chinese people, she was prepared "to leave the door wide open to all Powers and to welcome their economic and cultural co-operation" in the establishment of a new order in East Asia.[65] This was just the kind of assurance which appealed to Neville Chamberlain, who still clung to the vision of China as a great arena for British capital investment. In trying to answer criticisms of Britain's soft attitude in allowing Japan to close one of the largest potential markets in the world, the prime minister declared that it would be flying in the face of facts to believe that Japan would have sufficient capital on her own to monopolize the trade of China. It was quite certain, he told the House of Commons on 1 November 1938, that "when the war is over and the reconstruction of China begins, she cannot be reconstructed without some help from this country." Win or lose, whether in an independent China or China as a dependency of Japan, Britain and the interests Chamberlain represented, apparently, could prosper.

[63]Charles Wilson, *The History of Unilever* (London: Cassell, 1954), 2: 364-65.
[64]Nicholas Clifford, *Retreat from China* (Seattle: University of Washington Press, 1967), p. 66; J. S. Scott to G. W. Swire, 8 April 1938, Swire—D.N.O.E.
[65]Cited in Clifford, *Retreat from China*, p. 52.

8

Conclusion

Several recurring historical issues emerge from the study of these years of British diplomacy and enterprise in China. The interactions of finance, trade, high politics, and diplomacy in an area of the world which was not subject to direct colonial rule provide abundant materials for the continuing debate about the nature and changing methods of imperialism. Insights may also be gained from the tactics of collaboration and contention which rival imperialisms employed as they jockeyed for position in the China market. In addition, on the level of national politics, several themes are apparent: almost accidentally, personalities in the bureaucratic structure emerge as decisive factors in policy formation; the political lobby of a small group can achieve success, not in usurping the power of the nation but in turning it to the benefit of private ends; and never far below the surface of events exists the powerful thrust of nationalism. In protectionist Britain, the economic variety of nationalism was most pronounced, while in Japan political nationalism was prominent. In the case of China there was a mixture of mass nationalism stemming from pent-up feelings of political humiliation and an élite nationalism striving to win for itself a greater share of its domestic market.

The imperialisms associated with the high tide of Western expansion into Asia and Africa in the nineteenth and early twentieth centuries have been the subject of many explanations and interpretations. These range from the views of writers such as Joseph Schumpeter and, more recently, D. K. Fieldhouse who deny any necessary or inherent connection between capitalism and modern imperialism, to those who take an opposite view, shared by the present writer: imperialism in the era of capitalist ascendency cannot be understood apart from capitalism.

A popular idea of imperialism refers only to the acquisition of territory or colonies. It was in this sense that the Foreign Office claimed in 1930 that British policy toward China historically had "no territorial or imperialistic aims" and was concerned instead with trade and maintaining the "open door" and equal opportunity for all.[1] Professor D. C. M. Platt hailed this claim in 1968, saying there could hardly have been a better statement of British official motives toward China since 1834. According to Platt, who studied British finance, trade, and foreign policy between 1815 and 1914 and who is apparently more interested in motives than in results, the interests of the individual British capitalists "had very little, if anything," to do with the "scramble for concessions" in China at the turn of the century:

> This was no case of British capitalists pressing for Government assistance in obtaining concessions for their private enrichment; the British Government was pressing concessions on an often reluctant City in the political interest of the Empire and in the general interest of British trade.[2]

However, while he considers that the economic factor in the making of foreign policy during the period of his study had less importance than writers such as J. A. Hobson and V. I. Lenin attached to it, Platt also concludes that it had more relevance than their detractors over the past thirty years have admitted. After Britain's monopoly position in her most important markets was challenged by powerful competitors in the 1880's (which was, of course, the period about which Hobson and Lenin were writing), Platt argues that the evidence for finance and trade "as determining factors in extra-European diplomacy and imperialist expansion ('formal' and 'informal') becomes overwhelming."[3]

Although their conceptions were quite different, both Hobson and Lenin popularized the idea of economic imperialism in their famous works entitled *Imperialism*. According to Hobson imperialism resulted from a conspiracy of selfish financiers who usurped the power of the state, while for Lenin the interests of the finance-capitalist and a bourgeois state were synonymous and led to imperialism as soon as capitalism matured to the stage where monopolies predominated. Hobson's argument was weakened by his unrealistic picture of surplus capital and its owners pressuring the British government to annex colonies; Lenin's analysis was open to attack because his picture of imperialism was a composite one, drawing upon the

[1]Memorandum on China Policy, 8 January 1930, *DBFP*, Series 2, 8: 26.
[2]Platt, *Finance, Trade and Politics*, pp. 304, 284.
[3]Ibid., pp. 153, 366.

different aspects which he saw in Britain, Germany, France, and the United States. Lenin's thesis, the more formidable of the two, in brief holds that modern imperialism is a stage in the development of the world economy when: several advanced capitalist countries stand on a competitive footing; finance and monopoly capital play a decisive role in their economic lives, and the export of surplus capital assumes great importance; severe rivalry in the search for markets and raw materials leads to cut-throat competition, the formation of cartels, and the seizure of colonies or creation of zones of influence in underdeveloped or backward areas. The struggle between rival groups of finance-capitalists is so sharp that the peaceful division of the planet is impossible.[4]

A careful review of the workings of British imperialism for the period after World War I by the British scholar, Michael Barrat-Brown, concludes that while Lenin was wrong in predicting parasitic decay as the future for the centres of "over-ripe" capitalist empires, in many respects during the 1930's, when

> the control of finance-capital over industry [was] much greater and the influence of the representatives of the most powerful sections of banking and industry upon government policy much more profound . . . ,

the facts of British economic life corresponded to Lenin's picture of the tap-root of imperialism.[5] The present study of British policy, where finance and industry were successful in influencing the formulation of government action, suggests the continuing relevance of Lenin's basic insights on the subject of modern imperialism.

Other more recent insights, such as those by D. C. M. Platt, do not in fact penetrate the façades of imperialism. Overt political rule was only a special case in the broader spectrum of methods by which imperialist gains were made. Although the Philippines, the East Indies, Indo-China and Hong Kong were made into colonies, intruders from the West were never able to win hegemony over East Asia. Most never seriously tried. Instead, there was a general intermingling of trade and the flag; formal and informal methods were used to gain control of resources, influence markets, protect investments, bolster prestige, and enhance security. In addition to the seizure of territory, imperialist policies in East Asia ranged from temporary diplomatic or military interventions by governments to the less

---

[4]V. I. Lenin, "Imperialism, the Highest Stage of Capitalism," *Selected Works* (Moscow: Foreign Languages Publishing House, 1952), 1, part 2, pp. 433-568.
[5]Michael Barratt-Brown, *After Imperialism* (London: Heinemann, 1963), p. 97.

costly "imperialism of free trade"[6] and the "open door," whereby powerful corporate groups were able to penetrate the area and by monopoly practices shut out competitors or otherwise control the environment in which they functioned. Imperialism had many "weapons" at its disposal, but in essence it was the bargaining advantage which rich nations had over poor nations. It was the control and exploitation, direct or indirect, of one nation, people, or group over another. Whether conscious or otherwise, imperialism existed whenever norms of equality, mutual benefit, and non-interference (the hallmarks of ordinary commercial transactions) were not observed in relations between countries, peoples, and corporate groups.

It may be, as Professor Thornton has maintained, that imperialism is imbedded in the record of every nation which has an ascertainable past[7]—including the nations of East Asia. Thornton possibly intended this remark to have a sobering effect on those who wish to criticize or condemn imperialism. The discovery that imperialism, like the pox, is widespread, however, is not a great help to anyone not inclined to take refuge in a fatalistic philosophy of history. If anything is to be learned about man's destiny from a study of the past, it still seems imperative to distinguish between those who have the disease and those who do not at any given time.

The top echelon of British policy-makers in the 1930's—both politicians and civil servants—clearly believed that it was the overseas empire which gave Britain its great voice in the world and provided hope for Britain's economic revival. Lord Chatfield made a candid appraisal of Britain's position when he remarked to Sir Warren Fisher that ". . . we have got most of the world already or the best parts of it, and we only want to keep what we have got and prevent others from taking it away from us."[8] To British leaders it was self-evident that the preservation of their Empire was a legitimate, necessary, and strictly defensive operation. Unless they were prepared to see Britain become once more "nothing but an insignificant island in the North Sea," they could not willingly contemplate any diminishing of imperial power and prestige. To other nations, who were not so well placed, "defensive action" by Britain to ensure a monopoly of the best parts of the world was just as clearly an aggressive or oppressive operation. Rivals, or those people subject to British control, were in fact becoming increasingly restive, as troubles in Egypt, India, and the Far East bore witness. There could be no doubt about the growing signs

---

[6]See John Gallagher and Ronald Robinson, "The Imperialism of Free Trade," *Economic History Review*, 2d series, 6 (1953): 1-15, for a discussion of this aspect of British policy in the mid-nineteenth century.

[7]A. P. Thornton, *Doctrines of Imperialism* (New York: Wiley, 1965), p. 53.

[8]Chatfield to Fisher, 4 June 1934, Chatfield Papers.

of instability around the world, the cause for which, it may be suggested, was shared both by the "have" countries who wished to preserve the *status quo*, as well as by the "have not," aggressive countries who demanded alterations. To judge by their forward policy in China, over-optimistic British leaders believed that perseverance and flexibility would bring to pass brighter chapters in the history of empire. Thus, according to Sir Samuel Hoare, foreign secretary in 1935, those "foolish and malicious people" who said that the British Empire had passed its zenith made a grievous mistake.[9]

The British presence in China had always assumed an informal aspect, especially when compared to India. But even so, the merchant venturers who were the pioneers of British enterprise in the Far East had always been able to count upon effective military-diplomatic support to back their claims. Gradually over the years, as Britain's military capability became marginal relative to China and the other powers in the area, financial, political, and diplomatic methods, as well as bluff, had to be exercised and depended upon more and more. During the mid-1930's, however, there was still no apparent wavering in official resolve "to keep the flag flying" in China. This determination was reflected in continued use or threat of limited naval force along Chinese inland waterways: the H.M.S. *Sandpiper* was launched in 1933 and plans for another shallow draught gunboat for the Yangtze River Flotilla were projected for 1936. Furthermore, the cabinet continued to show its support for the China Houses by firmly rejecting any suggestion that extraterritorial privileges in China, enforced for almost a century, should be modified or abandoned. Apart from these defensive arrangements, the government supported efforts for the "rehabilitation of the Chinese government" through tutelage and control by British finance, and the creation of "spheres of influence." These policies, so prevalent before World War I, were a recognition of the fact that the Nine Power Treaty of 1922 was already moribund.

Seen in the perspective of a wider time span, therefore, the undeclared Sino-Japanese war which broke out in July 1937 and the Anglo-Japanese rivalry which preceded it were but further episodes in the century-old struggle of advanced countries to influence the politics and profit from the economy of China. The competitive struggle of the advanced countries in the years immediately preceding 1937 was, to be sure, not confined to China. But in the aftermath of the depression which struck the world-wide capitalist market system in 1929, rivalry in China was sharp because China was still open territory—outside the gates of any formal empire.

[9]Guildhall speech, 9 November 1935, Templewood Papers, 8: 2.

The British combined a new flexibility with old approaches. Apart from any moral scruples which they may have felt from their adherence to the Covenant of the League of Nations, they recognized perforce that in a country which had belatedly entered the age of mass nationalism, "gunboat policy" was largely counter-productive. Gunboats were retained, but the new approach was to search for special relations with the élite groups of Chinese nationalism—the Soong, Kung, and Chiang families—who controlled the bureaucracy and could silence popular nationalistic, anti-imperialist, protest movements. Vigorous efforts were therefore made to create an identity of British and Chinese interest by negotiating partnerships with such bodies as T. V. Soong's China Development Finance Corporation. Technical experts were recommended for employment in Nanking since, in the "peculiar conditions of Chinese public life," it was considered that private and reliable access to the administrative departments of the Chinese government had a decisive influence on the fortunes of business enterprise. Willingness to scuttle the international banking consortium at the prodding of the Chinese government was also indicative of the British government's mood. Rather than see opportunities go by default, Whitehall was prepared to encourage London financiers to run considerable risks in order to foster British investment and trade. The United States and Germany followed a similar policy of cultivating close relations with the leading groups in the Nanking régime, but less actively.

Japan, on the other hand, relied on the more obvious and cruder methods of imperialism. Unsuccessful in competing with the British for political influence in Nanking, the Japanese government sanctioned armed interventions to intimidate the central government. From 1931 on, attempts were made to create "reliable" local governments which could ensure law and order for Japanese investments as well as control raw materials in North China and provide access for the products of Japanese industry. Determined Japanese pressure was, in fact, the chief immediate obstacle blocking the success of Britain's aim to create a united, well-ordered, and prosperous market in China.

In retrospect it is clear that the only way Britain might have been able to "get anything out of the Japanese" at the time of the Leith-Ross mission would have been a willingness by the British Treasury to make a *bona fide* bargain on issues of concern to Japan outside the sphere of influence where Japan was already supreme. It has been argued elsewhere that the British government was prevented by strong currents of domestic liberal-socialist opinion from any compromise or bargains with the dissatisfied or aggressive powers.[10] In dealings with Japan this was not the case. The

---

[10]Medlicott, *British Foreign Policy*, p. xvii.

cabinet records show that Neville Chamberlain was not deterred by such opinion and was willing to go to Parliament with his plan—it was Japan and China who blocked his "bargain" over Manchukuo. Bribing some Chinese leaders to recognize the Japanese seizure of the four northeastern provinces of China while Britain controlled the expenditure of the bribe was no bargain for Japan, especially when the Kwantung army was already astride the Great Wall. The making of a bargain elsewhere in the world, which Japan might have accepted, was turned down by vested financial and trading interests and empire-minded politicians.

The unwillingness of the Treasury and the Board of Trade to consider accepting the cost of a bargain outside the confines of China was a notable failure of British realism. This failure occurred in spite of clear and repeated statements by the Japanese that the price of their co-operation in China was greater freedom for Japanese goods in the British Empire. The Japanese, perhaps not unreasonably, resented a British cabinet decision to limit their imports into India and West Africa in April 1934, the exclusion of Japan's immigration and trade from the sparsely settled Dominions, and the way high British officials came to the Far East to raise questions about the "open door" in Manchuria and to propose "co-operation" in China on British terms. The Japanese, who alternated between the soft-line "duck" and the hard-line "woodpecker" policies, made no secret of their fears that, by encouraging the "anti-Japanese faction" within the Chinese government, Great Britain was trying to drive Japanese trade from China.

The British Foreign Office itself had a decidedly more realistic assessment of the dangers in the Far East than most other departments of the government, but its difficulty lay in the lack of any imaginative or active policy to cope with a complex situation. The suggestions of the Northern Department of the Foreign Office that Britain make common cause with the Soviet Union against Japan were ignored, more for political-ideological than military reasons, and the view of Admiral Little, commander-in-chief of the China Station in 1936-37, that Britain might benefit by actively encouraging Chinese nationalists was rejected as absurd. Instead there was an air of universal benevolence in the Far Eastern Department's insistence that Britain should cultivate Chinese good will while doing nothing to antagonize Japan. Not strong enough to act alone in China in defiance of Japan and barred by world public opinion from going along with any Japanese re-ordering of the Chinese market, Britain, according to the Foreign Office scenario, would have to follow a passive, opportunistic policy and await developments. The test of any British initiatives in China would have to be their soundness from a strictly business standpoint; since the risks were great, such criteria were guaranteed to make British policy inconspicuous.

Historically, there was much to be said for the view that the rehabilitation of the Chinese nation was bound to be a slow process and that any British role would have to proceed piecemeal until greater administrative and political unity was achieved by the Chinese themselves. But in the face of the short term, day-to-day difficulties of the British interests involved, such a passive stance was rejected by the more ambitious and energetic politicians as drifting, defeatist, and muddle-headed.

The dynamism which Neville Chamberlain, as chancellor of the Exchequer, and his chief adviser, Sir Warren Fisher, were able to inject into British far eastern policy refutes any notion that foreign policy is the business of the Foreign Office. Through its own channels the Treasury was able to intervene in foreign policy when it lost patience with the hesitations and objections of the far eastern experts of the Foreign Office. Chamberlain's interest in the Far East arose in the first instance from political and strategic concerns: an understandable desire to reduce the possibility of conflict with Japan, the better to concentrate British defence resources against Germany. He was aware of the opinion that friendship with Japan would be difficult because Japanese ambitions in China were incompatible with Chinese independence to which Britain was committed by more than one treaty. But he had his own opinion, nurtured by a handful of favoured, pro-Japanese observers, that Japan could and should be appeased by recognition of her Manchukuo empire and that China could be pacified by a sterling loan. The idea that some dramatic gesture at someone else's expense would neutralize a dangerous aggressor foreshadowed the tactics which Chamberlain would try at Munich a few years later. A further aspect of a developing pattern was his style of work within the cabinet, which was to circumvent the opposing or disagreeable views of his colleagues by handling issues of great importance outside normal constitutional procedures.

A decade later, when Sir Warren Fisher wrote a brief memoir, he suggested that if the British Empire, the United States, and France had squarely faced the facts in unison, "the horrors which started up with the rape of Manchuria, followed by the outrage on Abyssinia, the all-out attack on China, the seizure of Austria and Czechoslovakia . . . could have been prevented" and that none of these countries could disclaim or escape a heavy measure of responsibility.[11] This observation was apt, but Fisher appeared to have forgotten the important fact that he and Chamberlain personally preferred *Japan* as an ally in the 1930's when these

---

[11]Fisher, "The Beginnings of Civil Defence," *Public Administration* 26 (Winter 1948): 211-16.

events were occurring and that they masterminded the prolonged British attempt to forge an alliance with that country during these years. The discovery that Chamberlain and Fisher engaged in conspiratorial methods to force an understanding with Japan upon unwilling colleagues underscores their responsibility for the disasters which took place.[12]

Under the influence of Chamberlain's dominating personality but unsteady hand, the priorities of British far eastern policy shifted, it seemed, almost imperceptibly. In the light of her weak military and strategic position, Britain should have remained on the defensive. But the active policy in China, associated with the Leith-Ross mission, deflected British activities onto a path which contradicted strategic security and political prudence. With the German menace increasing and an Anglo-Japanese understanding still eluding them, Chamberlain and his chief advisers were linking Britain and China by economic policies whose almost certain result would be, and were intended by the Chinese to be, the alienation of Japan.

The forward movement in China did not achieve the ultimate success to which its authors aspired, but neither was it a plan which remained on paper; its initial success had a definite bearing on the intensified friction between China and Japan. The key decision was Chamberlain's move, prompted by the China lobby, to find some way to renew the flow of British capital into the China market in 1936 following the successful currency reform of 1935. After that reform, there had been wide-spread industrial recovery in central China, with remarkable improvement over the corresponding period of the previous year: power consumption up 69 per cent, cement production 42 per cent, railway earnings 20-40 per cent, exports 45 per cent, and imports 32 per cent.[13] Japanese smuggling into North China had been curtailed and the sense of confidence which pervaded financial circles in London was reflected in the twenty-year high for quotations of Chinese bonds. The entanglements of the international banking consortium in China had been sidestepped by the British groups and negotiations had been completed for the flotation of large railway and currency loans beginning in the autumn of 1937. A special British

---

[12]D. C. Watt's article "Sir Warren Fisher and German Rearmament," in *Personalities and Policies*, pp. 110-16, gives a critical but sympathetic assessment of Fisher's role in the foreign policy-making elite in the 1930's. Writing before the archives were open, Watt mistakenly concluded that the notion of a separate Anglo-Japanese deal ended in December 1934 (ibid., p. 90), whereas, in fact, it continued in full vigour for at least another two years, perhaps to the neglect or alienation of other possibilities for international peace-keeping.

[13]G. E. Hubbard, *Eastern Industrialisation and Its Effects on the West* (London: Oxford University Press, 1938), p. 243; data from *Far Eastern Survey* (New York), 29 September 1937.

government agent was in Shanghai to prepare for a stream of medium term credits to China in support of the importation of British capital goods. With the well-calculated approval of the Nanking government, the practice, if not the principle, of British tutelage of China was re-asserted and a high official of the Bank of England, Cyril Rogers, was *de facto* adviser to the new Central Bank. This bank would control all currency and foreign exchange transactions. The security of foreign investments seemed to be further assured by the prospect that a British subject would remain as head of the Chinese Maritime Customs and by the resumption of the recruiting of foreign personnel in the Customs and Salt Administrations. In addition, W. H. Donald, a British subject, had been able to maintain his potition as the personal adviser of Generalissimo and Madame Chiang Kai-shek.

A British policy of such dimensions was obviously a challenge to the Japanese, who had announced their own exclusive programme for China. Since a challenge to Japan was contrary to the political desire of the Foreign Office as well as to the strategic requirements of the service chiefs and to the political and ideological sympathies of Neville Chamberlain, who wished to befriend Japan and saw her as a bulwark of order and civilization in Asia, the question remains: why was it adopted and followed with increasing vigour?

Senior members of the Far Eastern Department of the Foreign Office attributed an adventurous China policy to the lack of sound political judgment in the Treasury. There was some element of truth in this claim, which serves to illustrate the accidental role of strong-willed personalities in the bureaucracy as a factor in policy formation. For his part, Sir Warren Fisher returned the compliment when he told Chamberlain that "our amateurs at the F.O. are a source of danger."[14] But on the whole, Leith-Ross, who was the instrument of the forward policy, was not lacking in a sense of political realities. He had been sent to China with instructions to combine a political understanding with Japan with the rehabilitation of the economy of China. He did not have detailed knowledge of far eastern politics, but he soon singled out the central fact that British and Japanese interests in China were, at this stage, irreconcilable. And without the fear of disapproval which would have inhibited a weaker personality, he clearly warned his masters in the Treasury of the unpleasant reality that, if Britain wished to persist, the only language which Japanese leaders understood was that of big guns. From their failure to heed the advice of their

[14]Fisher, Minute, 23 February 1937, T 188/53.

political experts, the inference may be, and has been drawn, that key British leaders during these years were incompetent or irresponsible.

Another, and possibly more plausible explanation for their actions is that British leaders were acting in response to stronger pressures and forces within British society which were pushing for a more lively economic policy from the government. In the case of China policy, such pressure found expression through the China lobby—the chambers of commerce, the "common platform" which the bankers gave to Leith-Ross, the China Association and its *ad hoc* groups such as the "China Committee" and the "McGowan Committee" of the Board of Trade, the British Residents Association of Shanghai, and, in Parliament, the China Sub-Committee of the Foreign Affairs Committee of the Conservative party. A man like Sir Victor Wellesley, who spent several decades working within the Foreign Office bureaucracy and was deputy permanent under-secretary of state until 1936, was in a favourable position to sense some of the pressures emanating from these social forces. Writing his memoirs in 1944, Wellesley observed that in Britain, as in all other great industrial states where individual activities had become collectivized, "big business, finance and vested interests often dominate, not only legislatures but also domestic and foreign policy." He also warned that the interests of industry and finance, which "by no means always coincide with those of the nation," were sometimes so powerful that the policy of the government was dominated by private rather than national interests.[15]

Warnings such as Wellesley's, which in some respects echoed the critiques of capitalist imperialism by J. A. Hobson and Lenin, have prompted studies of the role of organized pressure groups and lobbies in British politics. These studies show that the lobby is "a great fact," as S. E. Finer wrote in *Anonymous Empire*, "pervading the whole of British political life."[16] But because other institutions, procedures, and beliefs which provide for full consultation, public disclosure, and the pinpointing of moral responsibility, also pervade British political life, Finer concluded that the lobby is not generally a corrupting influence in public life and does not engender erratic or grossly inconsistent policies. The main effects of the lobby are that it "cloys, clogs, enmeshes, slows down the conduct and decisiveness" of the administration and that it gives party governments a distinctive bias: they lean towards one set of interest groups or another depending on whether Labour or the Conservatives are in power. In spite

---

[15]Wellesley, *Diplomacy in Fetters*, p. 23.
[16]Samuel E. Finer, *Anonymous Empire: A Study of the Lobby in Great Britain*, rev. ed. (London: Pall Mall Press, 1966), p. 101.

of the checks on the sectional demands of the lobby, however, Finer found it necessary to warn against complacency, especially when the national consensus is on the wane: at such time the centrifugal tendencies of the lobbies are increasingly victorious.[17]

The depression days of the 1930's were a time when social cleavages and centrifugal tendencies were paramount in British society. And yet, because of the marginal nature of Britain's China trade, it might not be so easily admitted that a China lobby could influence high politics. However, can it be doubted that marginal economic questions can carry special weight at times—especially when they may be important to the plans of such giant corporations as Shell-B.P., British-American Tobacco, Imperial Chemical Industries, Unilever, and Sheffield steel interests, who were at the core of the China lobby? The concentration of economic power in the hands of these corporations, which remained for many years, gave them an inordinate possibility to influence public policy, especially at a time when the Conservative party was in power.

The trend of British policy in the Far East leads to the conclusion that the original concerns of Chamberlain and Fisher for strategic retrenchment and political prudence towards Japan were upset in favour of an increasing potential for the growth of British corporations. Again and again the China market was referred to as a place on which the future development of British trade and employment would depend. In this circumstance, the influence of British business and financial interests in the China trade became paramount. To use Sir Victor Wellesley's phrase, it was not difficult for them to present their "private interest" as a "national interest." It was the demand of these groups to keep the British flag flying in Asia, and the hoped-for benefit to the home economy, which seized the imagination of Neville Chamberlain and his closest colleagues. In view of Japanese displeasure, hopes were secretly placed in the growing strength of other forces in the Far East, particularly those of the Soviet Union, to keep Japan in check. But in any case Britain could not retreat. Those who walked the corridors of power in Britain were haunted by the thought that, despite the solid success of Britain in the East during two centuries, if British companies were forced to pull out of China, as they threatened to do unless the British government backed them up, the carry-over effect on India and the rest of the Empire would be incalculable. Britain's prestige had to be maintained, for it was on this national asset that possibilities for profitable trade and financial gain depended.

[17]Ibid., p. 111.

In part this has been an empirical investigation to find out what happened to British attitudes and fortunes in relation to China in a brief period of quiet during the drive of Japanese imperialism to dismember Chinese territory. It has also been an attempt to assess the significance of British actions and characterize their policy. It may be that some ambiguities about the actions of Britain and other nations towards China during the first half of the twentieth century, about the new meaning, methods, and results of imperialism and inter-imperialist rivalry in East Asia, remain to be unravelled. But it is clear that Western and specifically British imperialism in China was not yet a spent force. From the time of the Boxer uprising to the storming of the Hankow concession by the Chinese in 1927, the British in China were often on the run, and yet these energetic and resourceful people seldom felt themselves to be helpless objects buffeted about by unknown forces beyond their control as some apologists maintain. As the British oscillated between friendship with Japan and economic advance in China, between the rejection and acceptance of Chinese nationalism, they kept repeating to themselves the old adages of Queen Victoria's reign, that in China there was room for us all, and acted as if they still believed that the sun would never set on the British Empire.

Tables and Charts

TABLE 1

GREAT BRITAIN'S POSITION IN CHINA'S ECONOMY

	FIRMS			POPULATION	
	British Firms	% of Total Foreign Firms		British Population In China	% of Total Foreign Population
1899	410	(43.0)	1899	5,562	(32.4)
1913	590	(15.0)	1913	8,966	(5.4)
1930	1027	(12.4)	1930	13,915	(3.6)
1934	1021	(9.3)	1934	13,344	(3.6)

SHIPPING		
	British Tonnage (in millions)	% of Total Chinese & Foreign
1899	23.3	(59.4)
1913	38.1	(40.8)
1930	57.2	(36.8)
1934	58.8	(41.9)

SOURCE: *Far Eastern Survey*, vol. 6, no. 13, 13 June 1937.

CUSTOMS PERSONNEL				
	British		Japanese	Chinese	Total
1927	548	(47%)*	216	2050	3198
1937	390	(55%)	79	3109	3807

SOURCE: Annual Service Lists, Chinese Maritime Customs Service, 23 December 1937, FO 371/20990. Note: foreign staff predominated in higher ranks. *Per cent of foreign staff.

TABLE 2

TREND OF CHINA'S FOREIGN TRADE

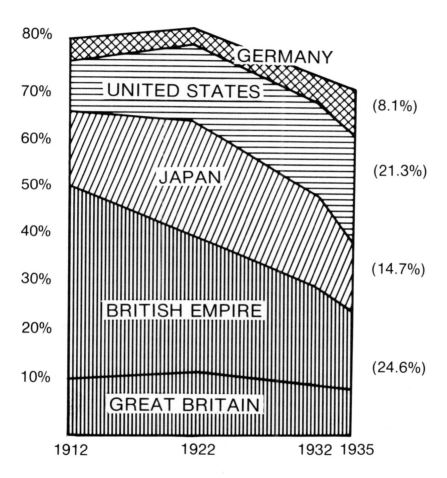

SOURCE: FO 371/18052, 20275, 1934 and 1936. *Large-scale Japanese smuggling in North China 1935-36 lowered customs figures, which if reported would have raised Japan's share.

TABLE 3

COMPARISON OF BRITISH FAR EASTERN EXPORTS

COMPARISON OF BRITISH FAR EASTERN EXPORTS 1928 - 1936

Exports to	1928	1936
	(£ millions)	
China	15.7	5.8
Hong Kong	5.5	2.1
Japan	14.5	3.6
Netherlands East Indies	9.6	2.8
Malaya and Straits	11.4	8.4
TOTALS	51.2	22.7

SOURCE: Foreign Office Memorandum, "British Policy In The Far East," 19 March 1937, Leith-Ross Papers, T 188/53.

TABLE 4

POSITION OF FOUR CHIEF COUNTRIES IN CHINA'S IMPORT TRADE 1933 - 1936

Year	Total Net Imports, Standard $'000	U.K. %	Japan %	U.S.A. %	Germany %
1933	1,345,567	11.4	9.7	22.0	8.0
1934	1,029,665	12.1	12.3	26.4	9.1
1935	919,211	10.7	15.2	19.0	11.2
1936	941,544	11.7	16.3	19.7	15.9

SOURCE: Board of Trade, notes for president of Board of Trade's speech to joint meeting of China Association and Federation of British Industries, May 1937, FO 371/20995/F2718/ 354/10. Note: large scale Japanese smuggling in North China 1935-37 decreased customs import figures and would have increased the Japanese share.

TABLE 5

PRINCIPAL ITEMS OF ANGLO-CHINESE TRADE

PRINCIPAL CHINESE IMPORTS FROM BRITAIN
(IN THOUSAND CUSTOMS GOLD UNITS)

Commodity	1932	1935
Metals	12,750	9,780
Machinery	10,308	7,930
Vessels & Vehicles	4,249	2,942
Linen Goods	974	2,941
Woolen Piece Goods	3,589	2,901
Cotton Goods	20,118	2,841

PRINCIPAL CHINESE EXPORTS TO BRITAIN
(IN THOUSAND CHINESE DOLLARS)

Commodity	1932	1935
Eggs & Egg Products	24,578	18,480
Bristles	2,966	3,307
Tea	4,573	2,961
Antimony	1,159	2,596
Wood Oil	539	2,118

SOURCE: *Far Eastern Survey*, vol. 6, no. 13, 13 June 1937.

TABLE 6

BRITISH INVESTMENTS IN CHINA

DISTRIBUTION OF BRITISH DIRECT BUSINESS INVESTMENTS ACCORDING TO NATURE OF
BUSINESS
(U.S. $ MILLIONS & % OF TOTAL)

	1930	1936
Banking and Finance	115.6	302.4
	(12.0)	(28.5)
Import–Export	240.8	243.9
	(25.1)	(23.0)
Real Estate	202.3	202.3
	(21.0)	(19.1)
Manufacturing	173.4	179.8
	(18.0)	(17.0)
Transportation	134.9	61.4
	(13.9)	(5.8)
Communications and Public Utilities	48.2	48.6
	(5.0)	(4.6)
Mining	19.3	15.8
	(2.0)	(1.5)
Miscellaneous	28.9	5.1
	(3.0)	(0.5)

SOURCES: *Far Eastern Survey*, (Institute of Pacific Relations, N.Y. vol. 6, no. 13, 13,6,37.
Hou Chi-ming, *Foreign Investment and Economic Development in China, 1840-1937*
(Cambridge, Mass.: Harvard Univ. Press, 1965), p. 226.

TREND OF INVESTMENTS
($ U.S. MILLIONS & PERCENT)

Direct Investments			Obligations of Chinese Government		Total	% of Total Foreign Investments
1902	150.0	(57.6)	110.3	(42.4)	260.3	(33.0)
1914	400.0	(65.8)	207.5	(34.2)	607.5	(37.7)
1930	963.4	(81.0)	225.8	(19.0)	1189.2	(36.7)
1934	1059.3	(86.8)	161.5	(13.2)	1220.8	(n.a.)

SOURCES: *Far Eastern Survey*, vol. 6, no. 13, 13 June 1937; Hou Chi-ming, *Foreign Invest-ment*, p. 225.

TABLE 7

QUOTATIONS OF CHINESE RAILWAY BONDS
ON THE LONDON STOCK EXCHANGE

LOAN
PRICE PER £100 BOND

	Oct. 14, 1935	May 31, 1937
Tientsin-Pukow Railway Loan (1908) ....£	22	£ 72
Hukuang Railways Loan (London issue)	39½	71
Honan Railway Loan	20-25	86½
Canton-Kowloon Railway Loan	10	54½
Lunghai Railway Loan	12	40¼

Data from Confidential Print, China, 8 June 1937, FO 405/276, no. 60.

TABLE 8

CHINESE NATIONAL RAILWAYS

CREDITS GRANTED FOR RAILWAY MATERIALS AND CONSTRUCTION

Loan	Amount in Sterling
Yushan-Nanchang (1934), Wolff (German) & Chinese Bankers Syndicate	£ 965,000
Nanchang Pinghsiang (1936) Wolff & Chinese Bankers Syndicate	1,200,000
Hangchow-Yushan (1936) Witcovice Iron & Steel Works	320,500
Paochi-Chengtu (1936) Belgian	3,000,000
Chuchow-Kweiyang (1936) Krupp, Wolff	1,800,000
Huang Ho Bridge (1936) Krupp, Wolff	600,000
Chengtu-Chungking (1936) French	2,080,000
Hsuchen-Kweichi (1936) Jardines (British)	450,000
TOTAL: .... Shanghai $173,290,300	£10,415,500

Data from Leith-Ross Papers, folder T 188/49, undated.

TABLE 9

Relative Strength of Foreign Navies on the China Station 1933

	Britain	U.S.A.	Japan	France	Italy
Cruisers, Large	5	2	—	1	—
Small	1	—	6	—	1
Aircraft Carriers	1	—	—	—	—
Destroyer Depot Ships	1	2	—	1	—
Sloops, Minesweepers, etc.	6	5	1	8	—
Destroyers	9	13	12	—	1
Submarines	11	12	—	2	—
River Gunboats	17	13	12	7	2
TOTAL: 150	51	47	30	18	4

Source: ADM 116/2984, Naval Intelligence.

TABLE 10

Diagram Illustrating
Structure of the Nanking Government

(in period of tutelage around 1935)

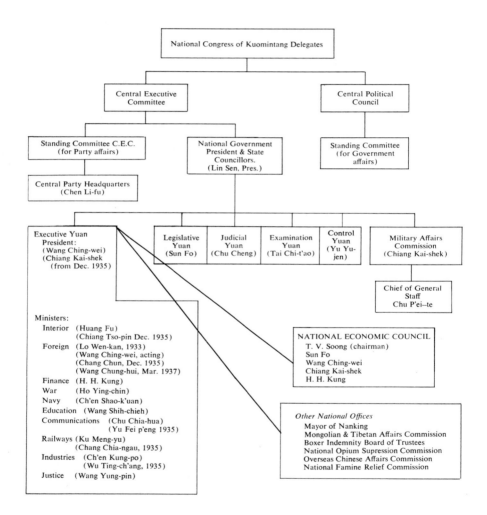

Source: List of "Chinese Central Government Officials As On 1st January 1935," FO 371/19307.

Selected Bibliography

Unpublished Sources

Cambridge. Cambridge University Library. Baldwin Papers. The papers of Stanley Baldwin, prime minister 1935-37, contain little on the Far East.

.... Templewood Papers. Letters, reports, and notes which contain little on the Far East during the six months Hoare was foreign secretary in 1935.

Edinburgh. Scottish Record Office. Lothian Papers. This prominent Liberal politician carried on a vast correspondence on many subjects, and together with his colleague, Lionel Curtis, he maintained close connections with the British merchant venturers engaged in the China trade.

.... Steel-Maitland Papers. The papers of this member of the World War I Coalition Cabinet contain useful material on the establishment and function of the Commercial Diplomatic Services of the British government.

London. British Museum. Cecil of Chelwood Papers. As honorary president of the League of Nations Union, Viscount Cecil was concerned with the League of Nations' efforts in China and carried on a voluminous correspondence on this and other topics with Chamberlain, Cadogan, Eden, Hoare, Simon, and others. See Special Correspondence, vols. 51080-89. Cecil complained to Eden that the "serried ranks of ignorant diehards" in the British Parliament rendered any attempt to speak of helping China against Japan "totally useless."

.... Cadogan Trustees. Cadogan Diary. The diaries of Sir Alexander Cadogan, 1938-45, edited by David Dilks, were published in 1971; the years 1933-37 remain unpublished and contain comments on Cadogan's political relationships while he was ambassador in China, 1934-36.

.... Chatham House. Royal Institute of International Affairs. Small files of the agendas and minutes from the Institute of Pacific Relations sub-committee of this unofficial but influential policy discussion organization are available.

.... Edinburgh House. Conference of Missionary Societies. This organization, representing a number of different protestant religious missions in China, kept in touch with the Foreign Office. Its officers forwarded letters which raised questions of a political nature, such as their attitude towards treaty rights in China or how to react to Japanese aggression. Much of this organization's archives on China have been transferred to the International Missionary Council (Geneva).

.... Hatton Garden. China Association Papers. The general committee papers of this long established organization are now available for study. The volumes covering the period from 1933-38 are primarily mimeographed material, including: quarterly reports by the secretary, E. M. Gull, on China's international policy, domestic politics, and trade; minutes of periodic meetings of the general committee, a body representing twenty or so of the most prominent China Houses (or Old China Hands) resident in London; translated extracts of the Chinese press; copies of correspondence to and from the Foreign Office; and circular letters to members of the executive committee on special topics.

.... Imperial Chemical Industries Ltd. This major British company has a large and mainly unorganized archive dealing with China. Mr. W. J. Reader, who is currently engaged in preparation of volume II of the company history, kindly located and allowed me to read documents on questions in which I was interested.

.... Imperial War Museum. International Military Tribunal Far East. Contains vast amounts of material on Sino-Japanese relations in court exhibits, transcripts, and summaries of defence. Important evidence about Japan's "Hands Off China" policy (Amau Doctrine) of 1934, which had an influence on the fortunes of British interests in China, is given, for example, in exhibits 3241 and 3243, and information on the evolution of Hirota's "Three Principles" in exhibits 3254, 3255, and 3257.

.... John Swire and Sons. Swire Papers. The archive of John Swire and Sons is an extensive collection of one of the great pioneer British shipping companies in the China trade, better known along the China coast as Butterfield and Swire, or Taikoo. This company also acted as Far East agents for the better-known Alfred Holt shipping company of Liverpool. The relevant material for this period is located as follows:

Private Office Papers: 1074-76 P Inland
                                        1082-84 P China
Director Now Out East: J. S. Scott and Warren
                                        Swire, 1932-34
                                        J. K. Swire 1935
                                        J. S. Scott 1935-36
                                        Colin Scott 1937
                                        Warren Swire 1938
China & Japan Letters: Boxes 47-51
China Navigation Co.,
Shanghai General Letters: Boxes 94-99

.... Port of London Authority. Simon Papers. The diary and personal correspondence of Sir John Simon, foreign secretary 1931-35, contain several important items on China, including a noteworthy exchange of letters with Neville Chamberlain, in a bundle marked Correspondence, Foreign Affairs 1934.

.... Public Record Office. Admiralty Papers. These papers, which include military intelligence reports, provide information on measures to maintain prestige and protect investments, on the degree of involvement in Chinese civil strife, and on divergent views for meeting the strategic threat from Japan. ADM 1, general correspondence, and especially ADM 116, with cases and reports of proceedings on the China Station and official minutes, are basic sources. In addition, ADM 12, indexes, ADM 53, ships logs, ADM 167, board minutes and memoranda, and ADM 176, Materials Department, were consulted for specific questions.

.... Board of Trade Papers. BT 11, Commercial Department, correspondence and papers; file 388 on the Chinese silver crisis, file 516 on the Leith-Ross mission, file 219 on cotton trade negotiations with Japan. BT 59, BT 60, Department of Overseas Trade, have minutes and correspondence of the Overseas Trade Development Council, including discussions on China.

.... Cabinet Papers. CAB 23 contains minutes and conclusions of full meetings of the cabinet; discussion of China arose in this body on some thirty occasions during these years. CAB 24 has the proposals and background papers for cabinet discussion. CAB 27 has full minutes of cabinet sub-committees, of which volumes 505-7 and 596 are of particular interest for this study. CAB 29, international conferences, has relevant papers on the World Economic Conference in London (1933), and the London Naval Conference discussions (1934-36). File 128 of CAB 32 provides background for the proposed Pacific Non-Aggression Pact, which was discussed at the Imperial Conference of 1937. CAB 2, 4, and 6 contain papers of the Committee of Imperial Defence (C.I.D.) and the Defence Requirements Committee—especially

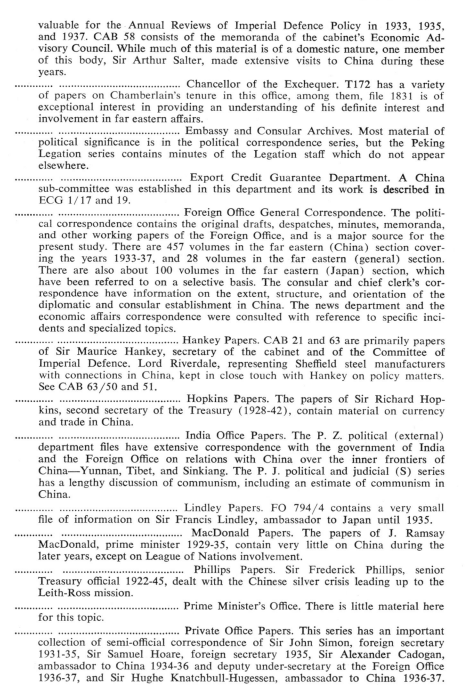

valuable for the Annual Reviews of Imperial Defence Policy in 1933, 1935, and 1937. CAB 58 consists of the memoranda of the cabinet's Economic Advisory Council. While much of this material is of a domestic nature, one member of this body, Sir Arthur Salter, made extensive visits to China during these years.

.... Chancellor of the Exchequer. T172 has a variety of papers on Chamberlain's tenure in this office, among them, file 1831 is of exceptional interest in providing an understanding of his definite interest and involvement in far eastern affairs.

.... Embassy and Consular Archives. Most material of political significance is in the political correspondence series, but the Peking Legation series contains minutes of the Legation staff which do not appear elsewhere.

.... Export Credit Guarantee Department. A China sub-committee was established in this department and its work is described in ECG 1/17 and 19.

.... Foreign Office General Correspondence. The political correspondence contains the original drafts, despatches, minutes, memoranda, and other working papers of the Foreign Office, and is a major source for the present study. There are 457 volumes in the far eastern (China) section covering the years 1933-37, and 28 volumes in the far eastern (general) section. There are also about 100 volumes in the far eastern (Japan) section, which have been referred to on a selective basis. The consular and chief clerk's correspondence have information on the extent, structure, and orientation of the diplomatic and consular establishment in China. The news department and the economic affairs correspondence were consulted with reference to specific incidents and specialized topics.

.... Hankey Papers. CAB 21 and 63 are primarily papers of Sir Maurice Hankey, secretary of the cabinet and of the Committee of Imperial Defence. Lord Riverdale, representing Sheffield steel manufacturers with connections in China, kept in close touch with Hankey on policy matters. See CAB 63/50 and 51.

.... Hopkins Papers. The papers of Sir Richard Hopkins, second secretary of the Treasury (1928-42), contain material on currency and trade in China.

.... India Office Papers. The P. Z. political (external) department files have extensive correspondence with the government of India and the Foreign Office on relations with China over the inner frontiers of China—Yunnan, Tibet, and Sinkiang. The P. J. political and judicial (S) series has a lengthy discussion of communism, including an estimate of communism in China.

.... Lindley Papers. FO 794/4 contains a very small file of information on Sir Francis Lindley, ambassador to Japan until 1935.

.... MacDonald Papers. The papers of J. Ramsay MacDonald, prime minister 1929-35, contain very little on China during the later years, except on League of Nations involvement.

.... Phillips Papers. Sir Frederick Phillips, senior Treasury official 1922-45, dealt with the Chinese silver crisis leading up to the Leith-Ross mission.

.... Prime Minister's Office. There is little material here for this topic.

.... Private Office Papers. This series has an important collection of semi-official correspondence of Sir John Simon, foreign secretary 1931-35, Sir Samuel Hoare, foreign secretary 1935, Sir Alexander Cadogan, ambassador to China 1934-36 and deputy under-secretary at the Foreign Office 1936-37, and Sir Hughe Knatchbull-Hugessen, ambassador to China 1936-37.

.... School of Oriental and African Studies. Maze Papers. Sir Frederick Maze
was inspector general of the Chinese Maritime Customs Administration after
1929. His Confidential Letters and Reports, vols. 9 to 13, cover the years 1933-
39 and are useful regarding trade and conditions in the Chinese treaty ports.
.... Treasury Chambers. Leith-Ross Papers. In the series T 188, files 23 to 75
are on China and are an indispensable source for this study. The numbering
of these files is provisional and subject to change when the documents are
transferred to the Public Record Office.
Oxford. Bodleian Library. Nathan Papers. E. J. Nathan was general manager of the
Kailan Mining Administration in Hopei Province. This archive is mainly correspondence with W. F. Turner, of the Chinese Engineering and Mining Co.,
London, which reputedly had an investment of £10 million in the Kailan coal
mines. Vols. C424-29 for the years 1933-37 show the close connection between
business and politics in Chiang Kai-shek's China.
Southampton. Southampton University Library. Chatfield Papers. As chief of naval
staff from 1933-38, Lord Chatfield's personal correspondence with Commander-
in-Chief, Admiral Dreyer, with Vice-Admiral Little, and with Sir Warren Fisher,
permanent under-secretary at the Treasury, are a useful supplement to the official
papers of the Admiralty.
Suffolk. Victor Rose, Framlingham. Rose Papers. Archibald Rose was director of the
British-American Tobacco (China) Co. Ltd. He made frequent business trips
to China and sent many reports to the Foreign Office. His diary and personal
papers for the 1930's are disappointingly sparse. The British-American Tobacco
Co., another of the largest British corporations, reports that the papers of its
Chinese organization have been destroyed "apart from a very few."

Published Sources

Abend, Hallet. *My Life in China, 1926-1941*. New York: Harcourt, Brace and Co.,
1943.
Allen, G. C., and A. G. Donnithorne. *Western Enterprise in Far Eastern Economic
Development*. New York: Macmillan, 1954.
Allen, Harry C. *The Anglo-American Relationship since 1783*. London: A. P. C.
Black, 1959.
Amery, Leopold S. *My Political Life*. Vol. 3. London: Hutchinson, 1955.
Angell, Norman. *The Defence of the Empire*. London: Appleton–Century, 1937.
Aron, Raymond. *Peace and War*. New York: Doubleday, 1966.
Ashton-Gwatkin, Frank T. A. *The British Foreign Service*. Syracuse: Syracuse Uni-
versity Press, 1949.
Avon, Anthony Eden, 1st Earl of, *Facing the Dictators: The Eden Memoirs*. London:
Houghton, 1962.
Bank of China. *Annual Reports*. Shanghai, 1934-36.
Barnes, Joseph, ed. *Empire in the East*. New York: Doubleday, Doran & Co., 1934.
Barratt-Brown, Michael. *After Imperialism*. London: Heinemann, 1963.
Bassett, Reginald. *Democracy and Foreign Policy*. London: London School of Eco-
nomics, 1952; reprint, 1968.
Baur, P. T. "The Economics of Resentment: Colonialism and Underdevelopment."
Journal of Contemporary History 4 (1969): 51-71.
Bergamini, David. *Japan's Imperial Conspiracy*. New York, Morrow, 1971.
Bertram, James. *First Act in China: the Story of the Sian Mutiny*. New York: Viking
Press, 1938.

Bishop, Donald G. *The Administration of British Foreign Relations*. Syracuse: Syracuse University Press, 1961.

Bisson, Thomas A. *Japan in China*. New York: Macmillan, 1938.

.... "Struggle of the Powers in China." *Foreign Policy Reports*, 1 August, 1936, pp. 211-16.

.... "The Communist Movement in China." *Foreign Policy Reports*, 26 April 1933, pp. 38-44.

Bloch, Kurt. *German Interests and Policies in the Far East*. New York: Institute of Pacific Relations, 1939.

Blum, John M. *From the Morgenthau Diaries*. Boston: 1959.

Borg, Dorothy. *The United States and the Far Eastern Crisis of 1933-1938*. Cambridge, Mass.: Harvard University Press, 1964.

Broad, Charlie L. *Sir Anthony Eden*. London: Crowell, 1955.

Buhite, Russell D. *Nelson T. Johnson and American Policy Toward China 1925-1941*. East Lansing, Michigan, 1968.

Butler, David and J. Freeman. *British Political Facts 1900-1967*, 2nd ed. London: Macmillan, 1968.

Butler, J. R. M. *Grand Strategy*. Vol. 2. London: H.M.S.O., 1957.

.... *Lord Lothian*. London: Macmillan, 1960.

Butow, Robert J. *Tojo and the Coming of the War*. Princeton: Princeton University Press, 1961.

Cable, James. *Gunboat Diplomacy*. London: Chatto and Windus, 1971.

Cairncross, A. K. "Did Foreign Investment Pay?" *Review of Economic Studies* 3 (1935-36): 67-78.

Carr, Edward H. *The 20 Years' Crisis*. London: 1962.

Cavendish, P. "Anti-Imperialism in the Kuomintang 1923-28." In *Studies in the Social History of China and South-East Asia*, edited by Jerome Ch'en and N. Tarling. Cambridge: Cambridge University Press, 1970.

Cecil, R. A. J. Gascoyne-, 5th Marquess of Salisbury. *A Great Experiment*. London: Oxford University Press, 1941.

Chang Kia-ngau. *China's Struggle for Railway Development*. New York: J. Day, 1943.

Ch'en, Jerome and N. Tarling, eds. *Studies in the Social History of China and South-East Asia*. Cambridge: Cambridge University Press, 1970.

Ch'en, Jerome. "Historical Background." In *Modern China's Search for a Political Form*. Ed. Jack Gray. London: Oxford University Press, 1969.

Cheng, Lin. *The Chinese Railways, Past and Present*. Shanghai: China United Press, 1937.

Chiang Kai-shek. *Soviet Russia in China: A Summing-up at Seventy*. Revised, abridged edition. New York: Farrar, Strauss and Giroux, 1965.

.... and Madame Chiang. *Sian: A Coup D'Etat. A Fortnight in Sian: Extracts from a Diary*. Shanghai: The China Publishing Co., 1937.

Ch'ien Tuan-sheng. *The Government and Politics of China 1912-1949*. Cambridge, Mass.: Harvard University Press, 1950; reprinted 1970.

China Quarterly. London: University of London, periodical.

China Reconstructs. Peking: China Welfare Institute, monthly.

China, Republic of, Ministry of Industries. *Silver and Prices in China*. Shanghai: Commercial Press, 1935.

China, Republic of, National Economic Council. *Annual Report, 1935*. Nanking, 1936.

Clifford, Nicholas R. *Retreat from China*. Seattle: University of Washington Press, 1967.

Cohen, Warren I. *America's Response to China: an interpretative history of Sino-American Relations*. New York: Wiley, 1971.

Collier, Basil. *The Defence of the United Kingdom*. London: H.M.S.O., 1957.

Collis, Maurice. *Wayfoong: The Hongkong and Shanghai Banking Corporation*. London: Faber and Faber, 1965.

Colvin, Ian. *The Chamberlain Cabinet*. London: Gollancz, 1971.
.... *Vansittart in Office: The Origins of World War II*. London: Gollancz, 1965.
Cooper, A. Duff. *Old Men Forget*. London: R. Hart-Davis, 1953.
Craig, G. A., and Felix Gilbert. *The Diplomats: 1919-1939*. Vol. 2. Princeton: Princeton University Press, 1953.
Craigie, Sir Robert. *Behind the Japanese Mask*. London: Hutchinson, 1946.
Crowley, J. B. *Japan's Quest for Autonomy*. Princeton: Princeton University Press, 1966
Curtis, Lionel. *The Capital Question of China*. London: Macmillan, 1932.
Degras, Jane, ed. *The Communist International 1919-1943*. Volume 3. London: Oxford University Press, 1956-65.
Dilks, David, ed. *The Diaries of Sir Alexander Cadogan 1938-1945*. London: Putnam, 1971.
Dirksen, Herbert von. *Moscow, Tokyo, London*. London: Hutchinson, 1951.
Drage, Charles. *Taikoo*. London: Constable, 1970.
Dreyer, Admiral Sir Frederick. *The Sea Heritage*. London: Museum Press, 1955.
Dull, Paul S., and Michael Umemura. *The Tokyo Trials: A Functional Index to the Proceedings of the International Military Tribunal for the Far East*. Ann Arbor: University of Michigan Press, 1957.
Eastman, Lloyd E. "Fascism in Kuomintang China: The Blue Shirts." *China Quarterly* 49 (1972): 1-31.
Fairbank, J. K. *The United States and China*. Revised edition. New York: Viking Press, 1966.
Far Eastern Survey. New York: Institute of Pacific Relations, periodical.
Feiling, Keith. *The Life of Neville Chamberlain*. London: Macmillan, 1946.
Ferrell, R. H. *American Diplomacy in the Great Depression*. New Haven: Yale University Press, 1957.
Feuerwerker, Albert. *The Chinese Economy, 1912-1949*. Ann Arbor: University of Michigan Press, 1968.
Finer, Samuel E. *Anonymous Empire: a Study of the Lobby in Great Britain*. Revised. London: Pall Mall Press, 1966.
Fishel, Wesley R. *The End of Extraterritoriality in China*. Berkeley: University of California Press, 1952.
Fisher, Sir Warren. "The Beginnings of Civil Defence." *Public Administration* 26 (1948): 211-16.
Frankel, Joseph. *National Interest*. London: Pall Mall Press, 1970.
.... *The Making of Foreign Policy*. London: Oxford University Press, 1963.
Friedman, Irving S. *British Relations with China: 1931-1939*. New York: Institute of Pacific Relations, 1940.
George, Margaret. *The Warped Vision: British Foreign Policy 1933-1939*. Pittsburgh: University of Pittsburgh Press, 1965.
Germany, Auswartiges Amt. *Documents on German Foreign Policy 1918-1945*. Ed. U.S. Dept. of State Series C, Vols. 1-6, 1933-1937. Washington, D.C.: Government Printing Office, 1949-64.
Gilbert, Martin. *The Roots of Appeasement*. London: Weidenfeld & Nicolson, 1966.
Gompertz, G. H. *China in Turmoil: Eye Witness 1924-1948*. London: Dent, 1967.
Great Britain. Department of Overseas Trade. *Economic and Trade Conditions in China, Reports*. London: H.M.S.O., 1933-1937.
Great Britain, Foreign Office. *Documents on British Foreign Policy*. 2nd Series. Vols. 8-10. London: H.M.S.O., 1960, 1965, 1970.
Great Britain. Foreign Office. *List and Diplomatic and Consular Year Book*. London: H.M.S.O., 1930-1939.
Great Britain. *Parliamentary Debates. House of Commons*. 5th Series. London: H.M.S.O., 1933-1937.
Great Britain. *Parliamentary Debates. House of Lords*. London: H.M.S.O., 1933-1937.

Great Britain. Public Record Office. *The Records of the Foreign Office 1792-1939.* London: H.M.S.O., 1969.

Grew, Joseph C. *Ten Years in Japan.* New York: Simon & Schuster, 1944.

.... *Turbulent Era: A Diplomatic Record of Forty Years, 1904-1945.* Ed. Walter Johnson. Boston: Houghton, 1952.

Gwynn, General Sir Charles. *Imperial Policing.* London: Macmillan, 1934.

Hamilton, Sir H. P. "Sir Warren Fisher and the Public Service." *Public Administration* 29 (1951): 3-28.

Hao Yen-p'ing. *The Comprador in Nineteenth Century China.* Cambridge, Mass.: Harvard University Press, 1970.

Harcourt-Smith, Simon. *Japanese Frenzy.* London: Hamilton, 1942.

Harvey, John, ed. *The Diplomatic Diaries of Oliver Harvey, 1937-1940.* London: Collins, 1970.

Hewlett, Sir William Meyrich. *Forty Years in China.* London: Macmillan, 1943.

Higham, R. *Armed Forces in Peacetime; Britain, 1918-1940.* London: G. T. Foulis, 1962.

Hindle, Wilfrid H. *The Morning Post, 1772-1937: Portrait of a Newspaper.* London: Routledge, 1937.

Ho Kan Chih. *A History of the Modern Chinese Revolution.* Peking: Foreign Languages Press, 1959.

Hobart, Alice T. *Oil for the Lamps of China.* London: Grosset & Dunlap, 1934.

Hongkong and Shanghai Bank. *Reports of Annual Meetings, 1933-1937.* The *Economist.*

Hou Chi-ming. *Foreign Investment and Economic Development in China, 1840-1937.* Cambridge, Mass.: Harvard University Press, 1965.

Hsu Shu-hsi. *The North China Problem.* Shanghai: Kelly and Walsh, 1937.

Hubbard, G. E. *British Far Eastern Policy.* New York: Institute of Pacific Relations, 1943.

.... *Eastern Industrialization and Its Effect on the West.* London: Oxford University Press, 1938.

Hudson, G. F. *The Far East in World Politics.* 2nd ed. London: Oxford University Press, 1939.

Hughes, Ernest R. *The Invasion of China by the Western World.* New York: Macmillan, 1938.

Hull, Cordell. *The Memoirs of Cordell Hull.* Vol. 1. New York: Macmillan, 1948.

Hyde, Francis E. *Shipping Enterprise and Management.* Liverpool: Liverpool University Press, 1967.

Iklé, Frank W. *German-Japanese Relations 1936-1940.* New York: Bookman Associates, 1956.

Imperial Chemical Industries Ltd. *Annual Reports of the Directors of. . . .* London, 1927-1940.

Institute of Pacific Relations. *Problems of the Pacific 1933.* Chicago: University of Chicago Press, 1934.

.... *Problems of the Pacific 1936.* Chicago: University of Chicago Press, 1937.

Iriye, Akira. *After Imperialism.* Cambridge, Mass.: Harvard University Press, 1965.

Isreal, John. *Student Nationalism in China 1927-1937.* Stanford: Stanford University Press, 1966.

James, Robert R. *Memoirs of a Conservative: J. C. C. Davidson's Memoirs and Papers, 1910-37.* London, Weidenfeld & Nicolson, 1969.

Jardine, Matheson & Co. *Jardine, Matheson & Co: An historical sketch.* Hong Kong, 1968.

Johnson, Franklyn A. *Defence by Committee.* London: Oxford University Press, 1960.

Jones, Thomas. *A Diary with Letters, 1931-1950.* London: Oxford University Press, 1954.

Journal of Asian Studies. Ann Arbor, quarterly.

Kawakami, Kiyoshi Karl. *Japan in China: Her Motives and Aims.* London: J. Murray, 1938.

Kennedy, Captain Malcolm D. *The Estrangement of Great Britain and Japan 1917-1935.* Manchester: University of Manchester Press, 1969.

Kirby, S. W. *The War in the Far East,* Vol. 1. London: H.M.S.O., 1957.

Knatchbull-Hugessen, Sir Hughe. *Diplomat in Peace and War.* London: J. Murray, 1949.

Langer, William L. *The Diplomacy of Imperialism.* New York: Knopf, 1935.

Lattimore, Owen. "Unpublished Report from Yenan 1937." In *Studies in the Social History of China and South-East Asia,* edited by Jerome Ch'en and N. Tarling. Cambridge: Cambridge University Press, 1970.

League of Nations. Council Committee of Technical Co-operation Between the League of Nations and China. *Reports,* April 1934 and May 1935. Geneva.

Lee, Bradford A. *Britain and the Sino-Japanese War, 1937-1939.* Stanford: Stanford University Press, 1973.

Leith-Ross, Sir Frederick. *Money Talks: Fifty Years of International Finance.* London: Hutchinson, 1968.

Lenin, V. I., "Imperialism, the Highest Stage of Capitalism." *Selected Works.* Vol. 1, part 2, pp. 433-568. Moscow: Foreign Languages Publishing House, 1952.

Levy, Roger, Guy Lacom, and Andrew Roth. *French Interests and Policies in the Far East.* New York: Institute of Pacific Relations, 1941.

Linebarger, Paul. *The China of Chiang Kai-shek: A Political Study.* Boston: World Peace Foundation, 1941.

Liu Chih-pu. *Military History of Modern China.* Princeton: Princeton University Press, 1956.

Louis, William R. *British Strategy in the Far East 1919-1939.* Oxford: Clarendon Press, 1971.

Luard, Evan. *Britain and China.* London: Chatto and Windus, 1962.

Mao Tse-Tung. *Selected Works.* Vols. 1-3. Peking: Foreign Languages Press, 1961.

Mathieson, F. C. and Sons. *Stock Exchange London and Provincial Ten-Year Record.* London: Mathieson and Sons, annual.

McAleavy, Henry. *The History of Modern China.* London: Weidenfeld & Nicolson, 1967.

McElwee, William. *Britain's Locust Years, 1918-1940.* London: Faber and Faber, 1962.

McLane, Charles B. *Soviet Policy and the Chinese Communists, 1937-1946.* New York: Columbia University Press, 1958.

MacNair, Harley F. and D. Lach. *Modern Far Eastern International Relations.* Revised ed. New York: Van Nostrand, 1955.

Medlicott, William N. *British Foreign Policy Since Versailles, 1919-1963.* London: Methuen, 1968.

.... *The Economic Blockade.* London: H.M.S.O., 1952.

Middlemas, Keith, and John Barnes. *Baldwin.* London: Weidenfeld & Nicolson, 1969.

Moore, Harriet L. *Soviet Far Eastern Policy, 1931-1945.* Princeton: Princeton University Press, 1945.

Morley, James W. *Dilemmas of Growth in Prewar Japan.* Princeton: Princeton University Press, 1971.

Morse, Hosea B., and Harley F. MacNair. *Far Eastern International Relations.* Shanghai: Commercial Press, 1928.

Murphey, Rhoads. *Shanghai: Key to Modern China.* Cambridge, Mass.: Harvard University Press, 1953.

Myrdal, Gunnar. *Rich Lands and Poor.* New York: Harper, 1957.

National Christian Council of China. *Bulletin.* Shanghai, 1930-1937.

Naylor, John F. *Labour's International Policy.* London: Weidenfeld & Nicolson, 1969.

Nicolson, Nigel, ed. *Harold Nicolson, Diaries and Letters: 1930-39.* London: Collins, 1966.

North China Daily News and Herald Ltd. *The China Hong List.* Shanghai, 1934-1939.

North China Herald. Shanghai, weekly.

Ogato, Sadako N. *Defiance in Manchuria.* Berkeley: University of California Press, 1964.

Oriental Affairs. Shanghai, periodical.

Pelcovits, Nathan A. *Old China Hands and the Foreign Office.* New York: King's Crown Press, 1948.

Piggott, Francis S. G. *Broken Thread.* London: Gale & Polden, 1950.

.... *Japan Again.* London: Japan Society pamphlet, 1940.

Platt, Desmond C. M. *Finance, Trade & Politics in British Foreign Policy, 1815-1914.* Oxford: Clarendon Press, 1968.

.... *The Cinderella Service: British Consuls since 1825.* London: Longmans, 1971.

Postan, Michael M. *British War Production.* London: H.M.S.O., 1952.

Potter, Allen. *Organized Groups in British National Politics.* London: Faber and Faber, 1961.

Pratt, Sir John T. *China and Britain.* London: Hastings House, 1944.

.... *Korea, the Lie that Led to War.* London, 1951.

.... *War and Politics in China.* London: J. Cape, 1943.

Purcell, Victor. *China.* London: E. Benn, 1962.

Reader, W. J. *Imperial Chemical Industries: A History,* Vol. 1. London: Oxford University Press, 1970.

Remer, C. F. *Foreign Investments in China.* New York: Macmillan, 1933.

Robertson, Esmonde M., ed. *The Origins of the Second World War.* London: Macmillan, 1971.

Robertson, John [Connell]. *The Office: A Study of British Foreign Policy and its Makers, 1919-1951.* London: A. Wingate, 1958.

Rose, Richard, ed. *Policy-Making in Britain.* London: Macmillan, 1969.

Rothstein, Andrew. *British Foreign Policy and Its Critics.* London: Lawrence & Wishart, 1969.

Royal Institute of International Affairs. *China and Japan.* London: Oxford University Press, 1938.

.... *Documents on International Affairs.* London: Oxford University Press, annual.

.... *Political and Strategic Interests of the United Kingdom.* London: Oxford University Press, 1939.

.... *Survey of International Affairs.* London: Oxford University Press, annual.

.... *The Problem of International Investment.* London: Oxford University Press, 1937.

Salter, Sir Arthur. "China and the Depression." The *Economist* Special Supplement, 19 May 1934, pp. 1-16.

.... *Slave of the Lamp.* London: Weidenfeld & Nicolson, 1967.

Selby, Sir Walford. *Diplomatic Twilight, 1930-1940.* London: J. Murray, 1953.

Selle, Earl A. *Donald of China.* New York: Harper, 1948.

Shen Po-chun. "The Sian Incident." *China Reconstructs* 11 (December 1962): 30-33.

Simon, John A. (Viscount). *Retrospect.* London: Hutchinson, 1952.

Slyke, Lyman P. Van, ed. *The Chinese Communist Movement: A Report of the United States War Department, July 1945.* Stanford: Stanford University Press, 1968.

Staley, Eugene. *War and the Private Investor.* Chicago: University of Chicago Press, 1935.

Steiner, Zara S. *The Foreign Office and Foreign Policy, 1898-1914.* London: Cambridge University Press, 1969.

Stimson, Henry. *The Far Eastern Crisis.* New York: Harper, 1936.

Stock Exchange Official Year-Book. London, 1935.

Strang, Sir William. *The Foreign Office*. London: Allen & Unwin, 1955.
Sun E-tu Zen. "The Pattern of Railway Development in China." *Far Eastern Quarterly* 14 (1954-1955): 179-99.
Tamagna, Frank. *Banking and Finance in China*. New York: Institute of Pacific Relations, 1942.
T'ang Leang-li, ed. *The People's Tribune*. Shanghai, periodical.
Taylor, A. J. P. *The Origins of the Second World War*. London: H. Hamilton, 1961.
Teichman, Sir Eric. *Affairs of China*. London: Methuen, 1938.
Templewood, Samuel (Viscount). *Nine Troubled Years*. London: Collins, 1954.
Thomson, Rear-Admiral Sir George Pirie. *Blue Pencil Admiral*. London: Sampson, Low, Marston and Co., 1947.
Thomson, James C. *While China Faced West*. Cambridge, Mass: Harvard University Press, 1969.
Thorne, Christopher. "The Shanghai Crisis of 1932: The Basis of British Policy." *American Historical Review* 75 (1970): 1616-39.
.... *The Limits of Foreign Policy*. London: Hamilton, 1972.
.... "The Quest for Arms Embargoes: Failure in 1933." *Journal of Contemporary History* (October 1970): 129-49.
Thornton, A. P. *Doctrines of Imperialism*. New York: Wiley, 1965.
Tilley, Sir John, and Stephen Gaselee. *The Foreign Office*. 2nd ed. London: G. P. Putnam, 1933.
The Times.
Toland, John. *The Rising Sun*. New York: Random House, 1970.
Union of Democratic Control. *Eastern Menace: The Story of Japanese Imperialism*. London: The Union, 1936.
United States, Department of State. *Foreign Relations of the United States: Diplomatic Papers, 1933-1937*. Washington, D.C.: Government Printing Office, 1949-1954.
United States, Department of State. *Papers Relating to the Foreign Relations of the United States: Japan 1931-1941*. 2 vols. Washington, D.C.: Government Printing Office, 1943.
Vansittart, Lord. *The Mist Procession*. London: Hutchinson, 1958.
Vital, David. *The Making of British Foreign Policy*. London: Oxford University Press, 1968.
Walters, Francis P. *A History of the League of Nations*. London: Oxford University Press, 1952.
Watt, Donald C. *Personalities and Policies*. London: Longmans, 1965.
Wellesley, Sir Victor. *Diplomacy in Fetters*. London: Hutchinson, 1944.
Williams, Francis. *A Pattern of Rulers*. London: Longmans, 1965.
Wilson, Charles. *The History of Unilever*. London: Cassell, 1954.
Woodhead, H. G., ed. *China Year Book*. Tientsin: Tientsin Press, 1926-1936.
Yin Ching Chen. *Treaties and Agreements between the Republic of China and other Powers 1929-1954*. Washington: Sino-American Publishing Services, 1957.
Yoshida, Shigeru. *The Yoshida Memoirs*. Boston: Houghton Mifflin, 1962.

Index

Addis, Sir Charles, 35, 36, 135, 142, 143, 166, 167
Admiralty, China station, 2-5, 76, 140, 154, 177, 179, 187, table 9. *See also* Gunboat Diplomacy
Aglen, Sir Francis, 7
Amau doctrine, 26, 45-50, 66, 87, 139
Amau, Eiji, 45, 46, 47; and the Amau doctrine, 45-50, 66
Anglo-American relations, 49-50, 59-63; financial rivalry, 60; naval talks, 60; Manchurian crisis, 61-62; Chinese silver crisis, 85-86; on Leith-Ross mission, 109; banking consortium, 143-44; Pacific neutralization pact, 164-65
Anglo-Japanese relations, preface, 4, 9, 11-12, 46-50, 63-81, 140; Defence Requirements Committee on, 63-64; trade rivalry, 66, 128; FBI mission to Japan, 73-74; Chamberlain-Fisher views on, xvi, 58, 64-65, 67, 71-73, 80-81, 97-98, 128, 163, 178-79; Edwardes's secret talks on, 74-77; Foreign Office views on, 56-57, 65-66, 67, 79, 114, 122, 124, 146-47; G. B. Sansom on, 78, 80; Japanese reaction to Leith-Ross mission, 113-14, 118, 126, 162, 179
Anglo-Soviet relations, 53-59, 148-49, 164
Anti-Comintern Pact (1936), 148-49
Appeasement policy, 57, 108, 112-15; Munich foreshadowed, 180
Araki, General Sadao, 75
Arita, Hachiro, 119
Ariyoshi, Akira, Japanese ambassador to China, 44, 45, 50, 120
Ashton-Gwatkin, Frank, 22
Asiatic Petroleum Co. (North and South China) Ltd. (a subsidiary of Shell B.P.), 30, 31n
Atherton, Ray, 143

Baldwin, Stanley, prime minister, 58, 70, 72, 125
Bank of China, 38
Bank of England, 36n, 82n, 92, 103, 106, 115, 182
Barratt Brown, Michael, 175
Barthou, Louis, 70
Beale, Sir Louis: as trade promoter, 6, 6n, 99, 131; on British business policy in China, 43
Bergamini, David, 117, 117n
Bingham, Robert Worth, United States ambassador to Britain, 49
Blue Shirt Society, 17
Boxer Protocol (1901), 27, 98-99, 135, 171
Britain: diplomatic, commercial, and consular services in China, 5-6, 42-44, 98-99; advisers to Chinese government, 10, 10n, 93, 97, 101, 112, 133, 157, 182; intelligence services, 2n, 45, 118, 119; missionaries, 23n, 154-55, 186; discussion of China in Parliament, 29, 50, 102, 103, 121, 151. *See also* Anglo-American relations; Anglo-Japanese relations; Anglo-Soviet relations; British business in China; British China lobby; British China policy
British-American Tobacco Co. (China) Ltd., 30, 184, 189; and Chinese managers, 40; use of Chinese capital, 44; China lobby, 89

Tariff and customs administration, 2, 6-8, 35
Thomas, J. H., 65
Thomson, Commodore, G. P., 4
Thornton, Archibald P., 176
Treaty of Nanking (1842), 8
Treaty ports, 2, 10, 24. *See* Map.
Treaty system, main characteristics, 2, 91. *See also* Extraterritoriality; Tariff; Treaty ports
Treaty of Tientsin (1858), article 52 (gunboat diplomacy) 3, 8
Treaty of Versailles (1919), 8
Tseng, T. K., 40
Tu Yu-sheng, 168
Twenty-One Demands (1915), 8, 46

Umetsu, General Yoshijiro, 186
Unilever Company, 172, 184
United Front, Kuomintang-Communist Party, 150, 154
United States: loans to China, 36, 46; on Japanese seizure of Manchuria and attack on Shanghai in 1932, 61-62; avoidance of joint action, 49, 62-63, 122. *See also* Anglo-American relations.

Vansittart, Sir Robert, (later Lord Vansittart), permanent under-secretary,

Foreign Office, 33, 38n, 53; on Sir Miles Lampson, 32; on Rajchman appointment, 38; and the Amau statement, 48; and Defence Requirements Committee, 53; on Anglo-Soviet relations, 58; on Anglo-American relations, 59; on Anglo-Japanese relations, 67, 73; on China policy, 89; on Leith-Ross mission, 103, 109; conflict with Treasury, 105n, 124; and League of Nations, 125
Wang Ching-wei, Chinese prime minister, 34; Wang-Ariyoshi conversations, 45, 50; and Japan, 26, 38, 45, 114
Wellesley, Sir Victor, assistant under-secretary of state: on business influence in politics, 22, 183, 184; on the Chinese worker, 24; on American foreign policy, 60; conflict with Treasury, 101n
Whyte, Sir Frederick, 10, 10n, 41n
Wilhelm II, Kaiser, 56
Winterton, Lord, 30, 30n, 31n
Woodhead, H. G., 28n, 29

Yamamoto, Mr., 12
Yin Ju-Keng, 124
Yoshida, Shigeru, Japanese ambassador to Britain, 145, 146, 147, 163, 165, 170
Yuan Shih-kai, 84, 168